WYNYARD HALL

THE HISTORY OF A GREAT HOUSE

With a foreword by Sir John Hall

Research and text by

Norma Neal, Barbara Leo and Haydn Neal

©Wynyard Hall Publishing, 2011

Published by Wynyard Hall Publishing

ISBN 978-0-9570114-1-0
Designed and Printed by **hpm**group 0191 3006941

Dedicated to all those people, past and present, whose enterprise, vision and craftsmanship created Wynyard Hall and its historic parkland. May future generations continue their proud tradition.

CONTENTS

FOREWORD BY SIR JOHN HALL

(Photograph courtesy of Holden and Jones)

The idea for this book has been in my mind for some time and now, thanks to the work, dedication and research of Norma, Barbara and Haydn of Sedgefield Local History Society, the dream has become a reality.

The privilege of living at Wynyard Hall is coupled with the great respect I feel for this beautiful place and the inspirational people who created it.

As the miner's son in the coal owner's house, I am very aware of the responsibility I bear for the future of this beautiful jewel in the Northern crown.

With continued economic investment, sensitive development of the hotel and gardens and the support of my family, I hope to leave an enduring legacy to my time at Wynyard Hall.

INTRODUCTION

Beyond the beauty of Wynyard Hall, evident at first glance, lies a fascinating history, enriched by a huge cast of characters, who all played their part in its remarkable story.

For generations, thanks to the considerable social and political influence of the Londonderry family and their circle of friends, Wynyard performed an important role on the world stage, playing host to royalty, aristocrats, politicians, diplomats, artists and writers.

As a country house hotel and restaurant, the splendours of Wynyard Hall can now be enjoyed by countless visitors and guests. As well as celebrating the artistry and skills employed in the design of the magnificent Hall and the surrounding parkland and gardens, our book also looks at the people beyond the portico.

Their lives and loves, triumphs and disasters, pleasures and pastimes illuminate this wonderful house, shedding light on a vanished world. The history of Wynyard is our history, too. We hope you enjoy discovering the life and times of this great house.

Norma Neal, Barbara Leo and Haydn Neal

CHAPTER 1

The History of a Great House

MEDIAEVAL ORIGINS OF WYNYARD

Excavations of an Iron Age village to the south of Wynyard Park show human occupation of the area since 700 B.C.

Anglo Saxon in origin, Wynyard means "enclosed meadow", a combination of winn (meadow) and yeard (enclosure). Spelling changed considerably during the middle ages, possibly because most people couldn't read or write. From Wyneiard in 1237 to Winherd only a year later, by 1311 it had become Wynhyard, changing again to Wyneyard by 1345. Not until the 16th century did we arrive at the modern spelling, Wynyard.

Chapells, de Lisles and Langtons

The Chapells, the earliest family known to occupy Wynyard, leased the land from Edward I in 1230. In return, the king expected them to provide soldiers when the need arose. Sir Hugh de Chapell (or Capel) and his wife Johane had no male heirs, so in 1265 the land passed to their five daughters. In 1283, land was given to Sir Henry de Lisle, knight and in about 1312, Katherina, daughter of Sir John de Lisle, married Alan Langton. Their son Simon and his wife Alice, daughter of John Carew of Seaton, inherited the house, which passed, in 1380, to their son, Thomas Langton. Later Chamberlain and chief officer to Henry Percy of Northumberland, he married Sibyl Laton and is said to have built a Manor House at Wynyard in about 1410. Wynyard ceased to be the property of the crown in Langton's time and, in 1433, Thomas granted the manor house to his wife Sibyl for life. They lie together under an alabaster tomb in the porch of the parish church of Redmarshall.

Conyers and Claxtons

In 1438, the male line came to an end and the property was inherited by Thomas' niece, another Sybil. She married Sir Roger Conyers and conveyed the manor to him. In 1454, she persuaded the Bishop of Durham to provide a chaplain for the services of the Wynyard household. Another clue to the size and significance of the house. There must have been a chapel on the estate in the fifteenth century. Estate records show that Sir Roger leased lands at the east end of Wynyard to John, Prior of Durham, for five years at 6d and 3 marks annual rent.

Langton of Wynyard. Argent a lion sable and a border gules engrailed - on a silver background, a black lion, a red scalloped border

Hereditary constables of Durham Castle, the family included Sir John Conyers, renowned for slaying the Sockburn Worm, back in the eleventh century. At the beginning of the 19th century, the last baronet, Sir Thomas Conyers, looked set to end his days in Chester le Street workhouse, until his dignity was restored by a generous donation from Sir Henry Vane-Tempest, a later owner of Wynyard.

Sir Roger Conyer's granddaughter inherited the property after her father's death. She married Ralph Claxton, the estate eventually passing to their son, William, in 1525. William Claxton leased Wynyard Mill, a workshop and grounds, annual rent £8, to Thomas Brasse. Originally from Trimdon, Thomas had to attend on Claxton in war time and present him with half the fish caught in the dam. William's male heir died at the age of fourteen, so, in 1595, he left the estate to his two daughters, Alice and Ann, and his granddaughter Cassandra Lambert. Alice married William Blackiston, Ann, William Jennison. No doubt in an attempt to continue the Claxton line, Cassandra married Lancelot Claxton.

Davisons

By 1633, Alexander Davison, a wealthy Newcastle merchant, had bought up all three parts of the estate of Wynyard, Fulthorpe and Thorpe Thewles, a total of 1,300 acres. The Davison family lived at Wynyard until 1702, when Thomas Rudd, counsellor at law bought the house. In 1742, the sale of Wynyard for £8,000 marked the beginning of an important connection with the Tempest family.

Davison. A fesse wavy between six cinqfoils gules - a wavy division between six red flowers

7

CHAPTER 2

THE TEMPEST CONNECTION

Since medieval times, the Tempest name has been linked to many historic events in the counties of York and Durham. According to the early records, the family left Normandy with William the Conqueror in 1066.

Encountering very stormy weather near the English shore, their small vessel was driven westwards along the coast. In consequence, they arrived too late for the battle of Hastings. As a reminder of their difficult arrival on these shores, the family adopted the name Tempest, their coat of arms consisting of three martlets, known as *'Les Oiseaux de Tempete'*. The heraldic representation of martins or swifts, the bird's inability to land symbolises the constant quest for knowledge, learning and adventure, as well as hard work and perseverance.

Tempest. Argent a bend engrailed between six martlets sable - on a silver background, a scalloped divider between six black swifts

The Northern Tempests

The Tempests quickly established themselves in England. In 1098, at Broughton, near Skipton in North Yorkshire, Roger Tempest founded a dynasty now unbroken through thirty one generations. Sir Piers Tempest of Bracewell, Yorkshire received his knighthood from Henry V at the battle of Agincourt in 1415. Other branches of the family were variously known as the Tempests of Hartford, Holmeside, Stella and Studley.

By the end of the 17th century, one of the Durham branches had settled near the city. Colonel William Tempest(1653-1700) served as Member of Parliament for Durham City in the reigns of Charles II and James II. His eldest son, John (1679-1737), the first of a series of family members so named, represented County Durham from 1705. Marriage to Jane, daughter and heiress of Richard Wharton of Durham, significantly expanded the family's coal mining interests, adding Houghton-le-Spring, Penshaw and Rainton collieries to their existing properties.

Tempests at Wynyard

The Wynyard connection began in 1742, when John Tempest (1710-1776), eldest son of John Tempest and Jane Wharton, bought Wynyard from Thomas Rudd, counsellor at law, for £8,000. Member of Parliament for Durham and Old Sherburn, John Tempest's extensive property included The Isle, Swainston, Kelloe, Dalton-le-Dale, Old Durham, Sherburn, Brancepeth Castle, Stainton, Thorpe Thewles, Carlton, Redmarshall, Broomhall and Offerton. The family also owned collieries at South Biddick, Rainton and Sunderland and were amongst the largest shippers of coal via Sunderland.

Their son, the next John Tempest (1739-1794), also represented Durham City. He married Ann Townsend of Warwickshire, but their only son, John Wharton Tempest (1772–1793) died tragically young as the result of a riding accident. Left without a male heir, on his death in 1794, John Tempest's Wynyard estate passed to his nephew, Henry Vane (1771- 1813), upon condition that he assume the name and arms of Tempest.

The Vanes

Only son of Sir Henry Vane, Bart, prebend of Durham and rector of Long Newton, the new owner of Wynyard also possessed a considerable family pedigree, distant forbears including Howell ap Vane, who was knighted at Poitiers in 1356 by the Black Prince (1330-1376), son of Edward III and father of Richard II.

Another ancestor, Sir Henry Vane the Elder of Hadlow, Kent and Raby, Co. Durham, (1589-1654) holder of several royal posts, including Secretary of State, became a

Parliamentarian in 1641, after being dismissed by King Charles I. His son, Sir Henry Vane the younger (1613-1662) of Raby,

Stewart, Marquess of Londonderry. A bend checky argent and azure between two lions gules - a checked divider, silver and blue, between two red lions

served briefly, from 1636-1637, as Governor of Massachusetts in North America. Like his father, a staunch Parliamentarian and supporter of Cromwell during the Civil War, he was executed for treason on Tower Hill in London in 1662, after the restoration of King Charles II. Second son, George Vane (1618-1679), knighted in 1640, married Elizabeth, daughter of Sir Lionel Maddison of Newcastle and produced *' thirteen hopeful children, viz foure sons and nine daughters.'* He acquired the estate of Long Newton near Wynyard, site of the family mausoleum, where an inscription declares :-

'His honour won in the field lies here in the dust,
His honour got by grace shall never rust.'

The Vane Tempests

In 1794, George's great great grandson, Henry Vane, inherited Wynyard from his uncle, John Tempest, becoming Sir Henry Vane Tempest. On his death in 1813, Wynyard passed to his daughter, Lady Frances Anne Vane Tempest. When, in 1819, she married Charles, Lord Stewart, Wynyard Hall began its long association with the Vane-Tempest-Stewarts, the Earls Vane and the Londonderry family.

Wynyard Families – mediaeval to modern

1230	Chapell
1283	de Lisle
1300s	Langton
c1438	Conyers
c1525	Claxton
1633	Davison
1702	Rudd
1742	Tempest
1794	Vane-Tempest
1819	Vane-Tempest-Stewart
1822	Londonderry
1987	Hall

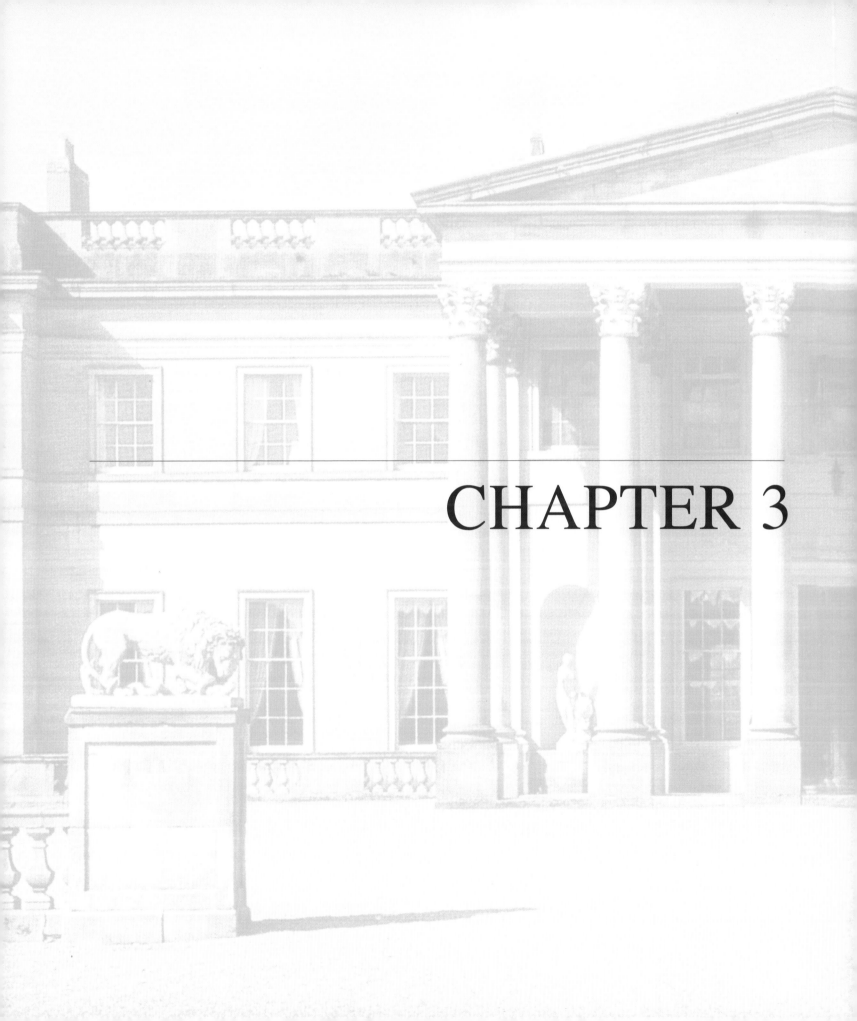

CHAPTER 3

FROM MANSION HOUSE TO PALATIAL HALL

Although the history of Wynyard stretches back to mediaeval times, the beautiful Park and Hall so admired today, now listed Grade II and II* respectively, did not come in to being until relatively modern times. In 1630, Newcastle merchant, Alexander Davison, bought the 263 acre Wynyard estate and mansion house. As well as a hall, parlour, kitchen, two butteries, a master bedroom, several more bedrooms, innumerable lofts and a study, he also acquired a chapel, stables, a dairy, an ox house, an apple loft, barns, a garden house, gardens and an orchard.

By 1742, when Durham MP John Tempest bought the estate for £8,000, Wynyard Hall had become a three storey building with Flemish style portico and entrance hall. The Lion Bridge, on the approach drive to the house, is the one unaltered survival of John Tempest's time. Portrayed in water colours of Wynyard dating from the late eighteenth century, the elegant bridge crosses a stream feeding a broad lake leading to a valley planted with evergreens.

New beginnings

However, the present building owes much to the Londonderry family, owners of Wynyard for several generations. In 1819, John Tempest's descendant, the wealthy heiress Lady Frances Anne Vane Tempest married Lord Charles Stewart. Together, they began repair and redecoration of the house, using local craftsmen where possible. Neglected during the lifetime and after the death of Sir Henry Vane-Tempest, father of Frances Anne, the house had developed cracks and fissures, preventing extensive repairs, as the whole structure was unsafe. As dry rot threatened as well, it was agreed to demolish part of the Hall and rebuild on the same spot. Rejecting an earlier plan to rebuild Wynyard on a larger site, according to Sir Archibald Alison, historian and friend of Lady Frances Anne, they planned ' *a splendid edifice … in the chastest style of Grecian architecture.'* A fine house befitting his new station became even more essential, when, in 1822, Charles Stewart succeeded to the title 3rd Marquess of Londonderry.

Wynyard Park - The seat of Francess Anne, Marchioness of Londonderry - Lithograph by W H James

Philip Wyatt, son of the renowned architect James Wyatt, was commissioned to redesign the house. Engaged to work on the Duke of Wellington's Apsley House (now known as Number One, London), Philip's brother, Benjamin Dean Wyatt, may have offered advice. The design for Wynyard Hall is based on plans drawn up but never used for Waterloo Palace, the house at Stratfield Saye in Hampshire, presented to the Duke by a grateful

The Original House from a painting by John Burlingham

nation. After Wellington's visit to Wynyard in 1827, the corridor of bedrooms overlooking the lake was renamed 'the Duke's Gallery', in honour of the distinguished guest. An obelisk 127 ft high was also erected, although the original inscription 'Wellington, friend of Londonderry' was shortened simply to 'Wellington' after his hero failed to offer the 3rd Marquess a cabinet post.

Philip Wyatt usually served as assistant to his older brother Benjamin Dean, making important contributions to many of the London houses built by the family firm. At Wynyard, however, he seems to have taken sole responsibility, after borrowing the unused plans for Wellington's house in the first place. Under Philip Wyatt's jurisdiction, about one third of the existing rooms at Wynyard were remodelled. The old dining room became the billiard room, the former drawing room a music room. Both were later combined to create the great drawing room, now known as the ballroom. Behind the remodelled rooms, Wyatt created a great gallery, an *enfilade* of rooms, running the length of the house, their doors opening to reveal the splendour of each one in turn. A series of smaller rooms to the west later became the chapel. On the north side of the house, Wyatt designed the magnificent entrance hall and statue gallery.

Making progress

The 3rd Marquess took a keen interest in the remodelling of Wynyard Hall, inspecting and initialling Wyatt's plans before handing them to Thomas Prosser, his executant architect and builder, who supervised the construction of the house, in the manner of a modern clerk of works. Despite the decision to build on to the existing house, rather than demolishing it entirely, the immense cost involved amounted to over £100,000, with further expenditure on the conservatory, hothouses, gardens and park. An additional sum of over £27,000 was spent on furniture. In 1825, Lord Londonderry wrote to his agent William Hawkes, ' *Every day I learn that this house was a concern too lightly engaged by me.'*

John Buddle, engineer, agent and viewer of the Londonderry estates, also kept a close eye on the progress of the building works. In 1822, after a meeting with Wyatt, he wrote that various rooms, mostly in the old part of the house, including the library, ante room, drawing rooms, various services and offices, part of the long gallery and one principal staircase should be completed by

May. Remaining rooms, the rest of the gallery and another staircase would be left as a shell, roofed in, to be completed later. The portico and colonnade would be added at a future date.

Progress continued slowly. By 1824, work had begun on fitting up the dining room and drawing room, but Wyatt requested a further £12,000 to provide a roof to cover the house. In 1828, the design for the floor of the entrance hall was agreed. By the following year, the conservatory, built at a cost of over £5,700, was being prepared to receive trees, work was proceeding on the portico, the gallery and the great drawing room, created from the old billiard and music rooms. Between 1829 and 1830, stables were built on lower ground to the east of the house, but plans drawn up for a riding school never materialised.

A splendid mansion

According to historian Nikolaus Pevsner, *'the most splendid 19th century mansion in the county'*, the Hall is dominated by a vast Corinthian portico, also known as a *porte-cochere*, after its original function as a covered entrance for horse-drawn coaches, allowing visitors to alight protected from the weather. Wynyard's portico is pedimented hexastyle, having a triangular roof supported at the front by six columns. Two columns deep, their capitals carved by C.Bielfield, in 1857 William Fordyce described the Wynyard portico as *'the finest in the north of England.'* The two large bronzes in front of the portico depict the Chasse du Cerf and the Chasse du Sanglier, representing hunting scenes from the time the 3rd Marquess spent in Vienna as British Ambassador.

The entrance is based on the Waterloo Palace design created for Wellington, with its rectangular balustraded shape, portico, end bays and high central hall, its dome visible from the exterior. Thirteen windows wide, the north front, the main entrance to the house, concludes at each end with a slightly projecting bay, each with a tripartite window, made up of three mullioned lights with a wider, central light.

The two storey building is constructed of ashlar, a type of dressed stonework. To the rear of the Hall, the south front, overlooking the terrace and gardens, is the 18th century house refaced. Three hundred feet in length, but relatively plain in comparison to the porticoed entrance at the north, the south front originally had wings one storey high projecting at each end. Lower in the 18th century design, Wyatt turned their canted windows (straight at the front with angled sides) into the pilastered segmental bow windows we see today, their shape gently curved. On each side of the south front, wings with quadrant-curved ends house the conservatory to the left, a private drawing room to the right. A giant colonnade, as proposed in the Waterloo Palace design, was never built, perhaps because it would have prevented light from entering the Hall.

Celebration

The foundation stone, laid on 3 April 1826, the seventh wedding anniversary of Lord and Lady Londonderry, sits upon coins of the realm. A large party of friends attended the official event and numerous tenants and tradesman were invited to a celebratory ball in the evening. Dancing

began at ten o'clock and the last guests left at six o'clock the next morning. A plaque at the foot of the rear left hand column of the portico commemorates the event. The inscription reads, ' *This mansion was erected by Charles Wm. Vane, third Marquis of Londonderry and the first Earl of Vane of the United Kingdom and Great Britain and Ireland and by Frances Anne Vane, Marchioness of Londonderry and Countess Vane, who was sole heiress to all the collieries in the County of Durham belonging to the Vane and Tempest families, inheriting the same from her father Sir Henry Vane Tempest Bart, who married Anne Countess of Antrim. This building was commenced in December Anno Domini 1822, the whole of the stone of this fabric was brought 26 miles from the quarry belonging to the family estate at Penshaw Colliery. Philip W Wyatt, Architect.'*

T. Allom.   W. Floyd.

Wynyard, Seat of the Marquess of Londonderry, Durham.
(DESTROYED BY FIRE IN 1841)

Wynyard by Thomas Allom (1804-1872) - hanging in Wynyard

Local coal mines owned by the Vane Tempests produced revenue to cover the rebuilding costs. The architect's fee alone was £4,000. As well as stone from the family quarry at Penshaw, marble was brought from Italy and France, wood shipped from Spain and interiors designed in the ostentatious style of Louis Quatorze. The 3rd Marquess soon became troubled by debts and expressed grave concerns about Wyatt's building estimates. Prosser, too, complained that work was often delayed while waiting for detailed drawings from the architect. In 1828, when the house was nearing completion, Lord Londonderry paid off Wyatt, finally finding him *'impossible to deal with'* and complaining of his *'extreme inconsequence.'* Work continued, however, through the 1830s, including the addition of marble doors to the great drawing room and gallery and the building of the chapel.

In 1832, writing in collaboration with the artist Allom, who produced a fine print of Wynyard Hall, Thomas Rose wrote *'It is difficult to say which is most worthy of admiration – the dignified simplicity exhibited in the exterior of the building, or the judicious arrangements of the interior, which combine the majesty of a palace with the comforts and conveniences of a domestic dwelling.'*

CHAPTER 4

FIRE AND RESTORATION

All the more tragic then, that the house was reduced to ruins so near to completion on 19 February 1841. Near Salter's House that Friday night at eleven o'clock, Linwood, the watchman and Dunn, the underkeeper were, as usual, patrolling the grounds of Wynyard Park, when they spotted smoke rising. Running towards the Hall, they saw flames darting out from the lowest window of the stone staircase, between the conservatory and the chapel, the final part to be completed of a mansion described in the press as "*an edifice fit for a monarch.*"

Fighting the flames

Wynyard's small extinguishing engine would not work, because the pipes were frozen, so Mrs. Edgar, the housekeeper, quickly organised Bailey, the gardener and Hikely, the steward with buckets from the kitchen and scullery. With the rest of the servants, they formed a human chain and, dredging water from the fish pond, did their best to douse the flames.

Lord Londonderry's huntsman, Cooper, leapt into the saddle and galloped off to summon the fire engines from Stockton-on Tees, about five miles away. En route, he alerted the whole neighbourhood and, when the Reverend Mr. Clarke of Wolviston ordered his church bell to be rung, the whole village turned out to help fight the fire. Cooper finally reached Stockton at midnight, a full hour after the flames were first spotted.

Three fire engines were dispatched, preceded by a detachment of rural police. By the time they reached Wynyard at one o'clock, the whole west wing was ablaze and a band of volunteers swarmed around the grounds. Servants, villagers from Thorpe Thewles and Wolviston and tenants from the surrounding farms were joined by tradesman from Stockton, arriving in carts and omnibuses. Some helped prepare engines to play water on to the house. Most were hurriedly removing valuables from rooms untouched by the flames. According to the Morning Post of 26 February 1841, many works of art were saved by the efforts of one Mr. Bell, a carver and gilder from Stockton, who '*directed his attention to this department*'. A Thomas Lawrence painting of King George IV, possibly from the Londonderrys' time in Vienna, was severely damaged when a chair leg was driven through it. Portraits of Queen Anne, George III and Queen Charlotte were lost, as well as all the Tempest family pictures, apart from a portrait of the young John Wharton Tempest. However, a marble chimney piece, possibly the antique Italian alabaster carving from the boudoir, highly prized for its sculpture, was saved.

Desolation

Lawns on the south side were soon covered in ornate mirrors, splendid chimney pieces, priceless works of art, costly furniture, silk hangings and immense chandeliers, some weighing a ton. About seventy beds were also rescued. Most of His Lordship's extensive library lay scattered, tumbled into a mangled heap. The construction of the hall, with its continuous roof space and stoothed walls, allowed the fire to spread rapidly. Despite the best efforts of the crowds and the fire fighters, most of the Hall was engulfed by flames. Only the east end of the building, including servants' quarters, the kitchen and stables were saved.

The magnificent drawing rooms, dining rooms, picture gallery, library, grand staircases and more than thirty bedrooms were reduced to rubble and smouldering ash. The still room, silver pantry and two footmen's rooms were also lost, along with the conservatory and its collection of exotic shrubs. Orange trees brought at great expense from the Empress Josephine's garden at Malmaison were reduced to charred stumps, only baked soil and the iron hoops from their tubs remaining. The chapel, too, the seat of the fire and intended to be the final jewel in this magnificent crown, lay charred and desolate in the early morning air. Marble columns in the entrance hall were nothing but pillars of dust, but the outer walls sustained little injury and the portico remained almost entire.

During the next two days, local people came from miles around to view the devastation. Rural police kept the crowds back, but all the valuables had, by then, been moved into the stables and only one woman was charged with stealing from the wreckage. Property saved from the fire was later insured for a sum approaching £18,000.

Golightly, the estate joiner, had battled the fire along with the rest, but his carelessness may well have been to blame. Working in the chapel, he had lit a fire to dry out the new timber. A stray spark could have lain smouldering amongst the wood shavings scattered on the floor. On the other hand, the conservatory was heated by steam and, in other parts of the building, hot air was conveyed through pipes. A faulty flue may well have caused the conflagration, but the 3rd Marquess certainly laid the blame on *'that blackguard Golightly.'*

Beginning again

On Saturday 25 February 1841, Lord Seaham, the Londonderrys' eldest son, arriving at Wynyard from Oxford, was despatched to Italy to break the news of the fire to his parents. The Marchioness became so ill she spent the next three weeks in bed. In his diary, the Marquess recorded *'the sad news that the Almighty had thought fit, in his wisdom and for purposes alone known to an inscrutable Providence, to allow my residence at Wynyard Park, in the county of Durham, to be utterly and entirely destroyed by fire ... To describe at all the manner this misfortune bent me to earth is a task beyond my pen.'*

Although fire insurance was a relatively new idea in those days, it seems that the 3rd Marquess had been covered, but was furious to learn from his agent John Buddle that insurance on the house and furniture had not been renewed since December 1832. The 3rd Marquess ordered rebuilding to begin at once. Lord Londonderry engaged Durham architect Ignatius Bonomi, in partnership with J.A. Cory, as well as John Dobson, now particularly renowned for his architectural work in the city of Newcastle. Using the 1822 designs produced by Philip Wyatt, who had died in 1836, it is thought that the new team reproduced the original layout.

Alteration

However, the statue gallery is not recorded in detail in plans drawn up before the fire and may have been altered. Neither is it clear whether the great central octagon replicates original designs. John Cornforth, writing in Country Life magazine in 1988, suggested that the Mirror Room, the Ball Room and the upper part of the gallery may have been altered after the fire, as they have decorative details in common, not seen in the rest of the house. He also suggests that the ceiling of the Ball Room

may have been raised after the fire, the removal of a bedroom above allowing an impressive increase in the height of the room, the existing marble pillars lengthened with wood, painted with a marble effect. Early plans show staircases at each end of the gallery, also shown in a drawing from 1839. No such staircases exist today. The oval staircase at the east end may have been installed in 1842, as a plan shows proposed alterations to such a staircase at that time.

Arising from the ashes

Restoration of the mansion after the fire cost under £40,000, much lower than the £100,000 already spent. The most severe damage was at the west end of the house, but, according to Bonomi, rebuilding was not required, just repair to the stonework. It appears that the house was gutted, rather than destroyed, by the fire. Two young workers left a note, recording their contribution to the rebuilding of the house. Addressed "To whom it may concern", carefully folded, and discovered decades later, it reads :- *Robert Robson Almond of Gateshead, aged 21, John Scott of Durham, aged 20, Plumbers, Laid this first gutter on the 16th day of October 1841.* The new house also benefited from one of the earliest local examples of central heating, a warm air system, installed by Thomas Mather. By 1846, restoration was complete, the new interiors even more ornate than those lost in the fire, complete with Turkish carpets, silk curtains and wall hangings, gilded and ornamental furniture and fifty one cases of stuffed birds.

All was not plain sailing, however, as the Marquess, dissatisfied with the restoration of the roof, took Ignatius Bonomi to court. Called in to arbitrate in the matter, fellow architects John Dobson and Anthony Salvin concluded that, while Bonomi's planning had been faultless, his superintending of the work was not. They ordered him to pay damages of £5. Reporting that the Marquess had to pay a further £160 to have Bonomi's faulty work remedied, the Morning Post of 21 October 1845, criticised *'the glorious uncertainty of the law'*. A year after his death, in 1855 the Marquess' opinion was vindicated when architect P.C. Hardwick assessed the dome, reporting the complicated timber trussing unsatisfactory and concluding that the rafters and slates should be entirely renewed. After two more fires, both beginning in the original chapel, entirely situated in the house, the Londonderrys installed a steam operated pump engine for fire fighting.

Completed in 1846, an official opening and consecration ceremony for the new Hall was held in the chapel in January 1849. Described by historian Archibald Alison, a friend of the family, as *'one of the principal ornaments of the north of England'*, the magnificently restored house attracted visitors from miles around. According to Victorian novelist Charles Dickens, a welcome guest at the house and journalist for the Morning Chronicle from 1834-1836, Wynyard had already been open to the public on Wednesday afternoons. In a letter of 1847, Benjamin Disraeli, a frequent visitor to Wynyard, commended the fortitude of his close friend Frances Anne.
'I admire your noble courage more even than your splendid taste', he wrote, clearly impressed by *'the unparalleled and, to me, startling resurrection of Wynyard.'*

A view across the lake, pictured in the 1800s

CHAPTER 5

A WALK THROUGH WYNYARD HALL

The Entrance Hall, pictured in 1988 (Country Life magazine)

The interior of Wynyard Hall reflects the opulent Louis Quatorze style characteristic of architects Philip and Benjamin Dean Wyatt and seen in many of their London houses. Throughout the house, the work of particular craftsmen, many of them local, is seen to impressive effect. Stained glass by William Wailes of Newcastle, gilding by James Lindsay of Sunderland, marble pillars by Thomas Scotson of Wolviston, carpentry and intricately patterned flooring by Robert Hardy of Stockton take their place alongside the delicate plaster carving of Daniel Nevin and the magnificent mahogany doors and buhl panels of Henry Burnell. The 3rd Marquess also used local suppliers, placing orders with Stockton timber merchants, the cement works of Lord Musgrave, the Northumberland Glass Company and Isaac Cookson, glassmaker of Tyneside.

Continuing this tradition, local craftsmen were used once again in the 1980s, during the refurbishment carried out by interior designer Rupert Lord. All the carpets were designed and created by Hugh Mackay of Durham City, which held a royal warrant from 1972 until its closure in 2005. W.H. Bonny from York was responsible for the decoration in the principal rooms, Hesp and Jones of Beningborough, Yorkshire, applying additional gilding. Dick Reid, also from York, made the torcheres, the carved candelabra in the four corners of the dining room, now the Wellington Restaurant. J.G. Gardiner of Bridlington repaired the marble chimney pieces, restoration of the chandeliers was undertaken by J. David Kelly of Knaresborough, while Neil Trinder of Sheffield brought specialised skills to the repair of the buhl bookcases in the library, as well as creating outstanding pieces of furniture throughout.

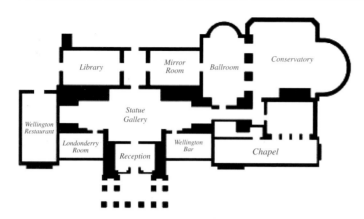

Ground floor plan of Wynyard Hall Country House Hotel

The entrance porch

A black and white marble floor, patterned in chequer board style, leads in to the entrance porch, now the hotel reception area. Originally white, the walls gained their warm orange tones during the modern restoration of the hall, continued in the ornate coffered ceiling, where a variety of flowers, carved and framed in white, stand out against the deep background. A pair of elegant pillars of pinkish marble, stand on square bases of black marble, completed with a scallop capital. The mahogany Henry Burnell door, 13 feet in height, is flanked by jasper pilasters surmounted by white Corinthian cornices.

Entrance porch coffered ceiling

Entrance porch fireplace

On either side of the door, mahogany pier tables with mirrors behind, 11feet 8inches high and 4 feet 7 inches wide, were created in 1987 by craftsman Neil Trinder of Sheffield. Formerly in that position, a pair of immense George III bookcases, containing handsomely bound copies of parliamentary records, now reside in another part of the hall. On opposite sides of the entrance porch, matching fireplaces are flanked by curved mahogany doors. Marble topped and with floral patterned surrounds to the front, the sides of the fireplaces bear coats of arms showing the family symbols of the gryphon and gauntlet beneath a pair of coronets representing the double title of Earl and Marquess.

The entrance hall

Modelled on that of Mount Stewart, the Londonderry's home in Northern Ireland, the entrance hall is dominated by the magnificent centrally placed statue gallery. Two smaller apses, or glazed domes, at either end of the entrance hall contain skylights of beautiful stained glass created by William Wales of Newcastle (1808-1881), responsible for much of the glass in the Hall. The ceiling, a coffered segmental tunnel vault, is decorated in the same way as the ceiling of the smaller entrance porch. The rose motif is repeated in the Durham carpet supplied in the 1980s by Hugh Mackay, responsible for all the carpets in the refurbished Hall.

The statue gallery

The statue gallery, 120 feet long and 58 feet high, is surmounted by a beautiful dome with a lantern of breathtaking stained glass, created by William Wailes of Newcastle, responsible for much of the beautiful Wynyard glass, as well as the painted glass in the family church at Long Newton. Around the walls, jasper pilasters stand upon black and gold marble bases, their plinths of Egyptian green. Daniel Nevin created the Corinthian capitals, with acanthus leaves and four scrolls, carved in plaster in 1847. A coffered cove forms a link with the clerestory, the octagonal balcony backed by long windows of beautiful stained glass. Pure white balustrading and pillars surround the upper gallery, which is supported by eight statues of Atlas, the god who, in Greek mythology, was condemned to hold up the heavens on his shoulders. The statues were designed by James Lindsey of Sunderland, employed for many years to carry out embellishments at Wynyard. The Henry Burnell mahogany doors leading from the statue gallery are surrounded by pillars of Siena marble made in about 1845 by Thomas Scotson of Wolviston, a village close to Wynyard.

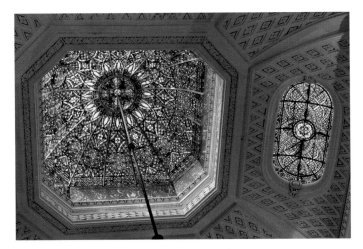

Statue Gallery dome lantern with stained glass by William Wailes

Gallery ceiling decoration with the Londonderry coat of arms

The present vibrant yellow of the walls replaced a cool blue used in earlier decoration, toning beautifully with the existing gold, bronze and pure white of the statue gallery. Above the entablature (the bronze coloured band connecting the upper and lower galleries), the Londonderry coat of arms, resplendent in gold and bronze, is repeated eight times. A gilded coronet, denoting a Marquess, above a pair of shields is flanked by bronze supporters. Soldiers in Hussar's uniform, distinctive cockades in their hats, are borne by two rampant horses. Beneath, a bronze ribbon carries the Londonderry motto *'Metuenda Corolla Draconis',* 'Fear the Dragon's Crest'.

All eight were expertly gilded and bronzed during restoration work in the 1980s. Around the outer edge of the central chandelier, the gilded gauntlet and dagger of the Vanes is repeated several times.

Octagonal in shape, the gallery forms the centre of the building and originally contained numerous statues of classical figures such as Hector, Paris, Venus and Mercury. Many were by Antonio Canova (1757-1822), a Venetian sculptor famous for his delicate realisation of nude flesh. His first sculpture of the Three Graces, created for the Empress Josephine of France in 1814, now stands in the Hermitage Museum, St. Petersburg. His 1806 sculpture of Napoleon as Mars the Peacemaker, given to the Duke of Wellington by a grateful nation, still stands in Aspley House, London, while his Theseus and the Minotaur is on display at London's Victoria and Albert Museum. Wynyard's statue gallery also originally housed several busts of friends of the 3rd Marquess, including the Dukes of Cleveland and Rutland.

The Londonderry coach, last used by the 7th Marquess for the coronation of King George VI in 1937 and beautifully restored recently at Mount Stewart, also resided in the Statue Gallery until the 1960s. On the wall to the left, a brass plaque records three recitals given at Wynyard in July 1986 by American concert pianist Earl Wild to commemorate the hundredth anniversary of the death of Franz Liszt, Hungarian composer and piano virtuoso.

Chandelier detail showing the Vane gauntlet

Gallery balustrade with supporting statues of Atlas

The Statue Gallery c. 1906 (Photographic Library Beamish Museum Ltd)

Londonderry coach, now at Mount Stewart
(with permission of the National Trust)

Londonderry family at the coronation of King Edward VII in 1902. The coach was also used at the coronations of George V and VI as well as royal weddings and great state occasions in London (with Permission of the National Trust)

Informal group during a house party at Wynyard. The 6th Marquess is on the extreme left of the front row and A.J. Balfour, with tennis racquet, on extreme right. From the Londonderry Album, with permission of Lord Londonderry.

Around the walls, photographs taken in the 1890s by Reginald Vane-Tempest and his mother Theresa, Marchioness of Londonderry, give a flavour of life at Wynyard in former times.

Wellington

To the left of the statue gallery, busts of the Duke of Wellington, former friend and comrade in arms to the 3rd Marquess, were acquired during the modern refurbishment, as were the Wellington coats of arms above the doors. Composed of lions and crowns, one bears the Latin inscription *'Virtutis Fortuna Comes'*, 'Fortune is the companion of honour'. Originating with the 3rd Regiment of Foot (the Duke of Wellington's), the motto has also been adopted by HMS Iron Duke, the Royal Navy frigate on which Prince William served briefly in 2008. On the second coat of arms, above the Londonderry Room, two coronets, one above the other, represent the titles emblazoned on the shield - Duc de Wellington and Prince de Waterloo.

The Londonderry Room

Transformed in the modern refurbishment, the Londonderry Room was, in recent years a kitchen, prior to that a breakfast room, containing, according to the Newcastle Courant of January 1884, several fine paintings, including a portrait of the Duke of Marlborough

Frances Anne in middle age

and a van Dyck painting of Cleopatra. The room also housed, at that time, paintings of family dogs and horses by John Frederick Herring, an eminent animal painter of the mid-nineteenth century comparable to Sir Edwin Landseer. Also on display was the outstanding George Stubbs painting of Sir Henry Vane-Tempest's famous racehorse, Hambletonian, now hanging at Mount Stewart, the Londonderry home in Northern Ireland, now a National Trust property.

Despite the loss of several major works of art, the Londonderry Room, now beautifully decorated and designed, contains fine portraits, some original to Wynyard, some acquired in order to honour the history and achievements of the 3rd Marquess. His own portrait above the fireplace is flanked by those of Wellington and

The Enfilade

One of a pair of fireplaces in the Vestibule

The Wellington Room

At the other side of the main entrance to the Hall, the Wellington Room, now used as a private dining room and bar, is constantly surveyed by the portrait of Frances Anne, Marchioness of Londonderry, renowned for her hospitality.

Reception rooms

Beyond the statue gallery, forming the south front of the mansion, a suite of reception rooms originally included the great ball-room, the drawing-room, the library and the billiard-room, which contained portraits of many illustrious military leaders in the Peninsular War. Fine works by Canaletto and Michelangelo, purchased during the time of the 3rd Marquess and his wife, originally hung in the vestibule. Linked by magnificent mahogany doors, each room opens into the next, an *enfilade* of rooms, giving an uninterrupted view from the conservatory to the library.

From the statue gallery, the vestibule, its floor an intricate design of polished oak, rosewood and satinwood by Robert Hardy of Stockton (1846), leads out on to the terrace, formerly known as the promenade. Flanking the doors from the statue gallery, a fine pair of corner fireplaces in cast iron, decorated with classical figures in bronze. To the right of the vestibule, magnificent Henry Burnell doors of Spanish mahogany, 13 feet in height, and surrounded by marble, lead to the mirror room.

The Mirror Room

Formerly known as the glass drawing-room, a plaque to the right of the door records the 1903 Privy Council meeting of Edward VII. Now carpeted, the floor of rosewood veneered on mahogany was designed by Robert Hardy. Fourteen mirrors 27feet high, the largest to be produced at the time, were supplied by Messrs Swinburne and Co. of Newcastle at a cost of £3,000. Their wide gilt frames, patterned with fleur-de-lys, were fixed and gilded by James Lindsay of Sunderland in 1848. He also applied gilding to the elaborate ceiling, each panel painted with mythological, pastoral and aerial subjects.

Pilasters of rare Piatle marble adorn the walls, while white marble was used to create a stunning fireplace, intricately carved with birds, animals, fruits and foliage. At either side, gilded figures of buxom beauty, winged and helmeted, adorned with fruit and foliage. In the centre,

Napoleon. Other paintings record the major battles in which they were engaged. By the window, near the bookcase, hangs a portrait of the Marquess of Anglesey, who served in the Peninsular Wars with Wellington. Despite losing a leg at Waterloo, he fathered eighteen children and lived to the age of eighty five. The people of Anglesey erected a monument to his heroism. The leg was accorded its own monument at Waterloo, before later being disinterred, the bones put on display.

The impressive glass fronted bookcase, which looks particularly fine when illuminated, was installed in the 1980s, along with the conference table and the wine red leather chairs. Neil Trinder of Sheffield, responsible for several pieces of fine furniture in the Hall, created the carved chandelier. A striking portrait of the 6th Marquess (1884-1915) in hunting pink adds the final touch to a room redolent of the history of Wynyard and its importance in the world.

The Mirror/Drawing Room before the 1980's refurbishment (with permission of RCHM)

The Mirror Room today, refurbished by Rupert Lord (Photograph courtesy of Chapman Brown Photography)

beneath the marble top, the fearsome gilded face of a minotaur, horned and bearded. The original Louis Quatorze style furniture, burnished and gilded, covered in pink and white satin damask, gave the room its alternative name, the pink drawing room.

The Ballroom

More mahogany doors by Henry Burnell lead in to the ball room, with its Siena marble pilasters, and elaborate vaulted plasterwork ceiling by Daniel Nevin. 86 feet long, 42 feet high and 36 feet wide, the room may have been heightened after the 1841 fire, a bedroom above removed to allow the increase in height.

The walls were originally painted to resemble lapis lazuli, a precious stone prized for its vibrant blue colour, retained in a more muted shade in the modern decoration. Large family portraits, now replaced with fine mirrors, originally hung above the two immense Florentine fireplaces of choice inlaid marble. In the centre, the crown signifying a Marquess is flanked by a dexter gauntlet erect holding a sword, symbol of the Vanes, while the Tempests are represented by the gryphon passant, signifying military courage, strength and leadership.

Expertly restored in the 1980s, the striking coat of arms above the door, emblazoned with the Londonderry motto

Mirror Room fireplace detail

Ballroom ceiling

Mirror Room fireplace detail

One of a matching pair of Florentine fireplaces in the Ballroom

The Marquess Coronet

The Tempest Gryphon

'*Metuenda Corolla Draconis*'
'Fear the dragon's crest', shows clearly the gauntlets of
the Vanes, the small birds or martlets of the Tempests and
the red lions of the Stewarts. Also incorporated is the

The Vane Gauntlet

Londonderry coat of arms above a Ballroom door

The Newcastle Courant of 18 January 1884 recorded that the ballroom ' *when completed, will be one of the most magnificent rooms in the kingdom.'* The Prince and Princess of Wales stayed at Wynyard in December 1883, at the invitation of the 5th Marquess, although he spent very little time at Wynyard, living mostly at his wife's family home in Wales. He died in November 1884, just a few months after the royal visit. Perhaps his son, the 6th Marquess and his wife Theresa, ensured completion of the work in the ballroom. During restoration in the 1980s, the immense chandelier was brought in from the family wing created in the 1960s. Robert Hardy designed the original windows, architraves and cornices, as well as the original doors, mahogany on the inside, deal on the reverse, now replaced with glazed doors, which lead in to the conservatory.

The conservatory

In the mid 19th century, building costs for the conservatory alone approached £6,000. A large Norfolk Island Pine, the first introduced into this country, took pride of place.

The Conservatory in current use

shield of the Talbots, family of Theresa Chetwynd-Talbot, eldest daughter of the 19th Earl of Shrewsbury, wife of the 6th Marchioness of Londonderry. Alton Towers in Staffordshire, the family seat from 1831, became a theme park in the 1980s. The coronet signifies a marquess. The figure to the left is described in heraldic terms as a moor, wreathed about the temples argent and azur (blue and silver) holding a shield of the last, garnished or (gold) charged with the sun in splendour. Harking back to the time of the Crusades, the Moor represents the antiquity and chivalry of the Londonderry family.

Filled with the scent of orange and lemon trees, choice exotics, rare and costly flowers such as magnolia, camellias and orchids, the conservatory provided beautiful cut flowers for the house and elegant corsages for the ladies. 27 feet high, 77 feet long, and 60 feet wide, in 1964, the conservatory was converted into an open air swimming pool. Its roof replaced as part of the major restoration work of the 1980s, the four cast iron pillars from the original conservatory remain. Near the modern

Picture postcard of the Conservatory (George Nairn's collection)

bar, a photograph taken in the 1890s shows how the conservatory would have looked in earlier days. The present pale green colour scheme, large stone vases and appropriate floral arrangements combine to restore the conservatory to its former glory.

The enfilade

From the conservatory, when the doors between each room are opened, the impressive *enfilade* of rooms envisaged in the 1822 designs of Philip Wyatt can be fully appreciated.

Returning from the conservatory, through the Ball Room and the Mirror Room, we cross the vestibule, with its intricately designed floor of rosewood and satinwood, to enter the library.

The library

Mahogany doors by Henry Burnell, their frames ornately gilded and carved with symbols relating to the arts and music, lead in to the library, where Burnell used ebony, ormolu and tortoiseshell to create the four magnificent bookcases, the gilding applied by James Lindsay. The remarkable boulle (or buhl) panels, sensitively restored in the 1980s, are named after Andre Charles Boulle (1642-1732), the French inventor of this type of marquetry. Very popular during the reign of the Sun King,

The Enfilade

The Library with its original decorative Burnell bookcases

of King George IV by Sir Thomas Lawrence, also surveyed the room. Between the windows, tall gilded pier glasses, topped with gilded coronets, increase the impression of space and light. As in the mirror room, the floor, designed by Robert Hardy, is bordered in rosewood veneered on mahogany, still visible beyond the Durham carpet. The vibrant pink decoration used previously was

Ornately decorated mahogany door frames by Henry Burnell

replaced in the 1980s by the present dark blue-green wallpaper designed by Rupert Lord and Norman Gibson of Sandersons.

Louis XIV of France (1638-1715), the style reflects the ostentatious Louis Quatorze designs beloved of Philip Wyatt, architect of Wynyard Hall.

The marble chimney pieces, carved with fruits and flowers, were originally topped by mantel mirrors, now replaced by fine portraits of General Sir Charles Stewart, later the 3rd Marquess of Londonderry, his wife Frances Anne and her close friend Czar Alexander I of Russia. Formerly, a splendid full length portrait

Boulle panel of bookcase with gilding applied by James Lindsay

The Library showing portraits of Czar Alexander I and Frances Anne

The ante room

From the library, a screen of marble pillars leads into the ante-room, now a small bar area. Built by Thomas Scotson of Wolviston, just a few miles from Wynyard, the pillars are surmounted with decoration carved by Daniel Nevin. Above the chimney piece, a stone arch, elaborately carved with the floral motif seen elsewhere in the Hall, surmounts a beautiful coloured glass panel, created in about 1849 by William Wailes of Newcastle, responsible for much of the stained glass in the Hall. Wailes' predilection for pink glass is seen clearly in the vase of flowers, while the circular panel above shows the Londonderry coat of arms. At the top, the dagger-clutching gauntlet of the Vanes and the gryphon passant of the Tempests flank the coronet of a Marquess. The two circular shields and their supporters echo those seen in the statue gallery, the medals and honours won by the 3rd

Marquess hanging beneath the shield on the left. At the base, the ever present Londonderry motto *'Metuenda Corolla Draconis', 'Fear the Dragon's Crest'*. William Wailes also designed the beautiful stained glass skylight, set into the ceiling.

A portrait of Emily Hobart, Marchioness of Londonderry dominates the room, while the gentleman in shooting gear is Lord Henry John

Ante-room stained glass window

Henry, younger brother of the 6th Marquess,
hanging in the Ante-room

Vane-Tempest, younger brother of the 6th Marquess. With youngest brother Herbert, both bachelors, he was a frequent visitor to Wynyard and appears in many photographs of shooting parties held during the 1890s.

The boudoir

Beyond the ante-room to the Wellington Restaurant and not open to the public, the boudoir, situated on the south side of the Hall overlooking the lake, is now used as an office. The beautiful ceiling, elaborately gilded, panelled and painted with classical scenes, is completed by a roundel of cherubs by George Jackson. Described on his

trade card as "Composition ornament manufacturer to His Majesty", granted a royal warrant by George IV in 1826, Jackson and his sons maintained the royal connection, in 1840 supplying Queen Victoria with several large frames for mirrors and pictures in Buckingham Palace.

From the French *'bouder'*, to sulk, a lady's boudoir was not a bedroom but a private drawing room, used for activities such as embroidery, letter writing or spending time with one's romantic partner. Resplendent in crimson and gold damask, in 1857, according to Fordyce, the room contained valuable miniature portraits of the family. Originally the private drawing room of Frances Anne, Marchioness of Londonderry, the boudoir was also devoted to the use of royal guests, including the Prince and Princess of Wales on their visit to the 5th Marquess and his wife, Mary Cornelia, in January 1884. In later years, estate children came to the boudoir for Sunday School lessons from Theresa, Marchioness of Londonderry.

We can now only imagine the superb cupboards with glass panelled doors of ebony and ormolu installed by Gillow and Co., who, throughout the 18th and 19th centuries produced furniture bearing the unmistakable characteristics of fine quality, simple designs and perfect proportion. Found in many stately homes, Tatton Park in Cheshire houses one of the largest collections of Gillow furniture. Still highly prized, a Victorian kidney-shaped pedestal desk sold at auction in 2006 for £54,000, more than twice the estimate. Amalgamation with the Liverpool company Waring in 1897 rather reduced the former quality and distinction. In 1822, furniture for Wynyard Hall was also supplied by Morant and Co., recognized throughout the nineteenth century as amongst the most eminent cabinet makers in England.

According to Pevsner, the scagliola, a form of imitation marble used to create the surround of the fireplace, was provided by William Croggan, who in the early 1800s, helped to manufacture and promote Coadstone. Used by Robert Adam (1728-1792), famous for his fireplaces, the material, also popular for coats of arms and outdoor sculptures, was very durable, having been fired in a kiln, like ceramics. Wynyard's designer Philip Wyatt also used a combination of brass and glass to design an unusual chimneypiece, framing old Italian alabaster carvings, possibly those which were saved from the 1841 fire. No longer present in the boudoir, according to Fordyce in

The Boudoir, pictured before the 1980's refurbishment (with permission of RCHM)

1857, the antique sculpture was created by the Baroque artist Il Fiammingo. Born in Belgium in 1597 as Francois Duquesnoy, Il Fiammingo gained his Italian name in Rome, where he spent most of his artistic career, collaborating with renowned artists such as Bernini and Rubens. His father Jerome produced, in 1619, the famous sculpture of the Manneken Pis in Brussels.

The dining room (Wellington Restaurant)

From the ante-room, Henry Burnell mahogany doors lead into the great dining room, 60 feet long and 30 feet wide, apparently an enlargement of the Benjamin Dean Wyatt

design for the dining room at Wellington's London home, Apsley House. Formerly very pale, the vibrant colour of the room was created in the 1980s by interior designer Rupert Lord. A Sanderson wallpaper design from the 1880s, recoloured in four shades of red, contrasts beautifully with the pale grey marble of the dado, the pilasters and the door frame and provides a sumptuous background for the immense portraits of the Londonderry family. Many were painted by Sir Thomas Lawrence (1769-1830), one of the most celebrated artists in Europe in the early decades of the nineteenth century and the greatest British portrait painter of his generation.

The Dining Room, now the Wellington Restaurant

In 1842, John Webb completed the plaster work and Robert Hardy the carpentry, while Frederick Dolman was responsible for the sumptuous gilding, the intricate ornamentation in the cove restored in the 1980s. Its ceiling ornamented in white and gold, the Wellington Restaurant, as the room is now known, originally contained a large chandelier rescued from the fire in 1841, despite weighing about a ton. Corner marble tables supported by carved figures replicate those originally found in the room, when antique tables of green Verde marble were supported by full sized figures of Neptune on a sea horse, his tridents richly burnished in gold. Upon the tables, in the four corners of the room, carved wooden torcheres or candelabra were created by Dick Reid of York for the modern restoration. Facing each other across the dining room, a pair of impressive black marble fireplaces still provide a stunning focal point.

Above the fire place on the right, a superb equestrian portrait shows the 3rd Marquess of Londonderry in the uniform of the 10th Hussars, as worn at the Battle of Benevente, when he '*with a very inferior force, charged and overthrew one of the best corps of cavalry in the French army.*' The extract on the splendid scroll beneath the portrait was written in December 1808 by Sir John Moore, killed at the battle of Corunna in 1809. To the left of this portrait, the 3rd Marquess is portrayed wearing the robes of the Order of the Garter, conferred in 1853, just a year before his death.

To the right, a 1904 portrait by John Singer Sargent shows the 6th Marquess of Londonderry carrying the Sword of State at the coronation in August 1902 of King Edward VII. The page, the Hon. Wentworth Henry Canning Beaumont (1890-1956), later became 2nd. Viscount Allendale and Lord Lieutenant of Northumberland. Nephew to the 6th Marquess, his mother was Alexandrina Vane-Tempest, known as Aline, youngest daughter of the 5th Marquess and Marchioness. On the opposite wall, a central portrait of Frances Anne and two of her children is flanked by portraits of the 3rd Marquess and his sister-in-law Emily Hobart, wife of Castlereagh.

Restored to glory

In its heyday, a country house of some repute, Wynyard has seen many changes of fortune and occupation has varied considerably through the years. Although beloved by the 3rd Marquess and his wife, Frances Anne, their immediate heirs, the 4th and 5th Marquess did not live much at Wynyard, whereas the 6th and 7th Marquess

Torchere by Dick Reid

frequently enjoyed holidays and entertained eminent visitors at Wynyard. The 8th and 9th Marquess and their families clearly loved Wynyard, but changing times and family circumstances meant that the Londonderrys were finally obliged to leave their family seat in 1987.

Over the centuries much of the original furniture, valuable paintings and Londonderry heirlooms, including magnificent jewellery and glassware were lost to Wynyard. The Londonderry jewels are now in display in London's Victoria and Albert museum, a fine cut glass table service of over 200 pieces engraved with the Londonderry coat of arms has returned to a museum in Sunderland, the city where it was originally created. Requisitioned for use by the Ministry of Defence during World War II, the Hall became a teacher training college from 1946-1960, much of the Hall's finery removed or covered in plainer materials for safe keeping. In the early 1960s, the hall was adapted for the use of the young family of the 9th Marquess, living in one wing of the house. The conservatory was converted to a swimming pool open to the elements. In 1982, the main part of the ground floor, empty for many years, was redecorated and brought into use for conferences and dinners.

After acquiring Wynyard in 1987, Sir John Hall appointed designer Rupert Lord to begin the work of restoring the Hall to its former glory. Within three months, work was completed on the first phase of five rooms, including the chapel. A further three months saw completion of the remaining seven rooms, as well as bedrooms on the first floor. Responsible for all the decoration and furnishings, Rupert Lord and the superb team of craftsmen employed in the 1980s have restored Wynyard to the glory envisaged by the original team in the 1820s. Respect for the history of the hall, the achievements of the 3rd Marquess of Londonderry and his wife Frances Anne, the memory of their descendants and the talents of skilled craftsmen, past and present, are evident in every footstep of our walk though the magnificently restored Wynyard Hall.

Charles William Vane-Tempest-Stewart, 3rd Marquess, portrait in the Wellington Restaurant. Sculptor Raffaelle Monti is said to have used this image to create the bronze equestrian statue in Durham City

CHAPTER 6

THE MEMORIAL ROOM

A later addition to the house, the memorial room, constructed in honour of the 3rd Marquess after his death in 1854, is reached from the conservatory. Beneath a beautiful glazed skylight created by William Wailes, a Minton tiled floor, bearing family emblems, battle honours and the emblazoned motto of the Order of the Garter, *'Honi Soit Qui Mal y Pense'*, leads in to the memorial room. Frances Anne, Marchioness of Londonderry, commissioned her friend, amateur architect, the Hon. Thomas Liddell of

Ravensworth Castle to design the room, which celebrates the career and accomplishments of her beloved husband.

Constructed by Messrs. W. and C. Burnup of Newcastle, and completed in 1857, the memorial room measures 40 feet 9 inches long, 26 feet wide and 21 feet high. Between 1903 and 1910, when the 6th Marquess commissioned the extension to the chapel, the fourth wall was removed, replaced by a screen of six columns of Cipollino marble.

Tiled floor leading in to the Memorial Room. At the top, the coronet of a Marquess, decorated with strawberry leaves and silver balls, in the centre the motto of the Order of the Garter 'Honi Soit Qui Mal Y Pense'. From left to right, the medals and awards won by the 3rd Marquess.
Talavera medal, Knight of St George of Russia, Order of the Tower and of the Sword Commander's badge (Portuguese), Order of the Tower and the Sword Star, Hanoverian Guelphic Order, Peninsular War Medal beneath the Badge of the Order of the Garter, Knight Grand Cross of the Bath, Royal Order of the Black Eagle of Prussia, Royal Order of the Red Eagle of Prussia, Royal Order of the Sword

The memorial Room (with permission of RCHM)

Streaked white and green, Cipollino marble from Italy, was favoured by Hadrian for the building of the Pantheon in Rome. Purple tinted Pavonazza marble from Turkey, named after the peacock, completes the columns, their impressive bases large blocks of white marble.

The field of battle

The names and dates of battles in which Lord Londonderry fought are inscribed in letters of gold on the walls. From Douro, Corunna and Talavera in 1809, through Busaco in 1810 and Fuentes de Onor in 1811, the list is a triumphant roll call of battle honours. A plaque commemorating the battle of Badajos (1812) is set in to the floor leading in to the chapel. Presumably it would originally have been displayed on the north wall, along with plaques celebrating

the battles of Sabagal, Culm and Leipzig. More gilt engraved marble plaques record the regimental service of the 3rd Marquess, who, as Charles Stewart, had served as Colonel or Lieutenant-Colonel in the 2nd Life Guards, the 5th Light Dragoons, the 25th Dragoons and two regiments of Hussars, the 10th and the 18th.

The skylight by William Wailes (1808-1881)

The skylight, bright with heraldic glass designed by William Wailes of Newcastle, responsible for much of the stained glass in Wynyard Hall, celebrates once again the battle honours of the 3rd Marquess. One of the most noted stained glass designers in Victorian Britain, Wailes loved using rich red glass and other bold colours in his predominantly mediaeval designs, often combining them to great effect.

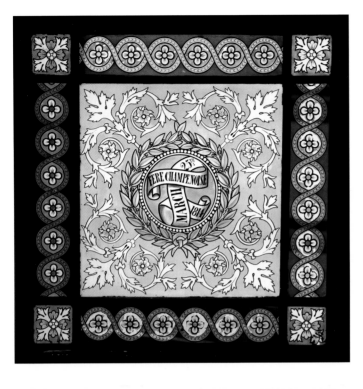 

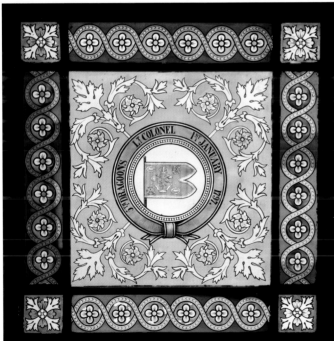 

Examples from the William Wailes skylight commemorating Peninsular War battles

Many of his windows contain a great deal of pink glass. One of twenty five stained glass artists who exhibited in the Crystal Palace Exhibition of 1851, Wailes designed windows for the cathedrals at Chichester, Peterborough and Gloucester, as well as many northern churches, including the Cathedral Church of St. Mary in Newcastle.

Memorial Room dedicated to the 3rd Marquess

The niches

Sixteen slender marble pilasters of the Corinthian order surround the room, each completed with an ornate capital decorated with acanthus leaves. The cornice, beams, and elaborate ceiling, now white, were originally painted and richly gilded by James Lindsay of Sunderland. Niches, with plate glass doors now contain richly gilded illuminated scrolls, many of them created by James Lindsay. The niches were originally created to display the various orders, trophies and objects of interest acquired during the eventful career of the third Marquess, including the Order of the Garter, the Grand Cross of the Bath, and the Russian medal awarded him on the capture of Paris. Many of the original objects were later removed, including the uniforms of the 3rd Marquess and the sword and cuirasse of Colonel de la Motte, vanquished and disarmed by Charles Stewart in single combat in 1811 at the battle of Fuentes de Onor.

Memorials of peace

In 1884, the Newcastle Courant reported the Prince of Wales most impressed by the room, which, at that time, also contained armour, weaponry and torn flags of campaign, as well as the writing desk and ink-stand used in 1815 at the Congress of Vienna, attended by Charles Stewart as British plenipotentiary. His half-brother Lord Castlereagh, as British Foreign Secretary, signed the treaties of Vienna and Paris, bringing peace to Europe at the end of the Peninsular Wars with Napoleon. Also on display originally were letters from such eminent figures as Louis Napoleon, Czar Alexander of Russia, the Kings of Sweden, Prussia, Portugal and Hanover, Prince Albert and Queen Victoria. The Congress of Vienna ink-stand can now be seen in London's Victoria and Albert Museum.

Celebrating the achievements of the Marquess after his fighting days were over, one glass niche contained the silver trowels used to lay the foundation stones of the new town, church and blast furnaces at Seaham Harbour, founded by the 3rd Marquess. Also on display was the spade used in February 1853 to cut the first sod of the Londonderry Railway, running between Seaham and Sunderland, as well as the wheelbarrow used to carry it away.

The marble sarcophagus

The empty white carved marble sarcophagus, with the recumbent figure of the 3rd Marquess in full uniform, was commissioned in 1854 from Raffaelle Monti, the Italian sculptor who also created the statue of the 3rd Marquess on horseback, in Durham City marketplace since 1861. Originally placed in the family mausoleum at Long Newton, the sarcophagus was moved to Wynyard in 1904. Above the monumental marble table on the wall behind the sarcophagus, a coat of arms bears the motto of the Order of the Bath (GCB), awarded to the 3rd Marquess as Sir Charles Stewart in 1813. *Tria Juncta in Uno* signifies the three countries of Great Britain united as one kingdom.

The plaque is inscribed thus :-

'This room is dedicated to the memory of Charles William Vane, third Marquess of Londonderry K.G., G.C.B., G.C.H., Grand Cross of the Black Eagle of Prussia, Grand Cross of the Sword of Sweden, Knight of St George of Russia, Knight of the Tower and Sword of Portugal, by his affectionate widow.

The rewards of his early achievements have been placed here, and will tell them late to posterity doing justice to heroism of the gallant soldier, of Peculiar fame, who nobly fought with the Duke of Wellington at Fuentes de Onor, Benevente, Talavera, Badajos, Busaco, and Corunna, and who at Leipsic, Gulm, and Fere Champenoise received the crowning honours of his military career.

Sheathing his sword he became no less distinguished as founder of Seaham Harbour and town which owed their existence to him; and his talent, energy and indomitable perseverance were as remarkable characteristics of his private life as his daring and bravery were conspicuous in the field of battle.'

Marble sarcophagus of the 3rd Marquess

CHAPTER 7

THE CHAPEL

Mediaeval records indicate a chapel of some sort within the manor of Wynyard in 1312. Over a hundred years later, Sybil, wife of Sir Roger Conyers, secured an agreement with the Bishop of Durham to provide a chaplain for the services of the Wynyard house. The first service took place on 3 November 1454. The present chapel owes its existence to three Marquesses of Londonderry, the 3rd, 5th and 6th, as well as numerous skilled craftsmen and designers, including those modern restorers who brought the chapel to its present glory.

Wynyard saw many changes over the centuries and, when the 3rd Marquess and his wife arrived in the early 1800s, the house changed considerably. Their original chapel, much smaller than the present building, was entirely contained within the house, behind the triple window visible from the exterior on the north wall at the front of the Hall. Rebuilt after the Wynyard Hall fire of 1841, the chapel was consecrated and opened for divine service on 16 July 1849. The chapel, in those days, would simply have been the part now known as the chancel, the eastern end of the present chapel, leading to the altar.

The nave, leading from the chancel, was constructed in 1880 by James Brooks, one of the foremost church architects of the time. The 5th Marquess commissioned Brooks to extend the chapel to the west, creating the long nave and incorporating the magnificent windows and organ. Between 1903 and 1910, during the time of the 6th Marquess, designer Henry Wilson incorporated quantities of marble and carved wood to create the ornate, Romanesque chapel we see today, using marble pillars to form a beautiful link with the memorial room, erected in 1857 in honour of the 3rd Marquess by his widow Frances Anne.

James Brooks (1825-1901)

The son of a farmer, Brooks invented a threshing machine and a new type of ploughshare before turning his attention to architecture. He designed many London churches, favouring the Gothic revival style, characterized by wide lofty naves, narrow aisles, raised chancels and lancet windows. As well as designing the Wynyard chapel, he also worked on Londonderry House, the family's sumptuous home in the capital.

In common with many other Victorian architects, Brooks insisted on being personally responsible for all the detailing in his buildings, including elements such as the woodwork surrounding the organ. In his design, beautifully grained solid Spanish mahogany gave the interior of the chapel an air of splendour, Corinthian columns of white marble supporting the gilded ceiling and its deep cornices. Although much of Brooks' original design for the interior of the chapel was altered in the early 1900s, carved capitals against the ceiling in the nave the only reminder of those original white marble columns, the exterior of the chapel remained unchanged. A fellow of the Royal Institute of British Architects (RIBA) from 1866, Brooks was awarded their gold medal in 1895.

EXTERIOR

The exterior of the chapel echoes the simple design of the memorial room alongside, with its quasi-blocked windows. Built in 1857, the moulded cornice and parapet of the memorial room, slightly lower than that of the chapel, continue the roof line of the conservatory. The nave, constructed in 1880, is single storey and rectangular in shape, faced with coursed ashlar, a type of dressed stone used throughout Wynyard. Slates cover the slightly pitched gable roof. The north side of the nave, facing the entrance court, has four stepped buttresses reaching half way up the wall, each one topped by a ball. Within the five bays thus created sit three rectangular windows, their stone frames topped with triangular pediments.

The entrance to the Chapel

At the west front, the entrance door is set in a slightly projecting central block, which rises above the parapet to end in a pediment containing a Greek cross. The round headed entrance arch is rusticated, that is, composed of large blocks of stone separated by deep joints. Its broad bevelled edge, or chamfer, surrounds a glazed tympanum and panelled wooden doors. This lower stage is topped by a moulded cornice with carved circular motifs or roundels in the spandrels, the roughly triangular shapes above and to either side of the entrance arch. In the upper stage, a large round headed window, framed by a delicately chamfered arch, is seen to stunning effect from the interior of the chapel.

INTERIOR

The Arts and Crafts screen

The entrance door leads in to a small vestibule, its panelled wooden ceiling simply adorned with one central carving. Double rectangular doors open into the nave, through a magnificent wooden screen, designed by artist Henry Wilson, commissioned by the 6th Marquess between 1903 and 1910. Exquisitely carved animals and foliage in the style of the Arts and Crafts movement decorate the wooden panels and doors of the screen, as well as its three round headed arches and the glazed tympanum above. Above the door, the central panel of the screen bears the coat of arms of the Bishop of York, while that of the Bishop of Durham appears in the two outer panels. According to the 1912 garden album of Theresa Lady Londonderry, the screen was created from a cedar tree, blown down in Wynyard Park after flourishing there for 200 years. Marble work executed by Messrs. Davison of Marylebone, London, patterned and veined in shades of green, brown and cream completes the stunning effect.

The nave

Black and white marble squares, laid chequer fashion, lead through the nave. A cornice of pale green marble contrasts with the vibrant blue of the walls, which provide a stunning background to the religious paintings, including

The Arts and Crafts screen

Studies of the Madonna and Child

*Moses taking down the Ten Commandments,
attributed to Andrea del Sarto (1486-1530)*

various portrayals of the Madonna and Child. Between the two windows on the north side of the nave, the portrait of Moses taking down the Ten Commandments is attributed to a major Italian artist, Andrea del Sarto of Florence (1486-1530). Two pairs of pink marble columns divide the nave from the chancel. A low screen, marble faced and set with three panels of differently coloured squares of marble on each side, leads in to the chancel.

The Chancel

*Above the altar, Madonna and Child with St Francis &
St Jerome, attributed to Francesco Francia (1450 - 1517)*

The chancel

The panelled barrelled ceiling is intricately painted,
intertwined patterning incorporating fruits and flowers.
Heraldic shields at the junctions include the Londonderry
coat of arms, the Vanes represented by three gauntlets, the
Tempests by three small birds or martlets and the Stewarts
by the red lion, repeated on the shield opposite. The
chancel is entirely faced in marble, veined in green and
purple, the floor composed of larger slabs of marble inset
with diamond shapes. A series of narrow pilasters in green
marble divide the upper walls, a contrasting pinkish
marble used to create a slight entablature at the top and a
dado at the base. The chancel arch concludes at the high
altar, above which hangs a painting of the Madonna and
Child attributed to Francesco Francia of Bologna (1450-
1517). Above the altar, the impressive baldachino (or
canopy), patterned on the underside in golden mosaic, is
supported by a pair of free standing marble columns with
scallop capitals set on tall pedestals. The marble
patterning of the pillars is repeated in those dividing
the chapel from the memorial room.

Henry Wilson (1864-1934)

Engaged by Charles
Stewart, 6th Marquess of
Londonderry, Henry
Wilson brought an Italian
Romanesque influence,
incorporating a great deal
of Italian marble within
the chapel and adding,
between the chapel and
the memorial room, six
columns of Cipollino
marble with bases of
Pavonazza marble. From
Italy, Cipollino marble,
favoured by Hadrian
for the building of the
Pantheon in Rome, is
streaked white and green.
Pavonazza, from Turkey,
contains many colours
and is named after the
peacock.

As chief assistant to the
renowned architect John
Dando Sedding, Henry
Wilson completed several
important commissions,
including Holy Trinity
Church in Sloane Street,
London. In 1891, Wilson
took over the business
on the sudden death of his
mentor, bringing together
the skills of an impressive
team of artists and
craftsmen in a common
creative cause. Henry
Wilson developed skills
in sculpture, silverwork,
church plate and jewellery,
as well as architecture and
served as President of the
Arts and Crafts Exhibition
Society from 1915-22.

St Cuthbert

*Memorial window
portraying St George*

St Hilda

Pre-Raphaelite style window bearing the initials LD

Stained glass by Louis Davis (1860-1941)

The chapel's stained glass windows, designed by Louis Davis, were installed between 1903 and 1910, when the 6th Marquess commissioned major redesigning of the chapel and memorial room. Described by historian Nikolaus Pevsner as *"the last of the pre-Raphaelites"*, the influence of artists such as Dante Gabriel Rossetti (1828-1882), founder of the pre-Raphaelite brotherhood, is obvious in Louis Davis' beautiful windows. An ardent

follower of the Arts and Crafts group, Davis also admired Edward Burne-Jones (1833-1898) and William Morris (1834-1896), who produced magnificent stained glass for churches as well as works of art. Louis Davis' wife, Edith, is thought to be the model for much of his work.

Originally a water colourist and book illustrator, Louis Davis became renowned for the translucent, glowing colours of his stained glass. He designed windows for many churches in the south of England, as well as Cheltenham College, Dunblane Abbey, St.Giles' Cathedral, Edinburgh, St. Patrick's Cathedral , Dublin and the home of the Duke and Duchess of Bedford, Woburn Abbey. Admired for moving away from the crude colouring of the Victorian period, Davis insisted that any window, coloured or otherwise, should admit light.

The window near the entrance porch depicts Durham Cathedral above the River Wear and the old Fulling Mill. The old style bishop's mitre and halo suggest Saint Cuthbert, possibly carrying the Lindisfarne Gospels. Violets symbolise watchfulness and faithfulness. The window portraying a young Crusader knight slaying a serpent, possibly Saint George and the Dragon, its motto *Deus Noster Refugium et Vertus,* was dedicated in 1905 by the 6th Marquess to the memory of his father, the 5th Marquess, who died in 1884. The next window shows Saint Hilda, the banner *'heruteum'* referring to the peninsula 'island of the hart' at Hartlepool, where she ran a monastery founded in 640. The lilies, often the symbol of the Madonna, also represent purity, chastity and Christianity.

The outstanding window at the east end of the chapel, to the left of the altar, the LD mark of Louis Davis clearly visible, vividly captures the pre-Raphaelite style in the beautiful face and tumbling locks of the girl, while the draughtsman-like depiction of the wooden organ reflects the artisanal influences of the Arts and Crafts movement. A plaque beneath the window records the dedication to Lord Henry John Vane-Tempest (1854-1905) by his mother Mary Cornelia, Marchioness of Londonderry, his sister Lady Alexandrina Beaumont and his brother Charles Stewart, 6th Marquess. Opposite this window, near the organ, a more recent plaque poignantly remembers Rupert Birley, *'whose spirit will remain at Wynyard forever'*. First-born son of Annabel, sister of Alastair, 9th Marquess of Londonderry, he disappeared in 1986, aged thirty, believed drowned off the coast of Togo

Foster and Andrews organ, built 1880

The organ

Mary Cornelia, Marchioness of Londonderry, presented the organ, built by Forster and Andrews of Hull, who made the case according to James Brooks' design. Completed on December 27th 1880 at a cost of £271.13.6, the organ was ordered by the Reverend H.A.V. Boddy of Wynyard Park. The design included a special concave pedal board, two composition pedals and a stool. The pipe work is of 'spotted metal' with burnished case pipes. Cleaned and overhauled in 1902, the organ was taken into storage for four months during 1903. D.W. Meiklejohn, estate manager for the 6th Lord Londonderry, ordered the work. Cleaned, tuned, fitted with new soundboards, motor and gearing at a cost of £192, it was restored to the chapel in August 1903. Twenty years later, an invoice itemized work to be carried out. *'To take the organ entirely to pieces, clean all the pipes and burnish the tongues of the reed, take the Swell, Great and Pedal Roundboards to pieces and repair them'* and much else. All for the princely sum of £85. According to Harrison and Harrison, organ builders of Meadowfield, Durham, *'as an unaltered Forster and Andrews instrument it certainly has historic value and deserves respect.'*

The chapel today

The 1923 invoice concluded, *'The work to be done in the best possible manner'*, an intention carried through to modern times, when extensive restoration work in the late 1980s produced the breathtaking chapel and memorial room we see today, at the beginning of the 21st century. During the time of the 8th and 9th Marquesses, the chapel regularly saw weddings of Wynyard tenants and their families, followed by a reception provided in the Hall by the Londonderrys. In its new guise as a fine country house hotel, Wynyard continues that tradition. The vision and determination of the 3rd Marquess, ambitious developments by the 5th and 6th, sensitive modern restoration coupled with outstanding craftsmanship combine in the Wynyard chapel to create a beautiful setting for the perfect wedding day.

in West Africa. Above the porch, a magnificent window, installed in 1907 to commemorate the wife of the 5th Marquess, is inscribed 'erected to the glory of God and in affectionate memory of Mary Cornelia 1828-1906.' The window portrays three women, one with a crystal ball, which may refer to Celtic legend, suggesting freedom from weariness or returning life to the dead. Another holds wheat and grapes, representing prosperity and fruitfulness, as well as the body and blood of Christ. The third, a garland of red roses in her hair, symbolises heavenly joy.

A view of the chapel showing the memorial window to Mary Cornelia, Lady Londonderry (Photograph courtesy of Holden and Jones)

CHAPTER 8

HENRY VANE TEMPEST

The Londonderry connection to Wynyard began in 1794, when Sir Henry Vane Tempest, father of Frances Anne, later wife of the 3rd Marquess of Londonderry, inherited the Hall and estate from his uncle, John Tempest. In the face of her parent's disapproval of the marriage, John's sister, Frances, had eloped with the Reverend Sir Henry Vane, prebend of Durham and Rector of Long Newton. Their son, also named Henry, born in 1771, was travelling abroad when he learned of his uncle's death and his own inheritance. His valet read a newspaper announcement requesting his master's immediate return. On arrival in England, Henry discovered that, during his absence, his own father had died too, thus making him Sir Henry Vane, 2nd Baronet. Adopting the name Tempest in accordance with his uncle's wishes, he became known as Sir Henry Vane Tempest.

Young, handsome and rich, Sir Henry soon left for London, enjoying a busy social life, usually accompanied by hard drinking. In 1837, long after Henry Vane's death, socialite Thomas Raikes described him as *'one of the handsomest men of his time, but one of the hardest livers... a very expensive man, fond of hunting, cock fighting and the Turf.'* Good natured, but by no means refined, Henry enjoyed the company of the Mohawks, fashionable young men about town known for their outrageous behaviour. Kind, generous and very popular with the ladies, the family of his future wife, aged eighteen when they met, did all they could to prevent their acquaintance developing.

Marriage to an heiress

However, Anne Catherine MacDonnell, Countess of Antrim, married Sir Henry, nine years her senior, at her mother's house in Hanover Square in April 1799. The marriage, adding to his own already considerable income the Glenarm property of his heiress wife, rendered him one of the richest commoners in England. 1800 saw the birth of their daughter, Frances Anne, who later described her parents as *'an ill assorted couple'*, who *'encouraged each other's follies and rushed into every species of extravagance.'* During his sojourns at Wynyard, he would remain at the dining table until five or six in the morning before putting on morning dress to accompany his bailiff walking over the estate. On October 25 1809, to celebrate the fiftieth year of the reign of King George III, he gave a great feast for 400 of his tenants, providing a large ox to be roasted, as well as bread and plenty of beer. Henry neglected his wife and daughter, leaving them for weeks at a time and spending vast amounts of money on theatres, hounds and racing. His illegitimate son, Jack Vane, later to become rector of Wigginton in Somerset and Chaplain to the House of Lords, was a regular playmate of the young Frances Anne at Wynyard.

Sir Henry Vane Tempest by P E Stroehling

Public life

A respected parliamentarian, Henry Vane Tempest served as mayor of Hartlepool in 1798 and 1806, as well as representing the County of Durham from 1807. In 1805, he was appointed High Sheriff of Antrim. In 1809, he laid the foundation stones for Durham Jail. Built to replace an earlier building, some of the expense was met by Shute Barrington, then Bishop of Durham, who pledged £2,000

The Vane Arms at Long Newton, showing the Vane coat of arms and motto Nec Temere Nec Timide – Neither rashly nor fearfully

towards the construction. On his death in 1813, an obituary recorded the valuable service of Sir Henry Vane Tempest under the administrations of William Pitt and Spencer Perceval, when *'such was the noble energy of his delivery and the masculine strength of his language that he governed the fixed attentions of his auditors and carried irresistible conviction to the mind.'* A far cry from the hard drinking dissolute young baronet of his early days.

The high living of his past had, however, taken its toll on his health. Suffering from gout, asthma and other ailments, as well as financial worries, he returned to Wynyard after the London season of 1813. Despite the best efforts of local physicians, a fit of apoplexy rendered him speechless and immobile. Two days later, he died, aged just 41, and was interred on 12 August 1813 in the family vault at Long Newton. In a crowded church, the tears and sighs of the congregation bore witness to the affection in which he had been held. *'It seemed as if everyone present had lost his dearest friend and nearest connection, so truly was he beloved and lamented'*, according to Edith, Marchioness of Londonderry, in her biography of Henry's daughter, Frances Anne. The young girl, aged thirteen at the time of her father's death, would eventually inherit a vast fortune as well as her ancestral home, Wynyard Hall.

The monument she erected in later years *'to the best and kindest of parents'* perhaps indicates a forgiving nature. Frances Anne, by then Baroness Stewart, records a man *'possessed of talents and interest, his career was marked by every trait of honour, manliness, integrity, generosity and liberality; lamented as much as he was revered and beloved, his loss is only justly to be appreciated by his numerous friends.'* The baronetcy inherited from his father became extinct on his death.

CHAPTER 9

HAMBLETONIAN

Hambletonian by George Stubbs 1800 (with permission of The National Trust)

In the nineteenth century, Wynyard boasted its own racecourse, a mile long, situated in the north west corner of the park to the west of North Lodge, complete with horse boxes and stables. Sir Henry Vane Tempest owned and bred many famous racehorses, kept at the racing stables of his paternal home, Long Newton. Sir Harry, as he was known, began racing soon after gaining his inheritance on the death of his uncle in August 1794. Just a few months later, in April and May 1795, horses ran under Sir Harry's name at Epsom and other racecourses. In 1798, he offered a reward of £100 for

the discovery of the person who had forced entry to his stables and attempted to strangle a valuable mare.

Sir Harry's most famous horse, Hambletonian, said to be one of the greatest racehorses of the 18th century, was sired by King Fergus, bred by John Hutchinson of Shipton-by-Beningbrough near York. Foaled in 1792, Hambletonian took his name from the racing area near Sutton Bank on the North Yorkshire Moors, where he won his first race in 1794. Racing for Sir Charles Turner of Kirkleatham Hall, he won the gold cup at Doncaster in

1795 and the St. Leger in 1796, beating Sir Harry's horse, Governor. Subsequently, in Sir Harry's colours, he won the Doncaster Cup and the Newmarket Craven Stakes.

Hambletonian won virtually all the races he ran in, the most famous being against Diamond at Newmarket on 25th March 1799. Unlike modern races, where several horses battle it out, in those days, horses were often put up against each other, one to one, by their owners. Sir Henry wagered 3,000 guineas on the outcome and could have lost his entire fortune and estate. Run over the Beacon course, a straight four miles and two furlongs, the race aroused enormous interest, more than a hundred thousand pounds placed in bets.

Hambletonian started at five to one on. After a hotly contested race, the leading jockey of his day, Frank Buckle, brought Hambletonian over the finish line, winning by half a neck. In recognition of the famous victory, Sir Henry commissioned George Stubbs, the renowned artist, to paint Hambletonian. One picture, later hung at Wynyard, vividly portrays the winning moment. The other, showing the horse being rubbed down after the race, is thought to be the finest Stubbs ever painted. Originally at Wynyard, the picture was taken in 1931 to Mount Stewart, the Londonderry home in Northern Ireland, now a National Trust property.

Wynyard's racing tradition

Unfortunately, Sir Henry was rather slower in settling his debts than Hambletonian had been in the race. In 1801, Stubbs sued him for non-payment. Hambletonian died on 28 March 1818, his body interred in Wynyard Park. The racing tradition established by Sir Harry continued at Wynyard well into the 20th century. The stallion Corcyra (1911-21), bred by the 6th Marquess, along with half-brothers Coup de Main and Benevente, raced regularly at Stockton and Newmarket, where he was narrowly beaten in the 2000 Guineas of 1914. The same year, he ran in the King Edward VI Stakes at the Ascot Derby before retiring to the Wynyard stud farm. Developed by Theresa, Marchioness of Londonderry, six paddocks, each surrounded by privet hedging, covered seventy acres of land. Polemarch, bred at Wynyard during the time of the 7th Marquess, won the 1921 St. Leger, the first Londonderry horse to do so for 125 years. Hambletonian's eleventh great grandson 'Fighting Charlie', named after the 3rd Marquess and owned by Lady Mairi Bury, daughter of the 7th, won the Ascot Gold Cup twice, in 1965 and 1966.

Hambletonian remembered

Local people commemorated the great horse, his name associated with several pubs in the area. White's trade directory of 1828 lists Horse Hambletonian, a public house, at Grindon, Thorpe Thewles, formerly part of the Wynyard estate. By 1851, it was known simply as Hambletonian, before becoming, in 1856, Hamilton Arms and in 1858, the Hamilton Russell Arms. Dispensing food and drink to this day, at the end of the 13th century, the land on which the pub stands was granted to the church to be 'kept in perpetual alms for the support of hospitality.' Amongst its many historic proprietors were Lord Boyne and the Marchioness of Londonderry. In Stockton High Street, the entrance to Hambletonian Yard is surmounted by a wrought iron outline of horse and jockey passing the winning post. The pub formerly situated in the yard and named after Hambletonian IV, a descendant of the original, is no more. The Hambletonian pub stood on the green in Norton, near Stockton from 1790-1935, the great horse a legend even before his momentous victory against Diamond.

CHAPTER 10

ROBERT HENRY STEWART
Viscount Castlereagh (1769 –1822), 2nd Marquess of Londonderry 1821

The Londonderry connection with Wynyard began in 1796, when, in the Irish peerage, Robert Stewart was created Earl of Londonderry, later raised to first Marquess of Londonderry in 1816. At that time, his son, Robert Henry, took the courtesy title Castlereagh, succeeding his father as 2nd Marquess of Londonderry in 1821. Only surviving son of his father's first marriage to Lady Sarah Frances Seymour, when his father married again, Robert acquired a half-brother, Charles, later to become the 3rd Marquess and husband of Frances Anne, heiress to Wynyard.

Marriage

In 1794, Robert Henry Stewart married Amelia (Emily) Hobart, daughter of John Hobart, 2nd Earl of Buckinghamshire, a former British Ambassador to Russia and Lord Lieutenant of Ireland. Emily's mother, Caroline, was granddaughter of William Conolly, Speaker of the Irish House of Commons in the early 18th century and one of the wealthiest landowners in Ireland. In 1796, whilst fighting in Ireland, Robert wrote home to his wife *'Remember you are a soldier's wife and must have no care now you are allowed fourpence a day in my absence.'*

Robert Henry Stewart, Lord Viscount Castlereagh from an original picture by T Lawrence RA, drawn by W Evans and engraved by H Meyer (© National Portrait Gallery, London)

Emily Hobart, Marchioness of Londonderry, 1772-1829 Portrait in the Wellington Restaurant

Noted in contemporary accounts for her attractiveness, volubility and eccentricities, well-known as a society hostess in Ireland and London, Emily Stewart provided vital support for her husband during some of his most important diplomatic missions. In later years, as one of the Lady Patronesses of Almack's Assembly Rooms, she took a leading role in the high society of Regency London. Devoted to each other to the end, the couple had no children, but cared for their nephew, the young Frederick Stewart, while the boy's father, Stewart's half-brother, Charles, later the 3rd Marquess, was serving in the army.

Political life

Early in his career, as Chief Secretary for Ireland, Stewart helped to put down the Irish Rebellion of 1798, granted

The Congress of Vienna by Jean Baptiste Isabey

The map of Europe redrawn at the Congress of Vienna 1815

Chairs from the Congress of Vienna, now at Mount Stewart, showing the Londonderry coat of arms (with permission of The National Trust)

the Freedom of the City of Dublin at the Easter Assembly of that year. Instrumental in securing the passage of the controversial Act of Union of 1800, marking the end of the Irish parliament, he was not popular in Ireland. As Secretary of State for the War Office from 1807-9, Castlereagh encouraged the advancement of Sir Arthur Wellesley, later Duke of Wellington, during the Peninsular War. Offered the post of Adjutant-General to the Duke, Charles Stewart received strong words of advice from his half-brother. *'The course of your future military life must materially hinge upon your present decision... make every other consideration subordinate to your fame as a soldier... I am confident of your energy and capacity. Resolve to rise, and you will succeed.'*

An argument over the deployment of troops led, in 1809, to a duel with Foreign Secretary George Canning. Castlereagh, regarded as one of the best shots of his day, wounded his opponent in the thigh, while Canning, who had never before fired a pistol, widely missed his mark. Both men eventually resigned from office, Castlereagh returning to the cabinet as Foreign Secretary in 1812, when he also became Leader of the House of Commons in the government formed by Lord Liverpool after the assassination of Spencer Perceval.

Diplomatic life

Central to the management of the coalition that defeated Napoleon in 1812, Castlereagh also played an important role as principal British diplomat at the Congress of Vienna of 1814 to 1815, where momentous decisions taken to redraw the map of Europe included the creation of the Netherlands. A noted statesman and diplomat, the 2nd Marquess is considered by many one of the most distinguished Foreign Secretaries in British history, serving in Lord Liverpool's government from 1812 to 1822. However, as Leader of the House of Commons, he was the target of much public dislike. Lines written by the poet Shelley, *'I met murder on the way, He had a mask like Castlereagh'*, refer to his responsibility for introducing The Six Acts, a measure which led, in 1819, to the bloody Peterloo Massacre in Manchester. In 1820, after an assassination attempt on the entire cabinet, Castlereagh took to carrying pistols in self-defence. Overwhelmed by the pressure of work and the fear that plots were being hatched against him, he committed suicide in 1822, just one year after succeeding his father to the title of Marquess of Londondery. At his country residence, Loring Hall in Kent, on the morning of August 12, taking a knife he had concealed in his dressing case, he cut his throat. The coroner's inquest recorded a verdict of Unsound Mind, but Charles Stewart considered *'the toils of office had become too burdensome'* for his beloved older half-brother.

Memorial

Granted a public funeral and burial at Westminster Abbey, a monument to his memory, not erected until 1850, occupies a commanding position in the north transept, ironically opposite that of his old enemy Canning, who died in 1827. The Newcastle Courant of 14 June 1850 described the life-size figure of Castlereagh in pure white Carrera marble, which *'well preserves the mien for which the original was*

Robert Henry Stewart, Lord Viscount Castlereagh, in Garter robes, originally painted 1821 by Sir Thomas Lawrence, engraved 1823 by C Turner (Sir John Hall's private collection)

distinguished.' One hand contains a scroll, inscribed 'Peace of Paris 1814', the other supports the garter robes, flowing around the figure. The marble pedestal beneath is inscribed, *'History will record the success and splendour of his public career during a period of unexampled difficulty in the annals of Europe, in which he successfully filled the highest offices under the crown; and Ireland will never forget the statesman of the legislative union.'*

The tribute *'to the best of brothers and friends'* was placed by Castlereagh's younger half-brother, the soldier, politician and diplomat Charles Stewart, who succeeded him as 3rd Marquess of Londonderry. Just a month after Castlereagh's death, his old political enemy George Canning was appointed Foreign Secretary. In protest, the 3rd Marquess immediately resigned his post as British Ambassador in Vienna.

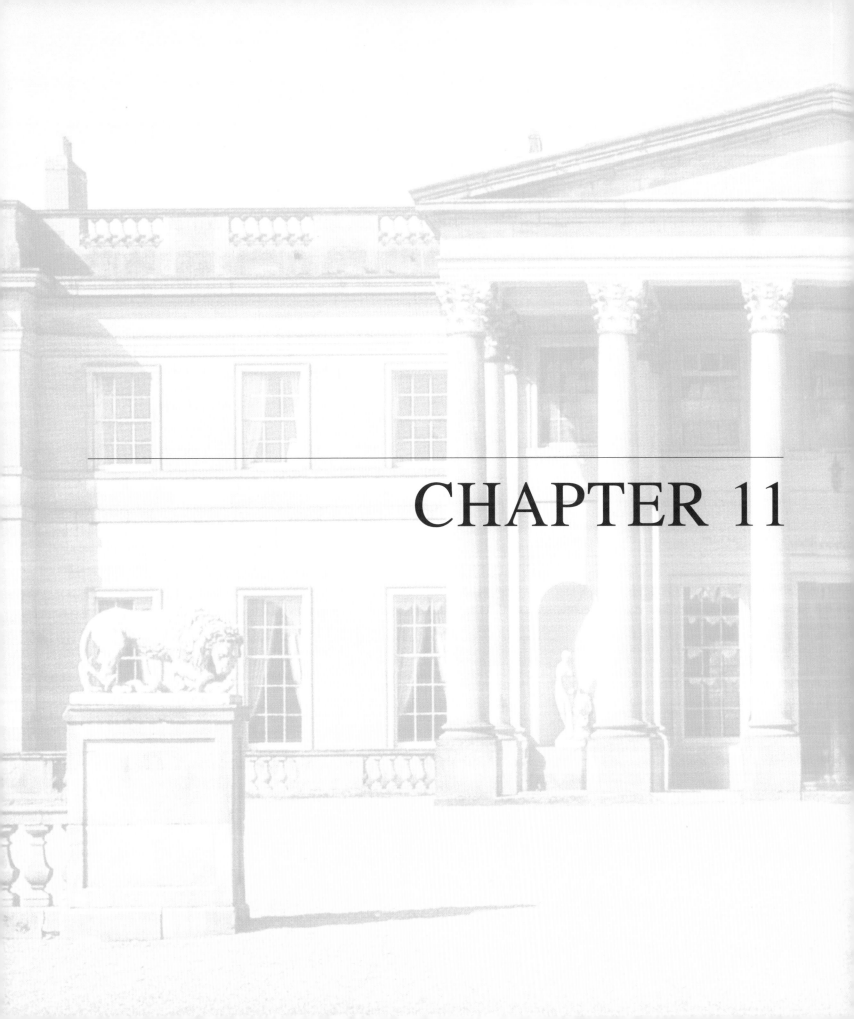

CHAPTER 11

CHARLES WILLIAM VANE-TEMPEST-STEWART
(1778-1854), 3rd Marquess of Londonderry (1822)

The Londonderry line

During the reigns of Queen Elizabeth 1 and her successor James 1, Catholic noblemen were ousted from their lands in Ireland and loyal Protestant subjects 'planted' in their place. Protestant John Stewart of Wigtownshire in Scotland, a kinsman of the Duke of Lennox, one of the King's favourites, was granted land in Ballylawn, near Moville in County Donegal, where he built a castle, Stewart's Court. In 1737, his descendant, Alexander Stewart married heiress Mary Cowan and purchased land in County Down, including the Newtownards estate, formerly called Mount Pleasant and later renamed Mount Stewart.

The Londonderry title originated in 1789, with Robert Stewart, father of Charles, who advanced quickly from Baron Londonderry, through Viscount Castlereagh (1795) and Earl of Londonderry (1796) to become 1st Marquess of Londonderry in 1816. When his son, Charles William Stewart, was raised to the peerage of the United Kingdom in 1814, he took the title Baron Stewart of Stewart's Court and Ballylawn in the County of Donegal. Despite the Londonderry title, most of the family estate was situated in County Down.

Political and military career

Born in Dublin on May 18 1778, Charles was the eldest son of Robert Stewart, 1st Marquess of Londonderry with his second wife Lady Frances, daughter of Charles Pratt, 1st Earl Camden, the distinguished Whig Chancellor of England. The couple produced three sons and eight daughters. Robert's son by his first wife, Lady Sarah Frances Seymour (1747-1770), later became Viscount Castlereagh, 2nd Marquess of Londonderry, half-brother to Charles. Educated at Eton, Charles William Stewart's early life combined politics and diplomacy with an impressive military career, particularly during the Peninsular Wars against Napoleon. At the age of 16, he was commissioned as a Lieutenant in the British Army.

After service in Flanders in 1794, he became Lieutenant Colonel of the 5th Royal Irish Dragoons and helped put down the Irish Rebellion of 1798. Elected to the Irish House of Commons in 1800, as Tory representative for Thomastown, County Kilkenny, after two months, he exchanged this seat for County Londonderry. The 1801 Act of Union, devised by Prime Minister William Pitt and foreign minister Castlereagh, brought together the Irish and British Parliaments. Charles Stewart continued to represent Londonderry in the reformed House of Commons until 1814.

'Fighting Charlie'

In 1803 Charles Stewart was appointed aide-de-camp to King George III. Four years later he became Under-Secretary of State for War and the Colonies, serving until 1809 under his half-brother Lord Castlereagh, Secretary of State at the time. These duties did not stop him from joining Sir John Moore's army corps in Portugal, where, during the Corunna Campaign of 1808-1809, he commanded a brigade of cavalry, playing a prominent role at the battle of Benavente. A portrait in the Wellington Restaurant at Wynyard records the appreciation of his commander, later killed at Corunna.

In April 1809, after the death of Sir John Moore, Charles Stewart became Adjutant General to Sir Arthur Wellesley, later the Duke of Wellington, and distinguished himself fighting with British and allied forces in the Peninsular War against Napoleon, particularly at the battles of Talavera (1809) and Busaco (1810). In 1810, he received the thanks of Parliament and was awarded the Talavera medal and star. Promoted to the rank of Major-General, he continued to serve in succeeding Peninsular campaigns before being invalided home for a short period in 1812.

In recognition of his military successes, in 1813, Charles was created a Knight Grand Cross of the Bath(GCB), an honour granted by the monarch since its inception in 1725

Charles William Vane-Tempest-Stewart, 3rd Marquess of Londonderry (1778 - 1854) by Sir Thomas Lawrence 1812 (© National Portrait Gallery, London)

In 1814, appointed Ambassador to Austria and created Baron Stewart, he took up residence in Vienna, where, in 1815, he served, alongside Lord Castlereagh and, later, the Duke of Wellington, as British plenipotentiary at the Congress of Vienna. A peace conference ending almost 25 years of continuous warfare, the final act of the Congress was signed days before Napoleon's ultimate defeat at Waterloo. Representatives from Great Britain, Prussia, Austria, Russia and France redrew the boundaries of Europe, creating a framework for European international politics which lasted until 1914 and the outbreak of World War I. Charles Stewart wrote histories of the Peninsular War and the War of Liberation, as well as accounts of his travels in Europe. He also edited the correspondence of Lord Castlereagh, his beloved half-brother, so important in promoting his political, diplomatic and military career.

by King George I. Appointed Colonel of the 25th Light Dragoons, returning to the fray, Stewart sustained severe wounds at the Battle of Culm in August 1813, earning the Russian Order of St. George and a letter of commendation from Czar Alexander I. Serving under Marshal Blucher at the Battle of Leipzig in October 1813, he received the Swedish Order of the Sword, while Prussia awarded him the Orders of the Black Eagle and the Red Eagle.

Diplomatic duties

From 1813-14, Charles Stewart lived in Berlin, appointed Military Commissioner with the allied armies by his half-brother Lord Castlereagh, by then Foreign Secretary. He was responsible for liaising with the Prussian and Swedish armies, both countries allied with Britain in the struggle against Napoleon, along with Russia, Austria, Spain and Portugal. Until the end of the war, with victory at Waterloo in 1815, Charles remained Envoy Extraordinary and Minister Plenipotentiary to Berlin.

General Sir Charles Stewart, portrait in the Library

3rd Marquess, portrait in the Wellington Restaurant

After the battles

Having received numerous foreign honours during the Peninsular War, in 1814 Charles became Baron Stewart of Stewart's Court and Ballylawn in the County of Donegal. The same year, Lord Stewart, as he was now known, received honorary degrees from Oxford and Cambridge, became a Lord of the Bedchamber to the King and was admitted to the Privy Council. In 1816, along with the Duke of Wellington and the Marquess of Anglesey, comrades in arms in the Peninsular War, he was appointed Knight Grand Cross of Hanover (GCH), an order of chivalry instituted in 1815 by the Prince Regent, later George IV.

Colonel of the 10th (The Prince of Wales' Own) Regiment of (Light) Dragoons from 1820-1843 and Colonel of the 2nd Regiment of Life Guards from 1843, Charles Stewart retained an abiding interest in military life. In 1840, he wrote an impassioned letter, printed in The Standard newspaper, in praise of the efforts of the British Legion in acquiring financial support for former soldiers who had fought in the Peninsular War. Condemning both the Spanish and British governments for their treatment of *'officers and soldiers who have fought and bled in their cause and under their orders'*, he commended the efforts of the British Legion in securing the military pay and allowances due.

A year earlier, the clergy of Ripon, Thirsk and neighbourhood received a sharp reminder of the Marquess' military background when he berated them for criticising his participation in a duel with Mr Henry Grattan, MP for County Meath in Northern Ireland. In a letter to The Morning Chronicle of 11 September 1839, referring to his reputation for *'candour and straightforwardness',* he advised them that, *'while you in the due exercise of your high calling are bound to preach the gospel and administer consolation to the repentant sinner, you must leave to the British soldier the unfettered right of being the best judge and arbiter of his own honour.'* Twenty years earlier he had fought a duel with a Mr. Battier, a member of the 10th Hussars, the Brigade under the command of Lord Stewart at that time.

Marriage and Family

Charles Stewart first married, at the age of twenty six, Lady Catherine Bligh, youngest daughter of the Earl of Darnley, but was abroad on active service for most of their married life. Their son Frederick, later to become 4th Marquess of Londonderry, was born in 1805, a year after their marriage. Catherine died seven years later, aged thirty seven, while her husband was with the army in Spain, leaving his half-brother and his wife, Lord and Lady Castlereagh, to look after his young son. In 1814, Charles Stewart took up a diplomatic post in Vienna, where the Austrian secret police kept records of his escapades and night-time visits. Although short in stature, a handsome man, extremely vain and a little eccentric, Charles was nicknamed 'Golden Peacock' and 'Lord Pumpernickel'.

On leave from Vienna in 1818, he was invited to dinner by the mother of heiress, Frances Anne Vane-Tempest, Lady Antrim, who thought Stewart would be a good match for her daughter. Mrs Angelo Taylor, Frances Anne's aunt and guardian, tried to prevent the marriage, on the grounds that Stewart had loose morals and insanity in the family, as well as being a fortune hunter. However, a marriage settlement was eventually drawn up and the ceremony took place on 3 April 1819. The Duke of Wellington, former companion in arms to Charles, gave away the bride. Charles Stewart's ostentatious life style continued after his second marriage, when, taking the surname Vane by royal licence, he became known as Charles William Vane-Tempest-Stewart.

Remaining as Ambassador in Vienna until 1822, Stewart occupied a prominent place in European society, developing a large circle of influential friends and acquaintances, many of them members of aristocratic, noble and royal families. He also amassed an impressive collection of paintings, including the first portraits by Sir Thomas Lawrence of the Duke of Wellington and King George IV and two Corregios now in the National Gallery, London. He also acquired several statues by Canova, including Theseus and the Minotaur, formerly on display in the statue gallery at Wynyard Hall. Having served for many years under King George III, Charles became instrumental in dealing with divorce proceedings instigated against Queen Caroline by her estranged husband when he came to the English throne as George IV in 1820. In 1822, on the death of his half-brother, Viscount Castlereagh, Charles Stewart became 3rd Marquess of Londonderry. Distressed by the suicide of his beloved half-brother and angered when George Canning, Castlereagh's sworn enemy, was invited to take over as

Foreign Secretary, Londonderry resigned his post in Vienna and returned to England. The following year, he was created Earl Vane and Viscount Seaham.

The Man of Business

His opposition to Parliamentary reform and Whig policy made the 3rd Marquess unpopular with many public figures and, disappointed not to be given a cabinet post in the Wellington government of 1828-30, he never held parliamentary office again. A return to diplomatic life was also thwarted when Londonderry was forced to decline the post of Ambassador to St. Petersburg, offered in 1834, by the new Prime Minister, Sir Robert Peel. The embassy position was taken up instead by John George Lambton, 1st Earl of Durham. However, the 3rd Marquess and his wife soon found the opportunity to visit that part of the world, described in the Russian Journal of Lady Londonderry 1836-37.

Durham Collieries

Building on the inherited wealth and properties of his wife, Londonderry became an astute man of business, devoting the rest of his life to the improvement of his estates, the development of the County Durham collieries and the erection of Seaham Harbour. Frances Anne had inherited considerable colliery property on the death of her father, Sir Henry Vane-Tempest. By 1819, the year of her marriage, Vane-Tempest collieries at Dawden, Framwellgate, Old Durham, Penshaw, Rainton, Pittington and Silksworth were at their peak of production, producing and selling a quarter of a million tons of coal per year. The marriage settlement drawn up by Frances Anne's trustees, her step-father Edmund MacDonnell, Sir John Beckett, an old family friend and Lord Dungannon, a political associate, ensured that her husband apply her fortune to the improvement of her inherited collieries.

During the first fifteen years of his marriage, determined to secure his wife's fortunes, Londonderry embarked on an ambitious programme of development and improvement of the family collieries, breaking free from the constraints of the church from whom he leased the Dean and Chapter Colliery. The terms of the settlement meant an annual outlay between 1819 and 1824 of about £28,000 annually. However, colliery profits fluctuated considerably in the 1820s, ranging from £46,000 to £22,000. In addition, allowances had to be paid to the

growing family, major expenditure was required on the restoration of Wynyard Hall, the couple's sparkling social life cost a further £14,000 a year and, in 1821, they bought Holdernesse House in London for £36,000. Despite the vigilance of the trustees, family debts rose to alarming proportions during the 1830s and Londonderry often exceeded the limits of his overdraft with bankers Backhouse and Co. of Darlington.

Seaham Harbour and Londonderry Railway

The largest producer of coal in County Durham, the family was the second largest exporter of coal from the River Wear at Sunderland, paying £10,000 a year in transport costs. Determined to bring an end to these high charges, Charles Stewart decided to build his own harbour and railway for the transportation of coal from the Vane-Tempest pits. In October 1821, he bought, for £63,000, the Seaham estate from Sir Ralph Milbanke, who had existing plans to build a harbour. Some funding came from the Irish property of Castlereagh, half-brother to Charles Stewart, but Londonderry agent, John Buddle, expressed concern at *'the expenses of an operation which could terminate only in disaster.'*

Work on the inner harbour began in 1828, when Lord Londonderry, using a silver trowel, the handle made of polished Rainton coal, laid the foundation stone of the north-east pier. Seven year old Lord Seaham, eldest son of Frances Anne and her husband, later to become 5th Marquess, used another silver trowel, this one with a handle of polished Seaham limestone, to lay the foundation stone of the first house in Seaham Harbour.

The Marquess of Londonderry commencing the Seaham and Sunderland Railway (©Photographic Library Beamish Museum Ltd)

Mount Stewart (with permission of The National Trust)

Officially opened on July 5 1831, the harbour cost a total of £162,000, much of the stone used coming from the family colliery at Penshaw, also used in the building of Wynyard Hall.

Adding to his already considerable colliery property, in 1849, at the age of 71, the 3rd Marquess began the sinking of Seaham Colliery, which, by 1854, employed 269 hands. On February 8 1853, he cut the first sod for the Londonderry Railway, connecting Seaham and Sunderland. Finally completed in July 1855, a year after the death of the 3rd Marquess, the project cost a total of £100,000. Both railway and harbour remained in the family's hands until 1900, when, during the time of the 6th Marquess, grandson of the 3rd, they were taken over by the North Eastern Railway and Seaham Harbour Dock Company.

Londonderry House, Park Lane, London

His obituary in the York Herald of 11 March 1854 stated that *'the responsibilities devolved upon Lord Londonderry by the management of the property of his bride, embracing a considerable portion of the County of Durham, and including some of the most important coal mines in the country, opened up a new field for the exercise of energies which the cessation of war had thrown into temporary inaction. His Lordship applied himself with a vigorous activity to the development of the vast resources of the estates, and exhibited an enterprise and sound judgement.'* The trustees may not have agreed entirely, as Lord Londonderry's incautious approach had created financial difficulties and embarrassment over the years, leading them to resume control of all his income from inherited properties in 1835. A new settlement, drawn up in 1842, aimed to ensure that his widow would inherit an estate free from debt.

Londonderry Residences

Charles Stewart brought great energy and enthusiasm to the refurbishment and ultimate rebuilding of Wynyard Hall, home to Frances Anne from childhood. In addition, the couple restored Mount Stewart, the Londonderry country seat in Northern Ireland and bought Holdernesse House on London's Park Lane, later renamed Londonderry House. In July 1839, Disraeli described Rosebank, their other London home, on the banks of the Thames, as *'but a beautiful cottage.'* However, the grandeur of the house may be assumed from the ensuing description of *'a grand conservatory more than sixty feet long, lofty and broad in proportion, and adorned with festoons of flowers.'* In 1850, they also built a summer residence, Garron Tower, in Carnlough, County Antrim, Northern Ireland, ancestral home of Frances Anne's mother. The 3rd Marquess and his wife also commissioned the building of Carnlough harbour and the Londonderry Hotel, which still welcomes visitors today.

The Belfast News of November 1828, wrote *'never did we meet a man of any rank, who, by his conciliating manners, his affability, his cheerfulness, his kind and unremitting attention to all, so effectually secured the esteem of all around him as the Marquis of Londonderry.'* By contrast, a letter from one of his tenants, appearing in the Belfast News of August 1849, complained about the doubling of his rent, the imposition of a fine and the lack of financial support after the potato famine of 1845. *'All I ask is fair play and my land at a fair rent'*, he continues, sure that the subject of his letter *'must be ignorant of the wrongs I have suffered'.* Despite his own problems, Agricola, as he signs himself, declares that *' your desire to see your tenantry prosperous, comfortable and happy does you infinite credit.'* In 1825, Lord Londonderry presided at a St. Patrick's Day dinner held in London in aid of poor Irish children. Speakers included Irish leader Daniel O'Connell and MP William Huskisson, killed in 1830 at the opening of the Liverpool-Manchester Railway. Members of the top table *'were much amused by a bottle of genuine (illegal) poteen, imported from the Emerald Isle.'*

The Great Man Remembered

Governor of County Londonderry from 1823, the 3rd Marquess was appointed Lord Lieutenant of Durham in 1842 and Colonel of the Second Regiment of Life Guards in 1843. He became a Knight of the Garter in 1853, just one year before his death at the family's London home, Holdernesse House, a victim of the influenza epidemic which ravaged the country during 1853 and 1854. The York Herald of March 11 1854 reported that *'the effects of a sudden attack of influenza proved too severe for a constitution already weakened by long service and the natural decay of age. His death was free from pain and his last moments were solaced by the presence of nearly all the members of his family.'*

After lying in state at the chapel at Wynyard Hall, his body was taken to the family vault at Long Newton, his hearse conveyed by the same black horses present at the Duke of Wellington's funeral sixteen months earlier. Although the family had requested a private funeral, the Morning Post of 18 March 1854 reported that, in three hours, *' upwards of a thousand people... chiefly the more respectable inhabitants of the county'* passed through the chapel to pay their respects. *'The chapel was hung with black cloth...the coffin covered in red velvet. A black velvet pall, ornamented with escutcheons of the family arms, was thrown partially over the coffin, upon the head of which rested the coronet and cushion, and at the foot the helmet, sword and sash worn by the deceased marquis.'* As a mark of respect, business was suspended in all the towns of the region, as well as works at the Londonderry collieries and quarries. The flags of vessels at harbour in Sunderland and Seaham were flown at half-mast and church bells tolled from an early hour. Soon

3rd Marquess, by George Gammon Adams 1854, portrait in the Wellington Restaurant

en route to the tiny church at Long Newton and the Londonderry family vault. Officers of the 2nd Life Guards had made a journey of 300 miles to pay tribute to their late colonel.

An obituary at the time spoke of *'the dashing Charles Stewart of the Peninsula, the princely dispenser of the hospitalities of Holdernesse House, Garron Tower and Wynyard Park. In Antrim, in Durham, as well as in Park Lane, there are many hearts which feel deprived of a true friend.'* The horrors of the Crimean War just beginning, the writer suggested England *'pause , amidst the preparations for the new contest before her, to drop a tear over the gallant soldier who served her so chivalrously in the last.'*

Memorials

Many memorials were erected in his honour, particularly by his grieving widow. Raffaelle Monti's renowned equestrian sculpture, central to Durham City marketplace since 1861, portrays the military hero and hussar. The superb Memorial Room created at Wynyard Hall in 1857 honours his achievements in war and peace. The magnificent marble sarcophagus, brought to Wynyard in 1904, was originally placed in the Vane-Tempest family vault at Long Newton, where an impressive marble plaque outlining his achievements remains. A quotation from Psalms XVIII, inscribed into the arched surround, offers a fitting epitaph to the determined man of action.

'I will not be afraid of thousands of people that have set themselves against me round about, For Thou hast girded me with strength unto the battle.'

Statue by Raffaelle Monti in Durham market place (© Marion Senior)

after daybreak, tenants of the Wynyard estate began to assemble, many on horseback, attired in deep mourning with black scarves and hatbands.

Before leaving Wynyard, the coffin paused for a moment beneath the beautiful central glass dome of the marble hall. The cortege, led by *'two mutes bearing wands',* left the mansion at 10 o'clock precisely. The hearse, drawn by six black horses, was followed by Lord Londonderry's favourite milk-white charger, his boots and spurs suspended from the saddle. His private carriage drawn by six grey horses followed the seven mourning coaches, bearing the immediate family and close associates of the Marquess. Silent crowds lined the streets as the funeral procession passed through the town of Stockton-on-Tees

Scrabo Tower near Mount Stewart, County Down

In Seaham, Frances Anne commissioned the building of Christ Church and in Northern Ireland, the people of Newtownards erected in his honour Scrabo Tower. Designed by Charles Lanyon, architect responsible for many buildings in Belfast, at 125 feet high (41 metres) the tower dominates the town. 122 steps lead to a viewing tower allowing panoramic views of the Isle of Man, the Scottish coast and the Mountains of Mourne. An inscription placed by his tenants and friends concludes *'Fame belongs to history, remembrance to us.'* Replying to a tribute from their Irish tenants in Carnlough, his widow noted that *'The same unconquerable energy that distinguished his military career was devoted to the improvements of the districts he became associated with, and his undertakings, both in England and Ireland, are lasting tablets recording that the desire to do his duty towards those amongst whom he lived was foremost in the impulses of his generous nature.'*

Succession

On his death at the age of 76, the landed estates of the 3rd Marquess were left to his widow, his personal property valued separately at £335,000, a huge sum in 1854. With an income of £75,000 a year, twice the sum he earned in the 1820s, he had become one of the richest men in Britain. In the year prior to his death, the collieries alone showed a profit of over £60,000. As well as the town and port of Seaham, he owned eleven pits, lime and stone quarries, 5,000 hectares of farmland in County Durham and estates in Northern Ireland.

Charles was succeeded as 4th Marquess of Londonderry by his son from his first marriage, Frederick William Robert Stewart, Viscount Castlereagh. Charles' eldest son from his second marriage, George Henry Robert Charles William Vane-Tempest (1821-1884), succeeded him as 2nd Earl Vane. On the death of his half brother in 1872, Henry became 5th Marquess of Londonderry.

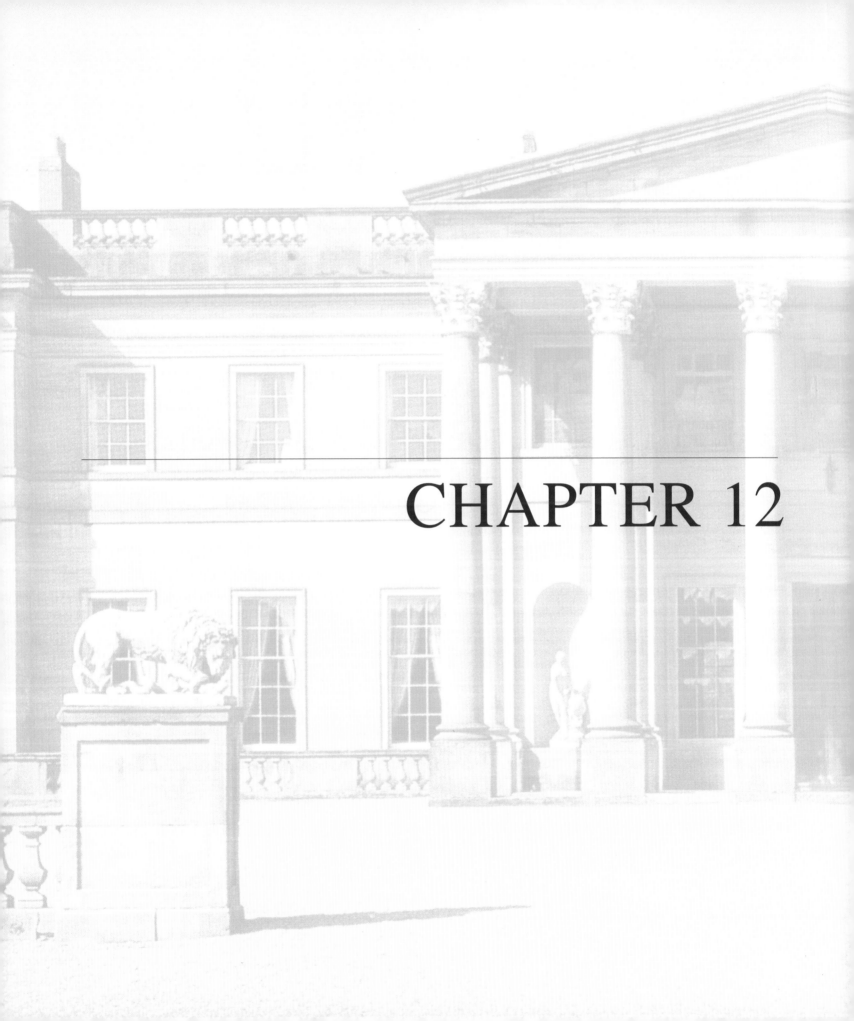

CHAPTER 12

FRANCES ANNE VANE-TEMPEST (1800-1865)

Marchioness of Londonderry 1822

Early life

The only child of Sir Henry Vane-Tempest of Long Newton and Wynyard and his wife Anne Catherine, Countess of Antrim, Frances Anne was born in 1800 in Lord Lichfield's house in St.James' Square. She records that both parents were disappointed, as they wished for a boy. Her young life was devoid of affection, except from her aunt, after whom she had been named. She recalled receiving parental kindness only when ill with scarlet fever. Perhaps a little harshly, she describes herself as ' *singularly ugly - broad, fat, awkwardly made, with immense feet, huge purple hands, greasy stubborn hair and a fixed redness in my face.*'

Despite his apparent neglect, Frances Anne's diary records her sorrow at her father's death. *'I certainly loved him better than my mother, but,'* she continues, ' *at 13 sorrow is not lasting and I soon began to find the difference in my situation. I was mistress of all around me. The cuffed child, whose mother had grudged her dresses and pocket money, was now an immense heiress.'* After her father's death in 1814, in order to protect the young girl and her inheritance, Frances Anne became a ward in Chancery, under the guardianship of her mother and her aunt, Mrs Angelo Taylor. At the same time, a manager was appointed to administer the increasingly valuable colliery interests.

Frances Anne continued to be educated privately and, for the next five years, spent more time in London than Wynyard, where, according to her diary, her mother had taken a lover. In1817, Anne Catherine MacDonnell, Countess of Antrim married Edmund Phelps, a music teacher she had known for under a month. He subsequently changed his name by royal licence to MacDonnell. Her daughter refused to attend the wedding.

Marriage

Frances Anne had become an attractive young woman as well as a wealthy one and received proposals of marriage from the Duke of Leinster and Lord O'Neill, members of

A lithograph of Frances Anne by Richard James Lane, 1843, after Sir William Charles Ross RA 1842

the aristocracy of Northern Ireland, her mother's homeland, before accepting Charles, Lord Stewart, later to become 3rd Marquess of Londonderry. At the time of her marriage, Frances Anne was nineteen, under the age of majority, which then stood at twenty one. Her husband, a widower, was considerably older at forty. His first wife, Catherine Bligh, died in 1812, after only four years of marriage, leaving a son, Frederick, Viscount Castlereagh, later 4th Marquess of Londonderry.

Charles met his new bride in 1818, when, on leave from Vienna, he was invited to dinner by Frances Anne's mother, Lady Antrim, who considered Stewart a good match for her daughter. However, Frances Anne's aunt Mrs Angelo Taylor, also her godmother and guardian, tried to prevent the marriage, appealing to the Lord Chancellor, Lord Eldon, on the grounds that Stewart had loose morals and insanity in the family, as well as being a fortune hunter. Far from being impoverished, with an income of £18,000 a year, he expected to inherit from his father estates valued at £8,000 and was also heir to the estates of his half-brother Castlereagh, worth a further £18,000.

Eventually a marriage settlement was drawn up and the couple were married on 3 April 1819 at Lady Antrim's Mayfair house in Bruton Street. Dr Pelham, Bishop of Exeter conducted the ceremony, witnessed by eighty relatives and friends. Wearing a superb bridal gown of Brussels lace, Frances Anne was given away by the Duke of Wellington. At about ten o'clock, *'a beautiful chariot with four horses'* took the bridal couple to a small country house at North Cray in Kent, lent by the Castlereaghs for the start of their honeymoon. On their arrival, local people followed the Kentish custom of strewing the ground with flowers to welcome the bride. Two weeks later, they journeyed on to the Pavilion at Brighton, where they were met by a large assembly of well-wishers, including the Prince Regent.

Returning north, the couple were received with great rejoicing and ringing of bells at Stockton and also paid visits to Durham and Sunderland, where they were greeted with equal enthusiasm. The couple gave a celebratory ball at Wynyard, although the Hall may not have looked quite as sumptuous on that occasion as it became later. Having left Wynyard at the age of 14, after her father's death, Frances Anne must have been dismayed, on returning with her new husband, to find the house almost unfurnished, most of it stripped and sold by her mother. However, the newly-weds stayed at Wynyard for a month, using the time to employ new agents and to put in order the estates, collieries and financial matters.

The wife of a diplomat

The couple returned to London before travelling to Vienna, where Lord Stewart was British Ambassador. En route, they spent three weeks in Paris, where they met King Louis XVIII, as well as visiting Geneva, Augsburg, Munich and Salzburg. Unfortunately, Frances Anne was unable to enjoy either the life style or the magnificent house provided for them in Vienna, as she felt ill from the moment she arrived and suffered a miscarriage towards the end of 1819. Returning to diplomatic duties in December of that year, she was presented to the Imperial family and undertook a round of parties, balls and dinners, interrupted in January 1820 by a period of mourning for the death of King George III. Lord Stewart was much involved thereafter with the divorce proceedings between Queen Caroline and George IV, who agreed to be godfather to Frances Anne's first child, a son, born on April 26 1821. In the same month, the baby's grandfather Robert Stewart, 1st Marquess of Londonderry, died at Mount Stewart aged 83, the title passing to Castlereagh, son of his first marriage.

Frances Anne's first-born, George Henry Robert Charles William, received the best of attention from three nurses sent from England, as well as a magnificent layette of baby clothes bought from Paris, London, Brussels and Vienna for a staggering £2,000. Over 120 guests were invited to the lavish christening dinner provided in the Viennese Embassy, where expert chef Careme catered for guests in the throne room and gallery as well as the dining room. In the latter alone, 48 visitors were offered a total of nine courses, including curried turtle soup, salmon, fillets of beef, pheasant, chicken, glazed ham, game pate, capons, stuffed quails and sturgeon. Desserts ranged from the relatively simple raspberry mousse, orange jelly and meringues to glorious concoctions described as a Venetian fountain, an Irish pavilion on a bridge and a Roman villa on a rocky outcrop. Lord Seaham, the subject of the christening, later 5th Marquess of Londonderry, blamed a lifetime of dental decay on the life style of his parents in Vienna. Thirty years after his own baptism, Lord Seaham engaged the same clergyman, the Reverend William Bradford, formerly chaplain to the British Embassy in Vienna, to officiate at the christening of his eldest son, subsequently the 6th Marquess.

Shortly after the birth of her first child, Frances Anne began a close platonic relationship with Czar Alexander I of Russia, later godparent to her daughter Alexandrina, born in 1823. The friendship was initiated by a portrait of Frances Anne painted by Sir Thomas Lawrence on the occasion of her engagement to Lord Stewart. Begun in London, taken to be finished at a studio in Aix-la-

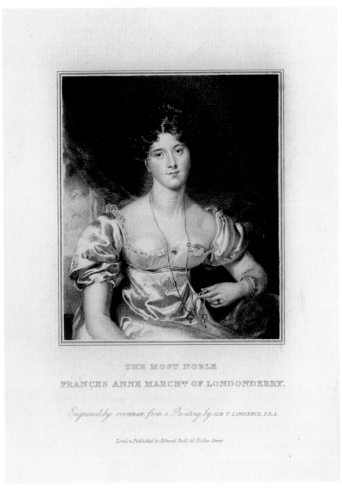

Frances Anne signed by Cochran from a painting by Sir Thomas Lawrence 1818 (© National Portrait Gallery, London)

bought in 1819, later renamed Londonderry House. At a cost of £200,000, the brothers Philip and Benjamin Wyatt who also worked on Wynyard Hall, installed a new entrance from Park Lane, a fine staircase, ballroom, gallery and banqueting hall. A housewarming party in the summer of 1825 was attended by guests including HRH the Duke of Gloucester and the Duke and Duchess of Wellington.

A lively member of London high society, Frances Anne counted amongst her friends some of the most important and influential people of the day, including several politicians. A close friend of Benjamin Disraeli (1804-1881), who once described her as *'half ruffian, half great lady'*, she is said to figure in his novel, *Sybil*. A frequent visitor to Wynyard, he enjoyed informal drives

Disraeli by Sir Francis Grant 1852 (© National Portrait Gallery, London)

and picnics with Frances Anne amidst *'all the splendid accessories of feudal life'*. In 1874, when Disraeli became Prime Minister, just as she had predicted, one of his first official acts was to the confer the order of St. Patrick upon the 5th Lord Londonderry, *'son of the grande dame who was so kind to me in my youth, though she was a tyrant in her way.'*

A great supporter to her husband, when, in 1834, he was obliged to turn down the post of Ambassador to St. Petersburg offered by Sir Robert Peel, Frances Anne accompanied him on a tour of that part of the world, publishing her *Russian Journal of Lady Londonderry 1836-37*. Touched to see the many memorials erected to Czar Alexander I, who died of a fever, possibly typhoid, in 1825, she was also impressed by the *enfilade* of rooms in Louis Quatorze style at his St. Petersburg palace, as well as huge mirrors and works of art by Canaletto, Canova and Andrea del Sarto in the Hermitage Museum. A keen traveller, Frances Anne published further journals, relating tours in Constantinople (1841) and Portugal, Spain and Africa (1843). Proceeds from the latter helped to fund an infirmary at Seaham.

Chapelle, the painting was spotted by Alexander, also having his portrait painted by Lawrence. He insisted the painting be placed in front of him during his sittings, the subject mysteriously dubbed Miss Stephenson. Two years later, now living in Vienna, Frances Anne became a close friend of the Czar, whose portrait hangs today in the library at Wynyard Hall, alongside those of the 3rd Marquess and his wife.

Return to London

After the death of his half-brother, Castlereagh in 1822, Charles Stewart inherited the Londonderry title, becoming 3rd Marquess. Leaving Vienna, the family travelled home via Verona, Florence and Rome, but the *'brilliant existence'* Frances Anne describes in her diary continued on their return to London in 1823. She directed the refurbishment of Holdernesse House which they had

The Irish Connection

Although both her mother and husband were Irish, Frances Anne did not visit Ireland until 1823, when the whole family crossed from Portpatrick to Mount Stewart, the family seat in County Down. Finding the house in a poor state of repair, the Londonderrys left orders for restoration work to be carried out, before travelling on to the home of Frances Anne's mother, Glenarm in County Antrim. Bonfires blazing, the town and castle illuminated, the entire population turned out to greet them.

Two weeks later, during a trip to Dublin, where the 10th Hussars, her husband's regiment, were stationed, Frances Anne enjoyed a busy round of entertainments and activities including a regimental review in Phoenix Park, a regimental dinner at Portobello Barracks and a trip to the theatre to see a musical romance 'Blue Beard'. According to a local newspaper, *'Applauded on her entrance, she wore a splendid diamond ornament at her waist of peculiar brilliancy and a beautiful ruby of very large size shone in each of her armlets.'* The splendid Londonderry jewels, now on display in the Victoria and Albert Museum, London, continued to attract attention throughout the lifetimes of subsequent Marchionesses.

The Londonderry Jewels

A great lover of priceless and elaborate jewellery, Frances Anne had a huge travelling trunk devoted solely to her collection, inviting favoured individuals to come and admire her jewels. At the christening of her first son, dressed in Brussels lace over white satin, she carried a jewelled bouquet of flowers and wore pearls bought in Vienna from Countess Fries, the widow of a German banker, at a cost of £10,000. Known as *gouttes* or teardrops, she had them mounted into a *parure* (or set), consisting of a tiara and comb, necklace, earrings and brooches, all framed in openwork diamond borders. At the christening, her husband Charles was no less resplendent, his scarlet hussar's uniform adorned with a gold chain clasped with a ruby and emerald slide and a diamond studded serpent.

Also in Vienna, Frances Anne bought a unique collection of turquoises collected throughout his life by Count Ferdinand Palffy, Chancellor of the Holy Roman Empire. Set into a *parure,* of which a necklace, earrings and two shoulder brooches survive, the turquoises were worn by

Frances Anne at the coronation of William IV in 1831. With them, she wore a suite of diamonds and an enamelled gold cross, set with pearls, emeralds and rubies, a gift from King George IV. In 1822, at the Congress of Verona, Czar Alexander presented Frances Anne with a collection of yellow diamonds, pink topaz and superb rubies, all mounted in diamonds. His gifts of Siberian amethysts mounted into shoulder brooches can be seen in the Thomas Lawrence portrait of Frances Anne with Lord Seaham as a small boy. Further amethysts, used to create a chain of six large settings alternating with diamond stars, could be worn either as a tiara or across the breast like the ribbon of an order.

Francess Anne dressed as Elizabeth I, published by Whittaker & Co 1830 (© National Portrait Gallery, London)

From her mother, the Countess of Antrim, Frances Anne inherited huge emeralds set with diamonds and rubies. Other jewels, including the Down diamond, had been passed down from the Stewarts, originators of the Londonderry title. On her travels around the world, Frances Anne bought more jewels, including African cornelian and Italian coral. After the Congress of Vienna, world monarchs grateful for his diplomatic expertise following the Napoleonic Wars, presented her brother-in-law, Castlereagh, the 2nd Marquess of Londonderry, with priceless gems some of which were originally set in to his hat badge, sword hilt and garter insignia. Included in the collection, a waistband three inches wide and set with 1225 diamonds was transformed, in 1854, into the famous Londonderry tiara. London jeweller Garrard used the diamonds to create a suite of jewellery which also included shoulder brooches, earrings and a magnificent cross. The set also contained items popular during the Victorian period - a bandeau or headband, a necklace named a riviere, composed of flowing rivers of diamonds and a stomacher, a triangular pane of jewels set in to the bodice of a gown.

During the lifetime of Frances Anne, the Londonderry jewels were displayed to great effect, often as part of elaborate fancy dress costumes. Disraeli described her dressed as Cleopatra, *'in a dress literally embroidered with diamonds from top to toe.'* Costumed as Queen Elizabeth I, wearing plush red velvet, she incorporated in to her design a throne embroidered with the monogram ER and three of her children as attendants. On her the death in 1865, her jewellery was dispersed, her will giving an idea of the variety and magnificence of the collection. Items included diamond bows set with black pearls, sets of diamond buttons, an emerald shamrock, a sapphire heart, sixteen diamond lilies set together in a band, two gold and diamond bracelets, one containing a lock of a child's hair, the other set with miniature portraits. All eighteen grandchildren received a ring, a pin or a brooch, while their parents' bequests reflected their position in society. The Londonderry jewels continued to appear at state occasions, worn with great pride by Theresa, 6th his wife of Londonderry and her daughter-in-law Edith, 7th Marchioness. Lady Annabel, daughter of the 8th Marquess, wore the Londonderry tiara, nicknamed 'the family fender', at a ball held in Windsor Castle in 1963 to celebrate the forthcoming wedding of Princess Alexandra and Angus Ogilvy.

The Children

The marriage of Frances Anne and Charles Stewart produced three sons and three surviving daughters. Their eldest son George Henry Robert Charles William, 2nd Earl Vane, Viscount Seaham (1821-1884), became fifth Marquess of Londonderry in 1872. He succeeded the 4th Marquess, his half-brother Castlereagh, eldest son of the 3rd Marquess by his first wife.

Frances Anne with two of her children, portrait in the Wellington Restaurant

Eldest daughter, Lady Frances Anne Emily Vane (1822-1899), married John Winston Spencer Churchill, 7th Duke of Marlborough. Their son, Randolph and his wife Jennie Jerome, daughter of an American business tycoon, produced the future wartime prime minister, Winston Churchill. Born in 1874 at Blenheim Palace, Churchill described his great grandmother, who died nine years before his birth, as *'a woman of exceptional capacity, energy and decision.'*

Second daughter of the 3rd Marquess and his wife, Lady Alexandrina Octavia Maria Vane (1823-1874), named in honour of her godfather Czar Alezander I of Russia, married Henry John Reuben, 3rd Earl of Portarlington. Youngest daughter Lady Adelaide Emelina Caroline Vane (1830-1882) disgraced herself by eloping at the age of 22 with her brother's tutor, the Rev. Frederick Henry Law. Their marriage lasted for thirty years, the family reconciled to the match, the youngest daughter providing great support during her mother's widowhood. Another daughter Hyacinthe Sophia Henrietta Charlotte Vane, born in August 1826, died of pneumonia just eight months later. A touching plaque in the family church at Long Newton remembers her as *'the blossom of an hour.'*

The couple's youngest son, Lord Ernest McDonnell Vane Tempest (1836-1885) served in the 2nd Life Guards and the 4th Light Dragoons, before leaving the British Army to join the Federal Army of the United States. He served for some time as assistant adjutant-general and was present at many battles of the American Civil War. After youthful high spirits and escapades, some of which landed him in court, he finally settled down and, in 1869, married Mary Townshend Hutchinson of Howden Hall, County Durham. Ernest died in 1885, his wife in 1891. Both are buried at Thorpe Thewles, near Wynyard. Their only child, Charles Henry Vane-Tempest, died in 1899 aged 27.

Adolphus (1825-1864), Frances Anne's favourite child, known as Dolly, served heroically in the Crimean War. He became Conservative Member of Parliament for North Durham in 1854, elected unopposed after the death of his father. Adolphus suffered severe bouts of mental illness, often being confined to hospital. In 1860, despite the protestations of her family, he married Lady Susan Pelham-Clinton, only daughter of the 5th Earl of Newcastle-under-Lyme. After the birth of their son in 1863, Adolphus had a severe relapse and died just a year later. His widow later became one of the many mistresses of the Prince of Wales, later Edward VII, allegedly giving birth to his illegitimate child in 1871. She died in 1874 and is commemorated in the family vault at Long Newton along with Adolphus.

Philanthropy

Mindful of the contribution of their extensive workforce to the success of their estates and business empire, Frances Anne and her husband awarded prizes for the efforts of their tenant farmers and made generous provision for the well-being and welfare of Londonderry workers and their families.

After providing a school in Thorpe Thewles, near Wynyard in 1844, in the 1850s Frances Anne endowed further Londonderry schools at East and West Rainton, Kelloe, Old Durham, Penshaw and New Seaham, which still stands. Her son Henry was later responsible for the Londonderry school at Silksworth, while the school in Wynyard Park, now demolished, was provided in 1895, by Theresa, Marchioness of Londonderry. Frances Anne personally paid the teachers' salaries and all other expenses and allowed the children of people not employed by the Londonderrys to attend. She spoke forcefully on the importance of education.

Adamant that boys should not be made to work in the pits *'till a certain amount of education has been acquired'*, she was angered to find her directive ignored, not only by government, but by her own colliery managers. On her final appearance speaking in public at a colliery school prize giving in 1862, she chastised parents for treating their children as *'slaves or mere makers of money.'* On the other hand, her husband once said that a boy of twelve should be learning a trade, not wasting his time reading and writing.

Memorial to Adolphus Frederick Charles William Stewart-Vane-Tempest, 2nd son of Frances Anne, in Long Newton church

The Marchioness of Londonderry School, Seaham Harbour 1858 (©Photographic Library Beamish Museum Ltd)

As well as providing access to education previously denied to the general population, the Londonderrys created *'institutions calculated to improve the physical well-being or elevate the moral character of its inhabitants',* as described in 1861 by historian and friend, Sir Archibald Alison. In creating the new town of Seaham, they provided housing for their workers and their families, as well as numerous schools, several churches, including Christ Church, in memory of the 3rd Marquess, a public hospital, an athenaeum, literary institute, public baths, gas and water works and many public seminaries.

In 1843, a bazaar organised by Frances Anne and patronised by the Dowager Queen Adelaide, raised over £1,200 to fund the building of Seaham Infirmary. The fund was further boosted by sales of Frances Anne's journal of her three month tour in Portugal, Spain and France, bought by over 1,000 subscribers, including members of the aristocracy, clergy and royal family. Lady Londonderry's Bazaar of September 1848 raised over £500 towards the building of Holy Trinity Church at Thorpe Thewles. *'Beautifully fitted up for the occasion',*

the new station of the Stockton and Darlington Railway provided the venue for the event, attended by Frances Anne's daughter the Countess of Portarlington, her daughter-in-law Viscountess Seaham, her sister-in-law Viscountess Hardinge and Viscountess Dungannon, wife of the MP for Durham. The Londonderry Band played at the two day event, which visitors attended by special trains from York, Newcastle, Sunderland and Shields.

At Seaham, Frances Anne started a needlework guild to provide warm clothing for the miners, their families and the elderly. She also strived to develop a sense of moral and social duty, often with a religious or military bent. Appalled by conditions described in letters she received from the front from her second son Adolphus, she launched a Patriotic Fund, which raised over £650 to provide comforts for the troops in the Crimea.

Frances Anne alone

After the death of husband in 1854, Frances Anne quickly gained a remarkable knowledge of commerce and industry, becoming a very successful business manager at a time when such work was not considered appropriate for women. Replying to a touching tribute to her late husband from the people of Seaham, she wrote *'whatever remains of life will be devoted to the accomplishment of all his plans and objects. Deeply do I feel the responsibility in succeeding to the management of these great concerns, and bitterly do I deplore my inferiority to the master mind that preceded me, but with God's help, I will do my best.'*

Under her husband's will, as well as retaining the use for life of Wynyard Park, Holdernesse House, Garron Tower and Seaham Hall, Frances Anne was left in complete control of the collieries. Mount Stewart and the Irish estates belonging to the 3rd Marquess in his own right were left to her stepson, Castlereagh, now 4th Marquess of Londonderry. Determined to continue the work begun by her husband, Frances Anne managed the Durham collieries left to her by her father, as well as the new colliery, brickworks and ironworks at Seaham. At first, the responsibility proved daunting. In July 1854, she wrote to Disraeli, *' I am turned into a clerk ... I could manage any one subject, but I have to go from estates to docks, from drainage to railways, quarries to timber ... till I get hopelessly bewildered.'*

However, she soon proved equal to the task, not only maintaining existing works but also instigating new projects. On a twenty acre site at Dawdon, near Seaham, she established four blast furnaces, planned and completed in about ten months, each capable of smelting 200 tons of iron a week, the fuel provided by 120 coke ovens. Resolute in her intention to protect the family empire *'bequeathed to me as a sacred charge to foster and watch over'*, she also planned ahead, confident that *' the present prosperous time should be seized to make money and pay off debt, so as to secure future large and certain income.'*

Chilton Moor celebration

In March 1856, Frances Anne dined 4,000 of her workforce in a large factory, loaned for the occasion, at Chilton Moor, right in the centre of the collieries inherited from her father. The total area then covered, including Seaham, represented the largest colliery property in England owned by a single individual, annual coal production amounting to one million tons. Although working conditions were difficult and uncomfortable down any pit, Londonderry mines were considered among the best for the time, miners preferring them to many others.

The Chilton Moor celebration, reported in the Illustrated London News 15 March 1856

The Chilton Moor celebration provided an opportunity to celebrate the development of the Londonderry empire, while offering thanks to the hundreds of workers involved in its success. The factory walls were hung with banners bearing the names of pits, including 'Londonderry', 'Lady Seaham', 'Adelaide' and 'Lord Ernest' and mottoes such as 'Success to the Coal Trade – England's Wealth'. Guests included the Bishop of Durham, whose cathedral choristers opened the proceedings by singing grace. On the centre table stood a huge baron of beef. Other provisions included eight fat bullocks, fifteen sheep, forty bushels of potatoes, a ton and a half of bread, a ton of plum pudding and fifty barrels of strong beer. The event cost over £1,000.

Frances Anne had invited everyone in her employ – pitmen, harbourmen, quarrymen and railwaymen. Thanking them all for their hard work, she particularly praised the pitmen for working on when other collieries were on strike. She urged them to be *'careful and watchful'* underground and exhorted them to *'frequent and support your reading rooms, your mechanics' institutions, your temperance societies and to avoid the public house.'* Clearly proud of her endowed schools, which she refused to submit to Government inspection, she reminded parents once again of their duty, saying *'it is your own fault if you take your children away too soon and thus deprive them of the benefit of the good education that is provided for them.'* Forster's Elementary Education Act, providing a framework for schooling of children aged five to twelve, did not come in to force until 1870, when factory owners expressed concern at the loss of cheap labour. Another ten years elapsed before attendance became compulsory and not until 1891 was education provided free by the state.

The devoted widow

After the death of her husband in 1854, Frances Anne commission several impressive monuments to honour his memory. In 1855, in Seaham Harbour, the town he created, she laid the foundation stone of Christ Church, paying the cost of building the church, which received free heating and lighting from the underground pipes of the colliery 200 yards away. At the family mausoleum at Long Newton, an elaborate Gothic arched recess with crocketed pinnacles and a gable with foliage carving is dedicated to Charles William Vane, 3rd Marquess of Londonderry. Installed by Frances Anne in 1856, a detailed

Frances Anne, photograph by Samuel Oglesby, albumen carte-de-visite, early 1860s (© National Portrait Gallery, London)

inscription bears witness to his military, political and philanthropic achievements, as well as the development of Seaham Harbour and railway. Describing *'the cheerful companion, steady friend, affectionate son, loving brother, fond parent, devoted and tender husband'*, Frances Anne fondly commemorates *'the idol of her life, the centre of her love and happiness, now the example for her future and the spirit that inspires her thoughts and actions.'*

The magnificent memorial room at Wynyard, completed in 1857, is further testament to Frances Anne's love, respect and admiration for her husband. The white marble effigy of the 3rd Marquess, brought to Wynyard in 1904 from the family mausoleum, was created by Raffaelle

Monti of Milan, also responsible for the famous equestrian statue of the 3rd Marquess as a dashing hussar. On 2 December 1861, in one of her final public appearances, his widow unveiled the statue in Durham City Market Place.

After her husband's death, Frances Anne lived mostly at Seaham Hall, spending summer and early autumn at Garron Tower in Ireland and Christmas at Wynyard Hall, staying in London only briefly, for the season. After the death of her beloved son, Adolphus in 1864, she wrote from Holdernesse House, later renamed Londonderry House, to Mrs. Benjamin Disraeli, '*I am going out of town and hope quiet and fresh air will do me good, for between ill health and sorrow, I have been well-nigh crushed.*'

After a long illness affecting her heart, Frances Anne died, on January 20 1865 at Seaham Hall. Family at her bedside heard '*the phantom coach*' drive up to the front door and, as she breathed her last, servants reported a piercing wail.

True to the tradition of the MacDonnells of Antrim, the howl of the banshee marked the passing of a chief. Escorted by the 2nd Durham Artillery Volunteer Corps, raised at Seaham and commanded by her eldest son, Frances Anne was interred in the family mausoleum at Long Newton.

Railway engineer George Hardy paid tribute to '*the splendid abilities of Frances Anne, Marchioness of Londonderry, who, after the death of the Marquess, so ably managed the various properties, including collieries, railways and, indeed, the whole interests of the estates belonging to her family.*' Her collieries, still protected by the conditions laid down when she inherited them as a girl of 13, passed to her eldest son Henry, Earl Vane, Lord Seaham, who as a small boy in 1828, laid the foundation stone of the first Seaham house. In 1872, he succeeded his half-brother Frederick, becoming 5th Marquess of Londonderry.

CHAPTER 13

THE VISIT OF THE DUKE OF WELLINGTON

Arthur Wellesley, 1st Duke of Wellington
by Henry Pierce Bone after Sir Thomas Lawrence 1822
(© National Portrait Gallery, London)

In September 1827, Commander-in-Chief of the British Army, the Duke of Wellington made a triumphant tour in the North, visiting York, Stockton, Newcastle, Durham, Sunderland and Ravensworth Castle, staying with his former comrade in arms, the 3rd Marquess of Londonderry at Wynyard. The day before his visit, the Morning Chronicle reported that the Marquess had *'summoned his tenants to go out on horseback to meet his noble visitant'*, anticipating *'full 500 horsemen, who will all be decorated with dashing cockades, and accompanied by a numerous body of torch bearers, also mounted.'*

As the Duke entered the County of Durham at Yarm, he was welcomed by about a hundred and twenty men. A carriage specially commissioned for the day, and drawn by six horses, bore the Marchioness, Lady Sophia Gresley and the young Lord Seaham. Two wagons carrying a band of musicians came next, followed by the 3rd Marquess, accompanied by his son Lord Castlereagh, Colonel Sir Henry Browne, author and Tory politician Sir Roger Gresley and others. A large party of guests, including Whig leader Lord Grey and artist Sir Thomas Lawrence, President of the Royal Academy, joined them for great festivities that evening in Wynyard Park.

In Stockton, a grand triumphal arch, decorated with evergreens and laurel, proclaimed "Welcome the Hero of Waterloo". Church bells rang throughout the day and the Post Office, the Town Hall and the Old Castle displayed flags and trophies. Two principal inns, the Vane Arms Hotel and the Black Lion, were bedecked with banners, flags, laurel and evergreens.

After replying to the addresses of welcome, the Duke resumed his journey in Frances Anne's open coach, escorted by Sir Henry Hardinge, Lord Beresford and Lord Londonderry, all former comrades-in-arms. Upwards of 150 tenantry on horseback accompanied the procession, rewarded on their arrival at Wynyard with a *'fat ox, divided into two halves, roasted for the occasion.'* During his visit, Wellington laid the foundation stone of a planned memorial arch, later changed to the obelisk which still stands in the grounds at Wynyard.

Visiting the Londonderry empire

The Duke also spent a night at Seaham Hall, where the plan of the proposed harbour was explained to him. He visited pits at Rainton and Pittington, where pitmen assembled to meet the Duke and colliery manager John Buddle, the best known mining engineer of his day, delivered a welcoming speech.

The Duke travelled the short distance from Pittington to Penshaw, then known as Painsher, in *'a triumphal car, mounted on springs, and built to run over the railway.'* Specially built for the occasion and resembling a boat

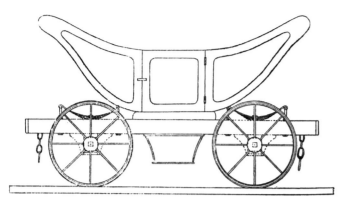

The Wellington Car designed and constructed at Chilton Moor Colliery Works, used to convey the Duke and Lord Londonderry from Pittington to Penshaw in 1822 (© Photographic Library Beamish Museum Ltd)

sitting on a coal wagon frame, the Wellington Car was preceded by another decked with banners bearing the names of the Duke's victories and carrying the colliery band, who played Handel's *'See the conquering hero comes.'* Although coal had been conveyed by rail from the pithead to the River Tyne for some time, the use of steam engines to haul wagons was relatively new. During his journey, Wellington was intrigued to see the locomotive engine or 'steam elephant' in motion, taking a close look at its construction and operation. On arriving at Penshaw, the gentlemen of the party accompanied the Duke to the staith, where wagons were lowered by machine to the keels for the unloading of coal. Returning to the town, the Duke was greeted by cheering crowds and the roaring of cannon.

The end of friendship

A few months later, in January 1828, Wellington became Prime Minister. Despite their former friendship, forged in the heat of battle during the Peninsular wars, political differences meant that Lord Londonderry was never offered a seat in Wellington's cabinet. The plaque on the Wellington obelisk at Wynyard, its foundation stone laid by the Duke himself in 1827, no longer bears the inscription 'Friend of Londonderry', placed there with such pride by his former comrade. The simple 'Wellington' a stark reminder of a broken alliance.

Nevertheless, Londonderry was very touched when, on the death of Wellington in 1852, he was awarded the Order of the Garter vacated by his late companion in arms. In a letter of congratulations, another old soldier Lord Anglesey, wrote, *'The value of it is much enhanced by its being worn by our late illustrious chief.'* The two men, both over 70, acted as pall bearers at Wellington's state funeral in November 1852. Although Londonderry had received many honours during his life, he told the Prime Minister Lord Derby *'To assure Her Majesty I value the bestowing on me the ribbon of Wellington as worth them all put together.'*

The Wellington Obelisk

CHAPTER 14

FREDERICK WILLIAM ROBERT STEWART (1805 - 1872)

Viscount Castlereagh (1822), 4th Marquess of Londonderry (1854)

Eldest son of the Hon. Charles Stewart by his first wife Lady Catherine Bligh, daughter of the third Earl of Darnley, Frederick was only seven years old when his mother died. As his father was serving in the army overseas, Frederick stayed with his uncle and aunt, Lord and Lady Castlereagh, before going to study at Eton in 1814. Styled Viscount Castlereagh from 1822, Frederick served as Member of Parliament for County Down from 1826 to 1852, holding junior office in the governments of both the Duke of Wellington and Sir Robert Peel. A Lord of the Admiralty from 1828 to 1830, appointed a Privy Councillor in 1835, he held the title of Lord Lieutenant of Down from 1845 till 1864.

Very popular in London society and known in his youth as "Young Rapid", Frederick often visited the Kensington home of Marguerite, Lady Blessington, an Irish writer, famed for her encouragement of literature, arts and science. A close friend of Benjamin Disraeli, who wrote 'Venetia' while staying at Lady Blessington's house, Frederick also loved music and the opera. After being introduced to famous opera singer Madame Giulia Grisi, he declared his love for her. In 1838, challenged to a duel by the lady's husband, Gerard de Melcy, Frederick was shot through the wrist, but survived otherwise unscathed.

Four years later, during an expedition to the Middle East, he had to be rescued when his boat ran aground and capsized in the River Nile. He later wrote an account of his journey through Egypt, Nubia, Petra, Palestine and Syria to Damascus and a volume of poetry, including 'El Tih' or 'The Wandering'. Published in 1849 and dedicated to his wife, the anthology also contains a poem written for her in Bellagio, Italy, in 1846, the opening lines a touching tribute to his love for her.

'Thou art become the essence of my soul,
From darker thoughts my heart for ever free,
Yields itself blindly to thy sweet controul;
I would not live could I not live with thee.'

At the British Embassy in Paris, in May 1846, Frederick married Elizabeth Frances Charlotte, widow of Viscount Powerscourt and daughter of the Earl of Roden. On his father's death in 1854, Frederick became 4th Marquess of Londonderry, but never inherited Wynyard, which went directly to his half-brother, son of Frances Anne, when he became 5th Marquess. In 1855 Frederick's wife became Roman Catholic, influenced largely by Cardinals Wiseman and Manning, both Archbishops of Westminster, and by Cardinal Newman, who converted to Roman Catholicism in 1845. All three were influential church men throughout the 1800s.

About the middle of 1862, Frederick began to suffer from mental problems and, medically certified as of unsound mind, was admitted to White Rock Villa, an infirmary in Hastings, Sussex. After a long seclusion in consequence of his mental disease, Frederick died childless in 1872, succeeded by his half-brother, the 2nd Earl Vane, as 5th Marquess of Londonderry. His widow died aged 70 on 2 September 1884 and was interred with him in the family burial place in Newtownards, close to Mount Stewart, the Londonderrys' home in Northern Ireland.

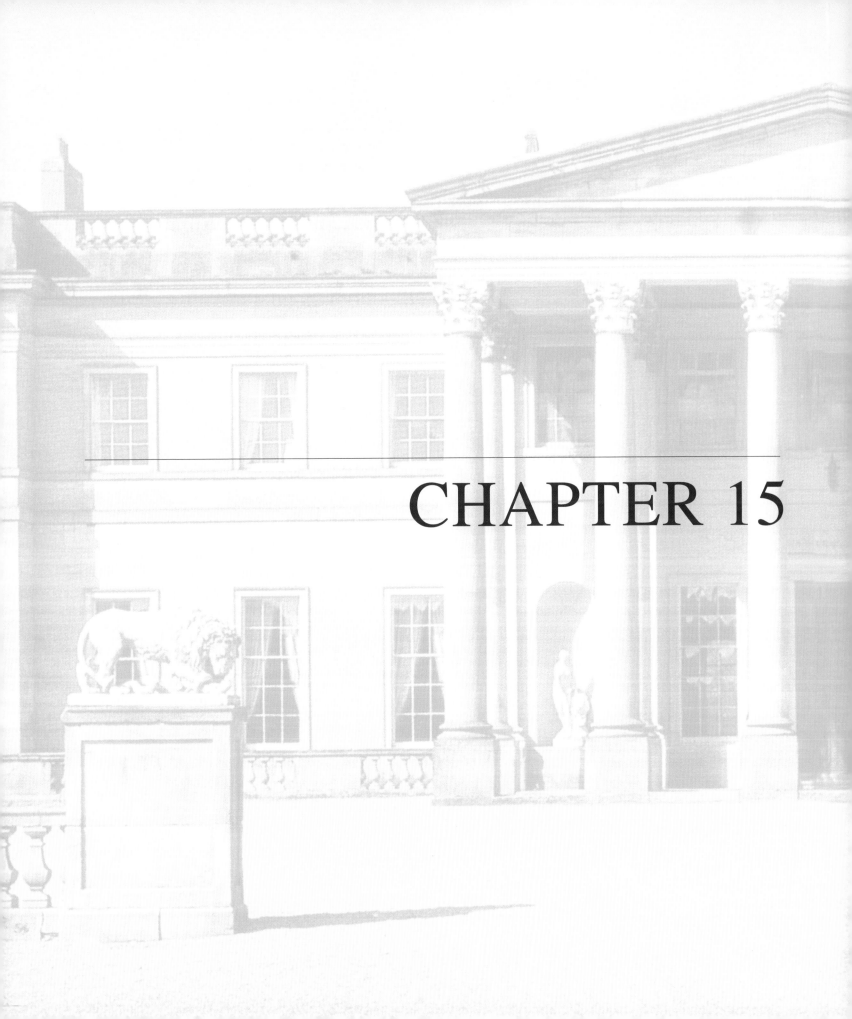

CHAPTER 15

GEORGE HENRY ROBERT CHARLES WILLIAM VANE-TEMPEST (1821–1884)

Viscount Seaham, Earl Vane, 5th Marquess of Londonderry (1872)

Frances Anne and Lord Seaham by Sir Thomas Lawrence c1828

Born in Vienna, where his father served as British Ambassador, Henry was the eldest son of Charles Stewart (later 3rd Marquess of Londonderry) and his second wife, Frances Anne. At the age of seven, Henry laid the foundation stone of the first house in New Seaham, the model town created by his parents for their colliery workers. He followed a military career, first as a lieutenant in the 1st Regiment of Life Guards, later as Colonel of the 4th Battalion of the Durham Light Infantry.

Conservative Member of Parliament for North Durham from 1847, after his father's death in 1854, he inherited the title Earl Vane and moved to the House of Lords. In 1867, he visited St. Petersburg in Russia, investing Czar Alexander II with the Order of the Garter on behalf of Queen Victoria. The Czar, in turn, conferred on him the Grand Cross of the Russian Order of St Alexander Nevsky. Thus continued the Londonderry family connection with the Russian royal family begun by his parents, the 3rd Marquess and Frances Anne.

Marriage

On August 3 1846, as Viscount Seaham, the future Marquess married Mary Cornelia Edwards, having met her during her coming out season just a little earlier that year. Only daughter of Sir John Edwards, Bart MP of Garth, Montgomeryshire in Wales and his wife Lady Harriet, Mary Cornelia and her new husband moved in to the Edwards' family home Greenfields, later renamed Plas Machynlleth. Known to later family members as 'Mummy Londonderry', Mary Cornelia was heiress to a considerable fortune, just like her mother-in-law, Frances Anne. Her father traced his ancestry to Ioworth, Prince of Wales and possessed 12,000 acres, including lead mines and slate quarries. Plas Machynlleth, the Edwards' family home, dating from at least 1653 and added to in 1820, contained 48 rooms.

In October 1846, shortly after their marriage, Viscount and Viscountess Seaham were received with great jubilation by the mayor and corporation of Stockton-on-Tees and by the local people. When the happy couple arrived at the new station at the terminus of the Stockton and Darlington Railway, the York Herald of October 3 1846 reported that they were '*greeted with a salute of cannon and three hearty cheers from the multitude assembled.*' Receiving congratulations and good wishes, Lord Seaham recognised the affection for his family, in particular his father, the 3rd Marquess, commending the people of Stockton for their help at the time of the catastrophic fire at the family mansion. Travelling on to Wynyard, at the village of Thorpe Thewles the couple passed through a triumphal arch, decorated with evergreens and flags. The Londonderry Colliery Band played, while on the village green, horsemen, neighbouring gentry, local farmers, Wynyard tenants and gaily dressed ladies in carriages cheered them on.

Family life in Wales

From 1846, Viscount Seaham managed the estates and slate quarries of his father-in-law, Sir John Edwards, as well as promoting the Corris Railway, created to carry slate from the quarries to the markets. As Earl Vane, the title he took in 1854 on the death of his father, he served, latterly as Chairman, on the board of Cambrian Railways.

It was not until 1872, when his half- brother, Frederick, 4th Marquess of Londonderry, died childless, that Henry inherited the title. With the addition of the Londonderry estates to his Welsh properties, he now owned a total of 27,000 acres in Ireland and 23,000 in England and Wales.

Like his father before him, from 1880-1884, the 5th Marquess served as Lord Lieutenant of Durham. However, after their marriage, the Vane-Tempests appear to have visited Wynyard rarely, spending most of their time at their Welsh home, becoming great local benefactors. In a reflection of the work of the 3rd Marquess and his wife at Seaham, as well as bringing the railway to Machynlleth, they also provided housing for local people, alms houses, an infant school and a hospital. They carried out restoration work at St. Peter's Church and, in 1874, erected the 78ft Castlereagh Memorial Clock to mark the coming of age of their eldest son, Charles (1852-1915). He succeeded his father as 6th Marquess in 1884 and left Machynlleth, spending more time at Wynyard as well as Londonderry House.

Children

The couple's youngest son, Lord Herbert Vane-Tempest (1862-1921), remained resident at Plas Machynlleth, served as Chairman of the Cambrian Railways and became JP and High Sheriff of Montgomeryshire. Created KCVO (Knight Commander of the Royal Victorian Order), a honour given for personal service to the sovereign, he was killed in

5th Marquess of Londonderry, Provincial Grand Master of the Masons 1880-84 (©Photographic Library Beamish Museum Ltd)

Memorial to Frances Vane Tempest at Long Newton church

Memorial to Avarina Mary Vane Tempest at Long Newton church

the Abermule train collision of 1921. Two daughters of the 5th Marquess and his wife, Mary Cornelia, died young, Frances Cornelia Harriet in 1872, aged 21, her sister Avarina Mary in 1873 at the age of 16. Commemorated in the family chapel at Long Newton, near Wynyard, both girls are buried with their parents and brother, Herbert, in the graveyard of St.Peter's Church, Machynlleth.

Their second son, Lord Henry John Vane-Tempest (1854 – 1905), a regular visitor to Wynyard during the tenure of

his older brother, the 6th Marquess, is commemorated in a stained glass window in the chapel at Wynyard and is portrayed in shooting gear in a painting in the ante-room beyond the library. Both Henry and his younger brother Herbert, known as Harry and Bertie, remained bachelors and figure in many photographs of Wynyard house parties in the 1890s.

Youngest daughter, Lady Alexandrina Louise Maud Vane-Tempest, born in 1863, was known as Aline. At the age of twenty six, she married Wentworth Canning Blackett Beaumont, MP for Tyneside, later 1st Viscount Allendale. Their eldest son accompanied his uncle, the 6th Lord Londonderry at the 1903 coronation of King Edward VII, portrayed in the dining room at Wynyard Hall, now the Wellington Restaurant.

Wynyard Chapel

Although the 5th Marquess and his wife Mary Cornelia lived most of their married life in Wales, their influence at Wynyard is still very evident. In commissioning James Brooks to extend and develop the original tiny chapel, they paved the way for the magnificent Romanesque building so central to Wynyard today. Mary Cornelia and her children were also responsible for installing the organ and the beautiful stained glass windows.

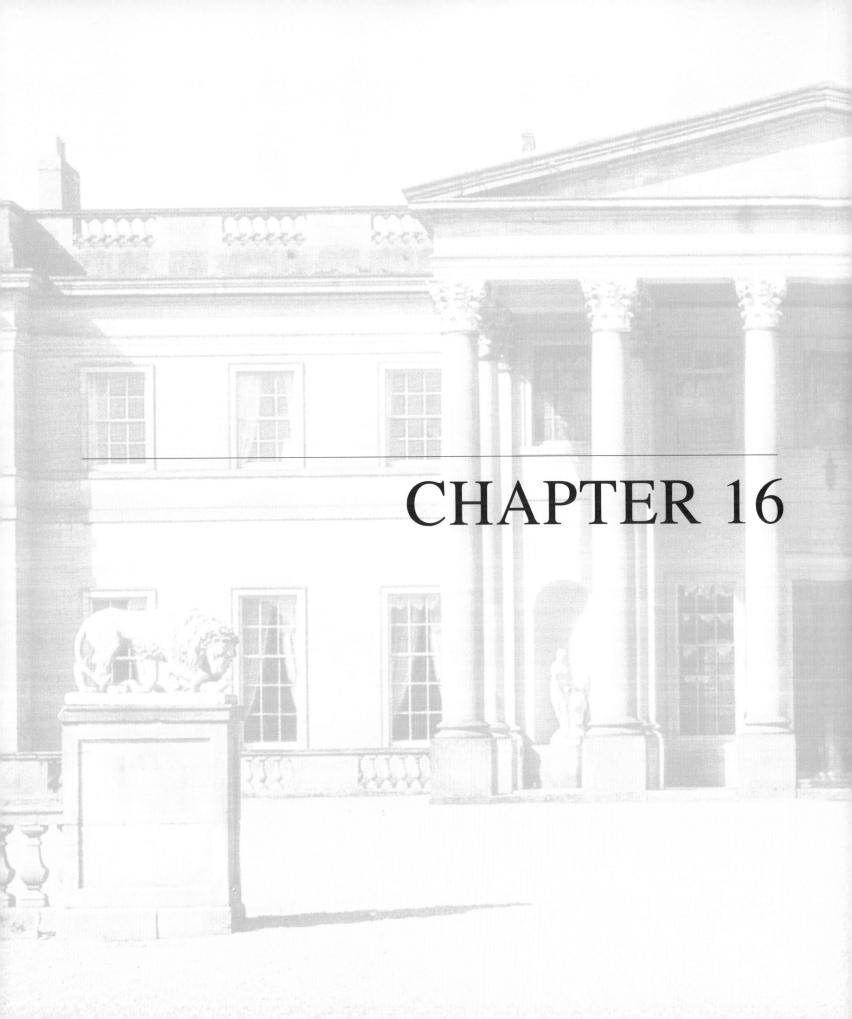

CHAPTER 16

CHARLES STEWART (VANE-TEMPEST-STEWART) 1852-1915

6th Marquess of Londonderry 1884

Life at Wynyard

In 1875, at the age of 23, he married Lady Theresa Susey Helen Chetwynd-Talbot, eldest daughter of Charles John Chetwynd-Talbot, 19th Earl of Shrewbury and Anna Theresa Cockerell. The wedding, attended by 1,000 guests, took place in the private chapel of the Chetwynd-

Charles Vane-Tempest-Stewart, 6th Marquess of Londonderry (©Photographic Library Beamish Museum Ltd)

Born at Holdernesse House in London on July 16 1852, Charles Stewart was the eldest son of Henry, 5th Marquess of Londonderry by his wife Mary Cornelia, daughter of Sir John Edwards, Bart., of Garth in Montgomeryshire. In 1884, on the death of his father, Charles became 6th Marquess of Londonderry, adding by royal licence the family name Stewart to that of Vane-Tempest one year later.

Charles Vane-Tempest-Stewart, 6th Marquess, painted by W W Hodgson (© National Portrait Gallery, London)

Talbots at Alton Towers in Staffordshire. The family of the 5th Marquess and his wife were born and brought up at Plas Machynlleth, the Welsh estate inherited by Mary Cornelia. Many of their children remained there until death. However, on their marriage, Charles and Theresa returned to the north of England, moving in to Kirkby Hall in Bedale, North Yorkshire. When Charles inherited the Londonderry title, they took up residence at Wynyard, where, by 1902, they had installed electric lighting and telephonic communication with Stockton-on-Tees.

Considered by many an ideal landlord, the 6th Marquess and his wife, Theresa renewed the habit of close association with their tenants, making regular visits to their homes and distributing gifts to the children on the estate. The 6th Marquess ordered the construction of a

reading room for the tenants, while Theresa provided a school on the estate and conducted Sunday School lessons in her own boudoir or study. She was also responsible for creating outstanding gardens at Wynyard. A keen sportsman, the 6th Marquess restored regular shooting parties to the estate, employing no less than eighteen gamekeepers, He also made considerable alterations to the Wynyard chapel between 1903 and 1910, incorporating the Arts and Crafts design entrance porch and a great deal of marble, including a screen of pillars leading into the memorial room.

Political life

Charles Stewart served as Conservative MP for the County of Down from 1878-1884, when he moved to the House of Lords as Earl Vane. In the governments of Lord Salisbury and Arthur Balfour, he was Chairman of the London School Board from 1895-1897, Postmaster-

Charles Vane-Tempest-Stewart, 6th Marquess of Londonderry, carrying the Great Sword of Occasion at the coronation of Edward VII August 1902 by John Singer Sargent RA 1904

Theresa, Marchioness of Londonderry, at the coronation of Edward VII 1902

A cartoon from The Westminster Gazette April 1912, showing the 6th Marquess, Bonar Law and Edward Carson

Theresa, Marchioness of Londonderry
(©Photographic Library Beamish Museum Ltd)

General in Balfour's Government from 1900-1902, serving as President of the Board of Education from 1902-1905 and President of the Council from 1903-1905.

Resident in Dublin from 1886-1889 as Lord Lieutenant (or Viceroy) of Ireland, he also served as Lord Lieutenant of Belfast from 1900-1904 and was Lord Lieutenant of Down from 1902 till his death in 1915. Created Knight of the Garter by Queen Victoria in 1888, he was appointed to the Privy Council after the accession of King Edward VII. A portrait in Wynyard's Wellington Restaurant shows the 6th Marquess of Londonderry carrying the sword of state at the coronation of Edward VII in 1902. A regular visitor to Wynyard both before and after his accession to the throne, in 1903 the King held a Privy Council meeting at Wynyard Hall, the first time the body had met outside London since the reign of King Charles I. A plaque on the wall in the Mirror Room commemorates the occasion, when the 6th Marquess was appointed Lord President of the Council.

Theresa, Lady Londonderry, an accomplished orator, gained prominence as a Conservative Party leader, forming the Ulster Women's Unionist Council in 1911, serving as President from 1913. The Londonderrys played a prominent role in the Ulster Unionist Demonstration held in Belfast at Easter 1912, when thousands gathered to hear Conservative leader Bonar Law and Irish Unionist leader Edward Carson speak against Home Rule for Ireland. Mount Stewart, the Londonderry home in Northern Ireland, provided hospitality for the two leaders, as well as other important politicians, aristocrats and family members. A few months later, in October 1913, the Londonderrys welcomed Lord Charles Beresford and Captain James Craig, members of the Ulster movement, to a shoot in Wynyard Park. In 1921, Craig succeeded Edward Carson as leader of the Ulster Unionist Party and became the first Prime Minister of Northern Ireland.

Theresa encouraged several parliamentary careers, including those of potential party leaders Walter Long and Edward Carson, who wrote in 1909, *'I am sure the most interesting chapter in my biography will be the one headed Visits to Wynyard and Mount Stewart.'* Acknowledging her great political influence, the North Mail of March 1914 suggested *'if she had been a man, she would have made a great political wire-puller.'* In addition, during World War I, Theresa supported the Red

Cross and the VAD (Voluntary Aid Detachments providing medical attention), establishing military convalescent homes at Mount Stewart, Londonderry House and Seaham Hall. She served on Durham Education Committee and the senate of Queen's University, Belfast, as well as being active in the Primrose League, the Victoria League and the Girls' Friendly Society. However, despite her political interest and influence, Theresa, known to the family as Guy, disagreed with universal suffrage and disapproved of the methods employed to obtain votes for women.

Social life and scandal

'Theresa lived and ruled at Wynyard like a very benevolent monarch. Once from there, I went to Stockton races with my hosts and our reception as we drove on to

Theresa Susey Helen Vane-Tempest-Stewart, Marchioness of Londonderry, by Lafayette, albumen cabinet card 1886 (© National Portrait Gallery, London)

the course was such as might be given to royalty.' Elizabeth, Countess of Fingall went on to describe Theresa, Lady Londonderry as *'a most dominant personality. The proudest face I have ever seen with a short upper lip and a beautifully shaped, determined chin.'* One of the most powerful society hostesses, both at Wynyard and at their London home, Londonderry House, contemporary accounts describe Theresa 'Nellie' Londonderry as irrevocably haughty. Socialite and wit, Margot Asquith, whose husband Herbert was Liberal Prime Minister from 1908- 1916, considered her *'arrogant and vulgar'*, while writer E.F.Benson (1867- 1940), creator of the Mapp and Lucia books, called her *'a highwaywoman in a tiara'*.

Vita Sackville-West's 'The Edwardians', written in 1930, is very critical of the aristocratic society of the time, when guests at magnificent house parties indulged in food, drinks, games and affairs. The book's Lady Sylvia Roehampton, said to be modelled on Theresa, Lady Londonderry, has an extra-marital affair with Sebastian, young heir to Chevron, an enormous country house. Fearing a scandal and wanting to maintain social standards, Lady Roehampton leaves Sebastian once her husband discovers the affair.

Theresa's younger son, Reginald, born in December 1879, is alleged to be the result of a similar liaison between Theresa and her brother-in-law, Reginald, Viscount Helmsley, one of the handsomest men of his generation. Son of the first Earl of Feversham and best man at the Stewart's wedding in 1875, a year later, Reginald Helmsley married Theresa's sister, Lady Muriel Chetwynd-Talbot. Although rumoured to have had dalliances with various men, including Lord Annaly and Henry Cust, noted socialite, womaniser and editor of the fashionable Pall Mall Gazette, the implied rift between Theresa and her husband, the suggestion that he refused to speak to her except in public, appears to be an exaggeration.

Family life in photographs

The Londonderry's third child, Reginald, suffered from congenital lameness and walked with crutches. After a lifetime of illness, he died aged nineteen of tuberculosis. His putative father Reginald Helmsley is thought to have died from the same disease in Madeira in 1881, at the age of 29. Known to the family as Rex, there has been some suggestion that Reginald's real father was King Edward VII himself. A keen engine driver, he travelled in the cabs of locomotives running on the Londonderry line and, by the age of fifteen, could drive the train single-handed from Wynyard to Seaham.

A talented photographer, the younger son left behind a wonderful pictorial legacy of his family's life at Wynyard, Seaham and Mount Stewart. In the 1970s, a Victorian darkroom, complete with porcelain sink, photographer's

Theresa and Reginald's dark room

Charles, Helen and Reginald, with 'Lina', taken by Theresa c1890. From the Londonderry Album, with permission of Lord Londonderry

bench and a Magic Lantern outfit, still in working order, was discovered in an upper room at Wynyard Hall. *'Scattered in profusion were porcelain trays, half empty bottles of photographic chemicals in all shapes and sizes, boxes of printing paper, in fact, all the wherewithal of the photographer's art.'* A leather camera case embossed with the initials T.L. bore witness to the fact that Reginald's mother Theresa was also a gifted photographer. Their collection of glass plates from the 1890s was used to produce the Londonderry Album, published by the 9th Marquess in 1978, *'a posthumous tribute to the memory of a brave and talented young man who departed this life all too soon.'*

The 6th Marquess and his wife had two other children. Lady Helen Mary Theresa Vane-Tempest-Stewart (1876-1956), known as 'Birdie', married Lord Stavordale, later the 6th Earl of Ilchester, and had two sons and two daughters. Sir Charles Stewart Henry Vane-Tempest-

Stewart (1878-1949) became 7th Marquess of Londonderry when his father died suddenly of pneumonia at Wynyard on 8 February 1915. Outside the Londonderry offices in Seaham, a touching tribute is inscribed, *'This statue is placed here by his son and daughter amongst those whom he loved so well and whose welfare and happiness were to him the principal objects of his life.'*

Despite the protestations of her family, Theresa, packed up her possessions in Londonderry House within weeks of her husband's death and lived in a suite of rooms in Seaham Hall before moving to live in Lumley Castle, ten miles from Seaham. She died in 1919 at Carlton House Terrace, her London home since 1917. Her funeral took place at Wynyard, coupled with a simultaneous memorial service at St. Peter's, Eaton Square in London, before she was laid to rest with her husband in the family vault at Long Newton.

Charles Vane-Tempest-Stewart, 6th Marquess of Londonderry, statue at Seaham Harbour

124

CHAPTER 17

CHARLES STEWART HENRY VANE-TEMPEST-STEWART (1878-1949)

7th Marquess of Londonderry 1915

Charles Stewart Henry Vane-Tempest-Stewart, 7th Marquess of Londonderry (©Photographic Library Beamish Museum Ltd)

Educated at Eton and Sandhurst, Charles Stewart Henry Vane-Tempest-Stewart was the son of Charles Stewart, 6th Marquess of Londonderry and his wife Theresa, daughter of Charles John Chetwynd-Talbot, 19th Earl of Shrewsbury. Styled Lord Stewart until 1884, when he took the title Viscount Castlereagh, Charles Stewart succeeded to the Londonderry title in 1915. Commissioned into the Royal Horse Guards in 1897, he was a natural cavalryman, winning prizes for horse riding and rising to the rank of Major during the war of 1914-18.

Political life

Entering Parliament in 1906, he served as MP for Maidstone in Kent until 1915 and as President of the

Charles Stewart Henry Vane-Tempest-Stewart, 7th Marquess of Londonderry, photograph by Mary Olive Edis (Mrs Galsworthy) 1920s (© National Portrait Gallery, London)

National Union of Conservative and Unionist Associations. Appointed Knight of the Garter in 1919, the 7th Marquess became leader of the Senate and Minister of Education in the newly formed government of Northern

Ireland in 1921. He steered through the controversial Education Act of 1923, known as the Londonderry Act, intended to secularise education in Northern Ireland.

An enthusiastic aviator, serving as Finance Member of the Air Council in 1919 and Under Secretary of State for Air from 1920-21, he encouraged the re-equipment of the Air Force after World War I. He was also responsible for the opening of Northern Ireland's first civil aerodrome at Newtownards, near Mount Stewart, the family home in Northern Ireland. In Ramsey MacDonald's National (coalition) Government of 1931, he served as Secretary of State for Air from 1931-35, promoting the development of radar, as well as the Spitfires and Hurricanes so crucial to Britain's aerial success in World War II.

During the 1930s, hoping to bring about Anglo-German understanding, Lord Londonderry, along with many other influential aristocrats, consulted with Hitler's associates Goering and Ribbentrop, the latter a frequent visitor to

Wynyard, although Lord Londonderry later described him as *'shallow, loquacious and self-opinionated'*. Singularly lacking in the diplomatic skills his position required, political cartoonist David Low dubbed Ribbentrop Ambassador Brickendrop. He also became known as the Londonderry Herr. Sir Eric Phipps, British Ambassador in Berlin found Ribbentrop *'irritating, ignorant and boundlessly conceited.'* On various trips to Germany during the 1930s, Londonderry also met Himmler, Rudolph Hess, Foreign Minister Neurath and Adolf Hitler himself, as well as visiting, with his wife and youngest daughter, the Berlin Olympics, tickets courtesy of Ribbentrop. Black American athlete Jesse Owens famously won four gold medals, confounding Hitler's Nazi belief in the superiority of the Aryan race. A stark memorial of this time, a gift from Ribbentrop in 1936, a porcelain figure of an SS man, known as 'The Storm Trooper' still stands on a mantelpiece in Mount Stewart.

Herr von Ribbentrop with the 7th Marquess at Wynyard, November 1936   (©Photographic Library Beamish Museum Ltd)

In 1938, in an attempt to explain his position, Lord Londonderry published a slim volume, '*Ourselves and Germany*', also produced in a German translation, despite opposition from Joseph Goebbels, Nazi Minister of Propaganda from 1933-45. In a final, possibly ill-judged bid to avert war, Lord Londonderry flew to Germany for brief talks with Ribbentrop and Goering the day before Prime Minister Neville Chamberlain's historic meeting with Hitler on 30 September 1938. The British leader returned with the infamous piece of paper supposed to guarantee the safety of the world. A year later, on 3 September 1939, Britain declared war against Germany. Londonderry failed to win a place in the new government formed in 1940 by his cousin Winston Churchill. Published in 1943, Lord Londonderry's memoir, '*Wings of Destiny*', reflected on his Air Ministry years, between the end of the first World War and the beginning of the second, when his determination to maintain an independent air force met with fierce opposition. The book's dedication, to Viscount Trenchard, known as the father of the RAF, speaks for itself.

Although Londonderry coveted the post of Viceroy and Governor General of India, for family reasons he turned down the post of Governor General of Canada, offered in 1931. In other areas of public life, he served as Mayor of Durham, Lord Lieutenant of both County Durham and County Down and as Chancellor of the Universities of Durham and Belfast. In 1924, he conferred honorary degrees of Queen's University, Belfast, upon the Duke and Duchess of York, the future King George VI and Queen Elizabeth, who stayed with the Londonderrys at their Irish home, Mount Stewart.

Marriage

In November 1899, Charles married Edith Helen Chaplin, daughter of Henry, 1st Viscount Chaplin, a friend of the 6th Marquess and frequent visitor to Wynyard. As their mother died when they were small children, Edith and her brother and sister were largely brought up by their Aunt Millicent, 4th Duchess of Sutherland, (married to Strath, their mother's brother) who ensured Edith's entry into London society. Close friends with Lady Helen Stewart, sister to Charley, as he was affectionately known, Edith often met the future 7th Marquess at social events. He proposed to her in the garden at Wynyard at his coming of age party in August 1899. On a trip to Japan in 1903, she acquired a snake tattoo on her ankle, her husband chose the insignia of his regiment, the Royal Horse Guards.

Edith, Lady Castlereagh
(©Photographic Library Beamish Museum Ltd)

Edith played an active role in numerous organisations and charities. In 1914, after the outbreak of World War I, she was appointed Colonel-in-Chief of the Women's Volunteer Reserve (WRV) and, in July 1915, founded The Women's Legion, serving as Director General from 1915-1918. Unpopular in some quarters for its apparent suffragette tendencies, tens of thousands of women joined the volunteer force, replacing men who left to fight in both World Wars. She became the first ever Dame Commander of the Order of the British Empire in the Military Division as well as, in 1918, the first woman Justice of the Peace for Durham. During World War II, Lord Londonderry was President of the Red Cross, purchasing a Belfast house to serve as headquarters. In July 1944, shortly after D Day, Lady Londonderry received a letter from General Eisenhower, Supreme Commander of the Allied

Edith, Lady Castlereagh, in uniform of The Women's Legion c1918 (with permission of The National Trust)

Expeditionary Force, expressing his appreciation for the work of the re-established Women's Legion, which she served as President from 1939-1945.

Political and literary entertaining

A powerful influence on her husband's political career, Edith, Lady Londonderry continued her predecessor's tradition of lavish political entertaining, particularly at their London home, Londonderry House, a sumptuous setting for the development of the careers of leading politicians. The magnificent staircase surmounted by a large skylight and rococo chandelier, provided a glittering platform where Edith, an outstanding political hostess, proudly wearing the Londonderry jewels, welcomed eminent visitors, presenting party leaders on the eve of the opening of Parliament. In 1919, 2,000 guests met Prime Minister Lloyd George and his deputy Bonar Law, while

the coalition government of 1931 saw Conservative Stanley Baldwin and Labour's Ramsey MacDonald, both extremely influential and important as party leaders and Prime Ministers in their own right, standing together on the Londonderry House staircase.

Although platonic, Lady Londonderry's relationship with Ramsey MacDonald caused outrage in some quarters, especially from the Labour party, who felt that he betrayed their cause by allying himself with such staunch Conservatives. Formerly MP for Seaham, Ramsay MacDonald became Britain's first Labour Prime Minister in 1924. In May the same year, the first signatories of the visitors' book at his official country seat, Chequers, were the Londonderrys. Many people considered that Edith's friendship with Ramsay MacDonald and other leading politicians enhanced the parliamentary career of the 7th Marquess. By 1933, he was increasingly described as husband of one of the most important political hostesses. F.E.Smith, later Lord Birkenhead, a frequent guest of the Londonderrys, alleged that *'Charley was catering his way to the cabinet.'*

In 1915, to provide an escape from the worries and pressures of World War I, Edith created an exclusive club known as The Ark, its eminent members named after animals, their leader, Lady Londonderry herself, known as Circe, after the mythological sorceress in Homer's Odyssey. Royal brothers the Duke of York (later King George VI) and the Duke of Windsor were invited to join, while literary visitors included John Buchan, George Bernard Shaw, Sean O'Casey, W.B. Yeats, Compton Mackenzie, Osbert Sitwell, Harold Nicholson and Vita Sackville-West. An able writer herself, Edith produced a memoir of Frances Anne, the Marchioness of Londonderry, a biography of her father Henry Chaplin and, in 1938, an autobiography *'Retrospect'*.

Her children's book, *The Magic Inkpot*, based on Celtic legends and influenced by Irish writer C.S.Lewis, was originally written, in 1928, as a series of letters to her youngest child Mairi. Later illustrated by artist Edmund Brock and Edith's older daughter Lady Margaret Stewart, all the stories feature Mairi and her brother Robin enjoying fantastic adventures together. First, they must take the plunge into the magic inkpot, based on the pot on their father's desk, used for the safe keeping of his Garter medal. In their mother's office, pencil marks on a door frame, still visible today, record the growing height of generations of Londonderry children, including grandchildren Annabel and, very high up, Timothy Jessel.

Relationships

During the course of their marriage, which lasted from 1899 until his death in 1949 and produced five children, Lord Londonderry had several mistresses, often with his wife's knowledge and support. Although he swore his undying love to Edith, Charley had relationships with Eloise, Countess of Ancaster, Ettie, Lady Desborough and American heiress Consuelo Vanderbilt, married to Charley's second cousin, the Duke of Marlborough. Shortly after Charley's marriage to Edith, his illegitimate daughter, Dorothé Mabel Lewis, was born to actress Fannie Ward. Edith offered to adopt the child and, in later years, became her close friend. Married at the age of seventeen, Dorothé was heartbroken when, just four months later, her husband, airman Jack Barnato, died in the Spanish flu epidemic of 1918. After a plane crash in 1938 tragically killed Dorothé and her second husband

Lord Plunket, Lord Londonderry became joint guardian to their three sons, Patrick, Robin and Sean. In an echo of Edith's young life, the boys were brought up by their paternal aunt, the Hon. Helen Rhodes. The Plunkets had been constant visitors at Londonderry House and Mount Stewart, the Londonderry home in Northern Ireland, and the children clearly considered the Londonderrys their grandparents.

Mount Stewart

During the 1920s, Edith, Lady Londonderry created gardens at the family's Irish home, Mount Stewart, County Down. Acquired by the Stewart family in 1744, the 18th century house and its contents, including Londonderry monogrammed glassware and china bearing the monogram Castlereagh, reflect the importance of the family in British social and political life. The twenty six bedrooms are all named after European capital cities. Chairs presented to Castlereagh by Prince Metternich after the Congress of Vienna of 1815 surround the dining room, their original upholstery of blue silk replaced by

Mount Stewart (with permission of The National Trust)

tapestry covers. Each one represents an eminent member of the Congress, including the Duke of Wellington and half-brothers Castlereagh and Charles Stewart, both subsequently holders of the Londonderry title. The chapel, where Edith and Charley married in 1899, contains the garter banners of several Lords Londonderry and an altar piece sent as a gift from the Vatican after Castlereagh had returned items looted by Napoleon.

Mount Stewart's ninety eight acre garden, now considered one of the best in the British Isles, contains an unrivalled collection of rare and unusual plants. Although laid out originally by Frances Anne and the 3rd Marquess, the gardens were transformed by Edith, who increased the size of the lake and laid out walks in the Lily Wood and the rest of the estate. Notable features of the formal gardens include the Shamrock Garden with its topiary harp and the Red Hand of Ulster portrayed in tulips. Edith also created a Fountain Pool, an Italian Garden and Spanish Garden with a mosaic tiled pavilion. She planted gardens to commemorate the Silver Jubilee of George V in 1935 and

A portrayal of Lady Mairi Bury, youngest child of the 7th Marquess, in the gardens of Mount Stewart

the coronation of George VI in 1937. The Dodo Walk with its carved stone animals and Ark refers to the social and literary clique she established during World War I.

The circular Mairi Garden centres on a beautiful statue, with a striking resemblance to Peter Pan, of the Londonderry's youngest daughter as a little girl. Around the base, mosaic tiles spell out 'Mairi, Mairi, quite contrary, how does your garden grow ?', while the silver and blue planting of campanulas, agapanthus, arum lilies, stachys and Perovskia 'Blue Spire' echoed the "Silver bells and cockle shells" of the answer contained in the nursery rhyme. Renowned garden designer Gertrude Jekyll created the Sunken Garden, planted with a wonderful combination of blue, purple, yellow and orange. In 1957, handing over the garden to the care of the National Trust, Edith, Lady Londonderry said, *'gardens are meant to be lived in and enjoyed. I hope they may long continue to be a source of pleasure to those who visit them.'* In 1977, the National Trust also accepted responsibility for the house and, with 50,000 visitors per annum, Mount Stewart is now the organisation's most popular property in Northern Ireland.

Children

Until her death in 2009 at the age of 88, Lady Mairi Bury, youngest child of the 7th Marquess and his wife, lived all her life at Mount Stewart. Born in 1921, ten years after their previous child, her mother described Mairi as *'the little star in our universe.'* In 1940, at the age of nineteen, Mairi married the Hon. Derek William Charles Keppel, later Viscount Bury, who had been invited to Mount Stewart as a young RAF officer posted to Northern Ireland during World War II. The couple had two daughters, Elizabeth and Rose, and divorced in 1958.

In 1920, at Durham Cathedral, the Londonderry's eldest daughter, Maureen, born in 1900, married the younger son of Lord Derby, MP Oliver Stanley, who became Secretary of State for War in 1940. The couple had a son, Michael Charles (1921-1990) and a daughter, who, as Lady Kathryn Dugdale, served as Lady-in-Waiting to Queen Elizabeth II from 1955-2002. Lady Maureen Stanley died from tuberculosis in 1942, aged 41.

The Londonderry's second daughter Margaret was born in 1910, followed a year later by Helen Maglona. A charming portrait of the two little girls painted in 1914 by

Margaret and Helen, children of the 7th Marquess, and Edith, Lady Londonderry painted by Mrs Young-Hunter c1914 (with permission of The National Trust)

Mrs Young-Hunter still hangs at Mount Stewart, while the sisters as young women can be seen in a 1930s photograph of Wynyard Hall amateur dramatics, now on display in the Statue Gallery. Both girls were married twice and divorced. In 1934, Helen was the only family member to attend Margaret's wedding to Alan Muntz, a divorced man, disapproved of by her parents. She later married Sir Hugh Falkus, but had reputedly been in love with the French airman and writer, Antoine de St.Exupery, killed during World War II.

In 1935, Helen married Edward Herbert, 2nd Baron Jessel, but the couple divorced in 1960 and she married Dennis Cecil Hartington Walsh. With her first husband, Helen had two daughters, Camilla and Joanne and a son, Timothy, who died in 1969, aged 34. Margaret had no children. A noted writer and war correspondent, she died in 1966 and is buried with her parents at Mount Stewart in a private part of the garden. Known as Tir na Nog, Irish for the Land of Eternal Youth, the burial ground is watched over by stone statues of Irish saints, created by Edmund Brock, the artist who painted the water colours for 'The Magic Inkpot', Edith, Lady Londonderry's children's book. In 2009, her youngest child, Mairi, for whom the book was written, was also laid to rest in Tir na Nog.

After suffering a stroke, following an earlier gliding accident, the 7th Marquess, always known as Charley, died in February 1949 at Mount Stewart, where, ten years later, on 23 April 1959, Edith died of cancer. A few months earlier, she celebrated her 80th birthday at Londonderry House, when guest of honour was Harold Macmillan, seventh in the long line of Prime Ministers Edith, Lady Londonderry classed as personal friends. On his father's death, son Robin succeeded to the title as 8th Marquess of Londonderry.

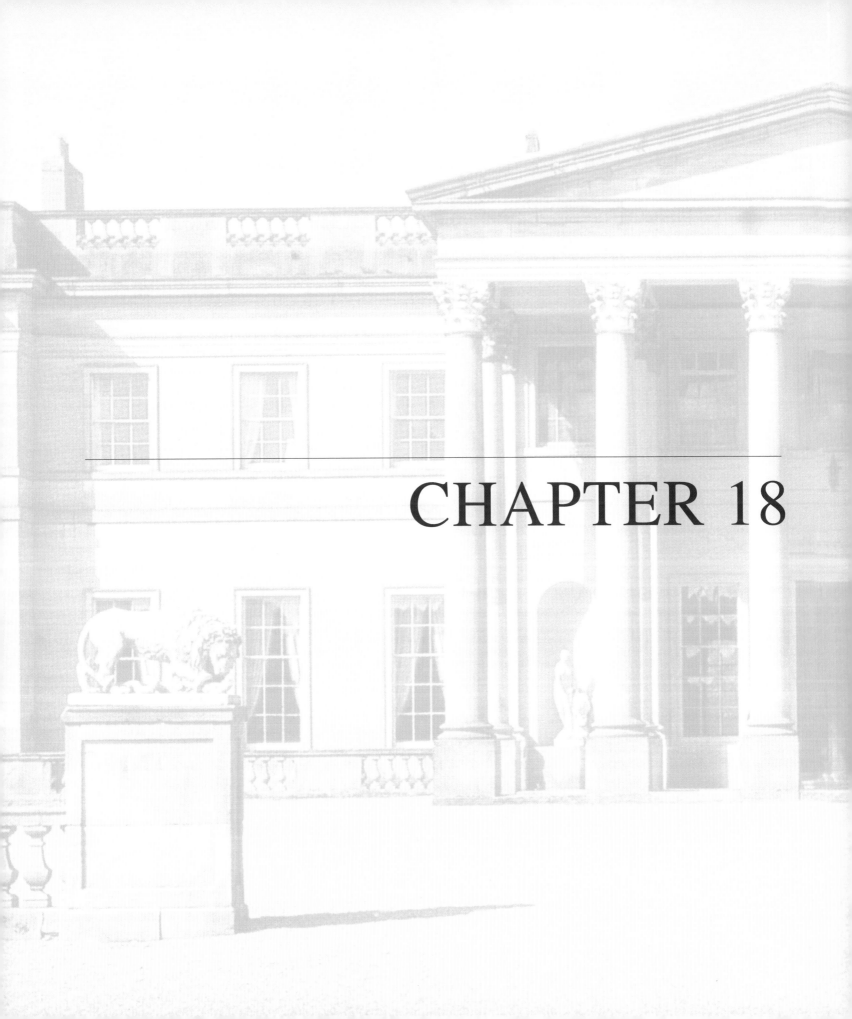

CHAPTER 18

EDWARD CHARLES STEWART ROBERT VANE-TEMPEST-STEWART (1902-1955)

8th Marquess of Londonderry 1949

Only son of the 7th Marquess and Marchioness, Edward Charles Stewart Robert Vane-Tempest-Stewart, born in November 1902, began life with royal connections. Known as Robin, godson to King Edward VII, as a small boy, in 1911, he was a pageboy at the coronation of King George V, his father one of the mantle bearers to the King.

The 7th Marquess and his wife, Edith lived mainly at Londonderry House and Mount Stewart, coming to Wynyard for Christmas and in May for Stockton Races. In addition to the huge outgoings on their other properties, annual costs of £7,649 to maintain a house they occupied only for a few weeks in the year made the Londonderrys first contemplate selling Wynyard in 1925. Assuming that their son would not be interested in farming there, they considered pulling the Hall down and building a smaller house in its place.

In the event, the 8th Marquess came to love Wynyard and developed a real sympathy with the mining community at Seaham. His difficult relationship with his parents, particularly his father, created friction during industrial disputes at the family's collieries and the General Strike of 1926, when father and son took opposing views. Unionist MP for County Down from 1931-1945, he succeeded to the Londonderry title on the death of his father in 1949. He also served as honorary attaché to the British Embassy in Rome and as a director of Londonderry Collieries and of Arsenal Football Club, acting as Chairman from 1939-1946.

Married in 1931 to Romaine Combe, daughter of Major Boyce Combe of Farnham, Surrey, and his wife Mabel Tombs, daughter of Major General Sir Henry Tombs VC, the couple had three children before her tragically early death from cancer in 1951. His wife's death plunged the 8th Marquess into deep depression and alcoholism and he died four years later, in 1955, aged fifty two.

Wynyard had been made over to the young family in 1945 and the children spent all their holidays there, one of them recalling tenants dropping curtsies to their mother. On her death, eldest daughter Lady Jane, born in 1932, assumed a parental role to her younger sister and brother and took over the running of Wynyard, even organising shooting parties. Maid of honour at the coronation of Queen Elizabeth II in 1953, she married Max Rayne, Baron Rayne in 1965 and has four children. Now a tireless charity worker, she is patron of Chicken Shed, the theatre company founded in London in 1974 to cater for children of all backgrounds and abilities. Lady Annabel, born 1934, later married to Sir James Goldsmith, gave her name to the fashionable London nightclub founded by her first husband Mark Birley in 1963. Her first born son, Rupert Birley, died tragically young and is commemorated in the chapel at Wynyard.

Alexander Charles Robert Vane-Tempest-Stewart, known as Alastair, born in 1937, became 9th Marquess of Londonderry in 1955 on the death of his father. He was eighteen. Buried together in the wild garden at Wynyard Park, Robin, 8th Marquess and Romaine, Marchioness of Londonderry, were reinterred in 1988 at the family vault in Long Newton.

Coming of age of Robin, Viscount Castlereagh, with his parents 1923

ALEXANDER CHARLES ROBERT VANE-TEMPEST-STEWART (Born 1937)

9th Marquess of Londonderry 1955

Inheriting the Londonderry title in 1955 at the age of 18, the 9th Marquess, known as Alastair, was a keen musician and gifted pianist. As a student, he ran a jazz band, The Eton Five. In 1958, he married Nicolette Harrison, daughter of Michael Harrison, a stockbroker, and his Latvian-born wife Baroness Maria Koskull. Aged 17 at her marriage, the bride wore a Norman Hartnell gown, embellished with five huge bows from waist to floor.

Aerial View of Wynyard Hall, 1950s (Ward Philipson Photographic Collection)

The couple had two daughters, Sophia, born 1959, and Cosima, 1961. During the 1960s, major performing stars appearing at local venues, such as Stockton's Globe Theatre and the Club Fiesta, were invited to Wynyard. Star guests included Mick Jagger of the Rolling Stones, Diana Ross and the Supremes, as well as members of the Tamla Motown tour of 1964, which included blues musician Georgie Fame. Nico, as she was known to family and friends, bore him a son, Tristan, subsequently divorcing Lord Londonderry in 1971.

On 10 March 1972, Alastair, Lord Londonderry married Doreen Patricia Wells, former principal ballerina with the Royal Ballet. When news of the forthcoming VIP wedding leaked to the press, arrangements were brought forward to 7.30 am. The ceremony took place at Durham Registry Office, in the presence of Sophia and Cosima, young daughters of the 7th Marquess. The following day, the couple invited everyone on the estate to Wynyard chapel for a Service of Blessing. Their first son Frederick Aubrey Vane-Tempest-Stewart, born 1972, assumed the title of Viscount Castlereagh. Lord Reginald, born in 1977, married Chloe Belinda Guinness and has a son Robin Gabriel (2004) and two daughters Amy Romaine (2007) and Violet May (2009). The second marriage of Alastair, Lord Londonderry ended in divorce in 1989, but his former wife retains the title Marchioness of Londonderry.

Aerial View of Wynyard Hall, 1950s (Ward Philipson Photographic Collection)

CHAPTER 19

ENTERTAINING ROYALLY

Wynyard Hall's reputation for generous hospitality and entertainment began in the early 19th century, when the 3rd Marquess and Frances Anne regularly invited eminent guests, including politicians, writers, artists, members of the aristocracy and royalty. *'No house in the north of England stands so pre-eminent for gaiety and good cheer as the mansion at Wynyard Park.'*

The Morning Post of 28 August 1828 goes on to report *'unequalled gaiety and hospitality during and preceding the Stockton Races.'* Guests included Frances Anne's mother, the Countess of Antrim, John Manners, 5th Duke of Rutland, the Lord Bishop of Bristol, author and Tory politician Sir Roger Gresley and Lady Georgiana Mitford, later to become great grandmother of the Mitford sisters, famed during the 1930s. Also present were Lord and Lady Ravensworth, their son, the Hon. Henry Liddell, M.P. for Northumberland, and their daughter Maria, with her husband Henry, 1st Marquess of Normanby. A Whig politician and author, Lord Normanby also served at various times as Governor of Jamaica, Lord Lieutenant of Ireland, Home Secretary and British Ambassador to France.

Visitors enjoyed concerts, balls and taking part in 'private theatricals'. Lord and Lady Normanby received particular praise for their excellent acting in 'A Day after the Wedding'. *'At Florence, Rome and Naples they have successively appeared and are established amongst the very first-rate amateurs of the drama.'* Commended for *'her extreme beauty and commanding person, with her talents and vivacity'*, Lady Emmeline Manners, daughter of the Duke of Rutland, played Lady Freelove. As Lady Clara in 'The Comedy of King Charles the Second', *'the Marchioness of Londonderry, on her first appearance, excited great and universal applause.'*

The 3rd Marquess and his wife entertained numerous foreign dignitaries, prime ministers and royalty at Wynyard Hall, as well as writers, scholars and soldiers. His Imperial Highness the Archduke Ferdinand of Austria, Prince Louis Napoleon, Sir Robert Peel, HRH Duke of Cambridge, portrait artist Thomas Lawrence and writers Charles Dickens and Sir Walter Scott were welcome guests. Encouraged by Frances Anne in his political ambitions, Benjamin Disraeli was a frequent visitor to Wynyard, both as a novice parliamentarian and later as Prime Minister.

Catering and household provision

Catering was often provided by Gunter and Co. of Berkeley Square in London. The menu for a ball supper on one occasion listed *'hot Soups, Cutlets, hot and cold Game, Raised Pies, Hams, Tongues, Galantines, Turkeys with Perigord, Roast Chickens, Lobster Salads, Cold Entrees, Babas, Gateaux, jellies, creams, pastry and other entremets, Pineapples, Grapes, first and second course Removes'*. In addition, guests were offered cream and water ices, orangeade, lemonade, tea, coffee, biscuits and bonbons. For this feast, Gunter's charged 7/6 per head (37p), which included transporting everything from London and providing twenty four waiters. The 3rd Marquess and his wife were used to entertaining up to 800 people at a time.

Providing for such a constant stream of visitors required a great deal of household equipment, as well as financial expenditure. In the 1840s, household bills at Wynyard averaged £200 a month. A Londonderry account of 1841 lists 68 mattresses, 136 pairs of blankets, 602 towels, 80 damask table cloths, 462 napkins, 910 pieces of china and 600 silver items. The silver service and plate Charles had brought home from Vienna in 1822, now in the Royal Pavilion, Brighton, was exhibited in the 1950s at Preston Hall Museum and Art Gallery, Stockton-on-Tees.

Tenantry entertainment and family celebrations

Festivities at Wynyard were not solely confined to the higher echelons of society. As long ago as 1802, the Morning Post and Gazeteer reported that Sir Henry Vane Tempest had *'entertained his numerous tenants at his seat at Winyard, with a ball and supper, during which he, as also his amiable lady, evinced that true affability, which rendered the hospitable entertainment doubly pleasing.'*

In December 1845, Freeman's Journal and Daily Commercial Advertiser reports *'a sumptuous entertainment in the splendid picture gallery'* when, on his Lordship's rent day, nearly 100 tenants sat down to table.

In April 1842, although rebuilding of the house was not yet complete, 700-800 tenants and estate workers were invited to a grand celebration, including an ox roast on the lawn, for the coming of age of the Londonderry's eldest son, Lord Seaham. There was also a plentiful supply of strong ale, brewed at the time of his birth, twenty one years earlier. Royalty was represented by Prince Adolphus, 1st Duke of Cambridge, son of King George III and great great grandfather to Queen Elizabeth II. During his visit, the Duke was also invited to dinner with more than 1,500 pitmen at Londonderry's Penshaw colliery, as well as dining with about 300 workers and ship captains at Seaham Harbour. In 1846, Wynyard received a visit from his sister, the Duchess of Gloucester.

In September 1847, former Prime Minister Sir Robert Peel was amongst guests invited to celebrate the marriage at Wynyard of the Irish peer, the Earl of Portarlington, to Alexandrina, the Londonderry's second daughter, goddaughter of the late Czar Alexander I. The huge house-party combined the event with a house-warming, as this was the first time the house had been fully opened to visitors since the fire. The next day, a deputation including the Mayor of Stockton came to Wynyard to present Peel with an address of thanks for his removal of restrictions on the corn trade.

In 1852, The Morning Post reported *'princely hospitalities dispensed during the past fortnight by the Marquis and Marchioness of Londonderry at Wynyard Park.'* The main event took place on January 17, birthday of Frances Anne, when a grand banquet was followed by a ball to which all the leading families of the county were invited. Guests included the Duchess de Coigny, the Duke of Cleveland, the Marquis and Marchioness of Stafford, the Earl and Countes of Glengall, Lord and Lady Londesborough, Lord William Powlett, His Excellency the Baron Brunow, Sir William and Lady Eden, Sir Thomas Monro, Colonel McDonald of the Second Lifeguards, Captain David Wood of the Royal Artillery and the Honourable Mr. Lascelles. Also in attendance were the couple's children Lord Adolphus, Lord Ernest and Lady Adelaide Vane plus their eldest son and his wife, Viscount and Viscountess Seaham.

In the splendid dining room, places were laid for 40 guests, the tables and sideboards adorned with gold and silver epergnes, dishes and plates in profusion. The culinary skills of the cook were compared to those of Alexis Soyer, chef to the Reform Club and London aristocracy. The dessert course consisted of fruits produced in Wynyard's own gardens. The Marquess' band played fashionable airs and polkas during the meal and afterwards at the ball, which opened with a quadrille, the Duke of Cleveland leading off with Lady Londonderry. The newspaper reports that *'the festivities were prolonged until a late hour on Saturday morning.'*

The 5th Marquess

Such lavish festivities did not appear to continue at Wynyard after the death of the 3rd Marquess in 1854. Frances Anne spent more of her time at Seaham Hall, where she entertained friends, including Czarewich Alexander, later Czar Alexander II of Russia, and Prince Louis Napoleon, later Napoleon III of France. A troubled soul, the 4th Marquess, eldest son of Charles Stewart, died childless in 1872, the estate passing to his half brother, Earl Vane. Although the 5th Marquess lived mostly in Wales and London, rather than at Wynyard, as Earl Vane he entertained some eminent visitors at Wynyard Hall, including Lord and Lady Randolph Churchill and Bismarck, the German Chancellor. On December 20, 1870, Prince Christian of Schleswig-Holstein, son-in-law of Queen Victoria, accompanied by a large party of noblemen, enjoyed an excellent day's shooting. In the evening, thirty gentlemen sat down to dinner, followed by a grand ball in the Pink Drawing Room, now known as the Mirror Room. Crimson cloth was laid on the floor leading from the statue gallery, where the band of the Seaham Artillery played selections of music, the opening dance, 'The Bonnie Pit Laddie'.

Towards the end of his tenure as 5th Marquess, in December 1883, the Prince and Princess of Wales, later King Edward VII and Queen Alexandra, stayed at Wynyard while on a royal visit to Stockton-on-Tees. Arriving on the royal train at Thorpe Thewles station, the Prince and Princess were welcomed by a guard of honour of the 2nd Durham Artillery. The 5th Marquess and his wife, accompanied by other eminent guests, escorted the royal couple to Wynyard, where they spent three days before discharging their public duty at Stockton.

At noon on Friday December 21, they left Wynyard in a state carriage with the Marquess of Londonderry and his eldest son, Lord Castlereagh, preceded by a bodyguard of the 5th Dragoon Guards. Other vehicles followed, carrying the Marchioness of Londonderry, Lord and Lady Zetland,

Visit of the Prince and Princess of Wales to Stockton on Tees and Wynyard, as reported by
The Illustrated Sporting and Dramatic News, 5th January 1884

Lady Castlereagh, Lords Herbert and Henry Vane, sons of the Marquess and Marchioness, and twenty year old Lady Aline, their youngest daughter. As reported in the Illustrated Sporting and Dramatic News of 5 January 1884, on arrival at Stockton, the royal couple were greeted by the Mayor and corporation, cheering crowds and pealing bells. The accompanying illustrations, hand-drawn by Horace Morehen from sketches by John Dinsdale, a guest at Wynyard, show the town decked out in style to greet the royal visitors, as well as providing a fitting tribute to the beauty of Wynyard Hall and Gardens.

The 6th Marquess

Just a few months after that triumphant royal visit, in November 1884, the Londonderry title passed, on the death of his father, to Charles Stewart. The 6th Marquess and his wife Theresa, Lady Londonderry, a very enthusiastic hostess, spent far more time at Wynyard than their immediate predecessors, bringing back to Wynyard the vibrant social life of previous generations. To ensure that the numerous guests arrived at the correct place at the appointed time, the Londonderrys employed a footman, known as a 'whipper-in', in hunting circles, the person who keeps the hounds from wandering.

Back row: Lady Coke (4th from left), Hon. James Lowther (next to her), Lord Coke (6th from left), Duke of Montrose (slightly behind Coke), Princess of Wales (6th from right), Lord Herbert Vane Tempest, Henry Chaplin, Count Herbert Bismarck, N. W. Apperley (2nd from right).

Middle row, seated: Prince of Wales (centre), Duchess of Montrose (next to him), Lady Randolph Churchill (2nd from right). *Front row*: M. de Falbe, 6th Marquess, Lord Randolph Churchill.

From the Londonderry Album, with permission of Lord Londonderry

The unique meeting of the Privy Council held at Wynyard on October 19, 1903. In his memoirs Sir Almeric Fitzroy, the then Clerk to the Privy Council, says that 'the last occasion on which a Council had been held in a country house belonging to a subject was in October 1625 when Charles II held one at Wilton, the Lord Pembroke of the day being his Chamberlain.

Lady Londonderry was greatly excited over the event and was particularly pleased to learn that the King desired the documents connected with the Council to be headed "at the Court at Wynyard", which is indeed the old style.'

The King also brought with him his mistress Mrs Keppel on this occasion. She is on the extreme left in the front row.

From the Londonderry Album, with permission of Lord Londonderry

The Prince and Princess of Wales, later to become King Edward VII and Queen Alexandra, continued to be frequent visitors. Their successors, the future King George V and Queen Mary were also entertained at Wynyard during the time of the 6th Marquess and his wife, noted for their hospitality. Other eminent guests included Lord Kitchener, Sir Charles Palmer, ship builder and Liberal MP for Jarrow, the writer Edmund Gosse and prominent politicians, such as Lord Curzon, Viceroy of India from 1898-1905, later Foreign Secretary.

On October 27 1890 at six o'clock, a large shooting party, including the Prince and Princess of Wales, Edward and Alexandra, arrived at Thorpe Thewles station. Decked out with flags and streamers, red and white flowers spelled out greetings, such as *'A Royal Welcome', ' Queen and Country', 'God Bless the Prince of Wales' and 'Londonderry'*. Although the royal party had requested no formal ceremony, a huge crowd gathered to greet them, including various railway officials. The Prince and Princess proceeded to Wynyard in Lord Londonderry's carriage, the road lit by twenty eight carriage roof lamps placed at intervals of thirty yards.

On arrival at Wynyard, the royal couple met up with other members of the house party, including the Duke and Duchess of Montrose, the Earl and Countess of Cadogan, Lord and Lady Randolph Churchill, Count Herbert Bismarck and the Right Honourable Henry Chaplin. Known as Squire Chaplin and instantly recognizable by his size and monocle, Henry's daughter, Edith, later married Charles, who became 7th Marquess of Londonderry. His Excellency M. Christian de Falbe, the Danish Minister in London, accompanied the royal couple, who expected their son Prince Albert Victor, known as Eddy, to join them a few days later. After three days shooting, the Prince visited Seaham Harbour to review the Artillery Brigade, before returning to Sandringham.

Further royal guests, the Duke and Duchess of York stayed at Wynyard in October 1893 while visiting the area to open Stockton's Ropner Park. In August 1899, a week-long house party held at Wynyard to celebrate the coming of age of Charles, eldest son of the 6th Marquess and his wife, became an engagement celebration, too, as Edith Helen Chaplin agreed to marry the man who would become the 7th Marquess of Londonderry.

On 20th October 1903, King Edward VII stayed at Wynyard with a party including the Duke and Duchess of Devonshire, the Earl and Countess of Shaftesbury and Lieutenant Colonel Frederick Ponsonby, the King's private secretary. Also among the guests were George Keppel and his wife Alice, the King's mistress, who,

ROYAL PARTY AT WYNYARD PARK.
Prince and Princess of Wales at Wynyard, Saturday Nov. 7th, 1908, before leaving for Sandringham for the King's Birthday.

Picture postcard of a Royal party at Wynyard Park 1908 (George Nairn's collection)

despite the twenty eight year age gap, was very good at defusing the royal mood swings. After dinner, in order to appoint the 6th Marquess Lord President to the Privy Council, the King held a Council meeting, the first held outside a Royal palace since 1625, in the reign of Charles II. A meeting was convened in the Mirror Room, where a plaque now commemorates the event. After looking at historical parallels, the King decided that the resulting document, should be signed 'Our Court at Wynyard', rather than 'Our Court at St James', still the only occasion in history when royal protocol was adapted.

The 7th Marquess

The 7th Marquess, Charles and his wife, society hostess Edith, took the Londonderry title in 1915. Renowned for entertaining at Londonderry House, their sumptuous home in the capital, they gave lavish parties, often with political intents. An ardent Conservative, Edith developed close relationships with both Neville Chamberlain and Ramsey McDonald, the Labour leader. The Londonderrys also spent much of the year at Mount Stewart, with its beautiful gardens and park land in an idyllic setting near Strangford Lough in County Down.

PRINCESS MARY AND VISCOUNT LASCELLES AND HOUSE PARTY AT WYNYARD PARK

Picture postcard of Princess Mary and Viscount Lascelles with the 7th Marquess C1921 (George Nairn's collection)

Although Charles and Edith lived at Wynyard only for certain parts of the year, they found opportunities to invite notable visitors such as Winston Churchill, Harold Macmillan, Lord Birkenhead and Anthony Eden. Wynyard also played host to Edward, Prince of Wales, destined to abdicate from his role as King Edward VIII for a life in exile as the Duke of Windsor. The Duke and

New Mayor of Durham, Lord Londonderry, with guests in the Mirror Room at Wynyard November 1936. Back standing, Lord Londonderry, Herr von Ribbentrop, Sir Ronald Graham, Mrs Roger Lumley, Mrs Kerr, Mr Roger Lumley (MP for York) Lord Durham, Sir Hedworth Williams, Robin Lord Castlereagh; front seated Lady Durham, Frau von Ribbentrop, Edith Lady Londonderry and Romaine Lady Castlereagh (Photographic Library Beamish Museum Ltd)

Duchess of York, later to become King George VI and Queen Elizabeth, visited in 1934, Princess Marina in 1945. A regular guest at Wynyard, on one occasion King Alfonso of Spain, exiled during the Spanish Civil war, visited Seaham Harbour and descended the mine shaft at Dawdon Colliery, 18,000 feet deep.

A notable, if controversial, guest, Joachim von Ribbentrop, personal envoy to Hitler from 1935-6 and German Foreign Minister during World War II, visited many aristocratic families such as the Londonderrys, attempting to create an Anglo-German alliance. Local man Robert Emmerson recalls his father, a chauffeur at Wynyard, driving von Ribbentrop from London up to the Hall, describing him as *'arrogant, aloof and very unfriendly'*. At a service in Durham Cathedral, a hymn with the same tune as the German national anthem prompted him to jump up and give the Nazi salute.

Amateur dramatics at Wynyard in the 1930s, on view in the Statue Gallery

Reviving a tradition begun by the 3rd Marquess and his wife, the family and friends of the 7th Marquess enjoyed amateur dramatics, performing on a stage, complete with footlights, formerly situated in the ballroom, to the right of the entrance. Estate workers were invited to see the plays and were given signed copies of the photographs as a memento. Probably taken in the early 1930s, this photograph, autographed by the participants, gives the character names as well as their own. On the far left, 'A late arrival', Lord Londonderry looks every inch the butler, while Edith Lady Londonderry in white overall and turban is Mrs Doddrell. Daughters Margaret and Helen Stewart play Winnie and Selina Morell and Edith's nephew, Anthony 3rd Viscount Chaplin, plays John Morel. Francis Vane Tempest, a male cousin, playing the part of Breese was grandson of Adolphus, second son of Charles and Frances Anne. His father, also Adolphus (1863-1932), made a career on the stage. The cast also included Conservative MP Anthony Eden and his wife Beatrice. British Prime Minister in the 1950s, Eden was born at Windlestone Hall in County Durham, not far from Wynyard. The signature at the top right is that of professional stage and film actress, Ena Grossmith, playing Warwick. In the part of Puddifer, Sir Hedworth Williamson was related to the Liddells of Ravensworth Castle, whose second son Thomas designed the memorial room for the 3rd Marquess. The *'gaiety and good cheer'* enjoyed by Lord and Lady Ravensworth and their son Henry, named in the guest list for 1828, was still going strong over 100 years later.

Welcome to Wynyard

Although lavish entertainments ceased in more recent years, Wynyard continued to provide hospitality of a different kind, the grounds opened to less exalted visitors as well as nobility. Many local cricket teams played on the estate pitch and local anglers were allowed to fish in the lake. At the turn of the 20th century, Wynyard became a popular venue for Sunday afternoon cycling, almost regarded as a public park by visitors from the local area. Keen cyclists themselves, the 6th Marquess and his wife were members of the local cycling club, whose members held their annual church parade at Wynyard chapel. In 1903, the service was held in a marquee, as the event attracted over 1,000 enthusiasts.

They were also keen supporters of the Primrose League, an organisation which held summer fairs at Wynyard. Founded in 1881 on the death of Disraeli and named after

Bicycling was the rage in the 90s: this group shows - (from left) Lord Castlereagh, Fraulein Sturmfels, Lady Helen in the centre, her father next to her, Reginald, and Mr Apperley the private secretary. Taken by Theresa 1892-3. From the Londonderry Album, with permission of Lord Londonderry

his favourite flower, vaguely political, the League believed in Empire, church, state, crown, patriotism and liberty, but mostly enjoyed Tory stately homes, dances and simple entertainments, such as magic lantern shows. Although ridiculed in its early days, by 1891, the League had a million members and survived until 2004. The Londonderrys encouraged groups in Seaham, Darlington, Stockton and Hartlepool, as well as Wynyard, the perfect spot for Primrose League picnics, complete with Lord Londonderry's Seaham Harbour Band, fortune telling, comedians and teas in the marquee. In 1903, eighty Germans, contracted to work on the docks at Seaham Harbour, were invited to lunch and a guided tour of the gardens, followed by a cricket match against forty young men from Theresa, Lady Londonderry's bible class in Seaham.

In a newspaper interview of 1949, Miss Holmes, daughter of Wynyard stonemason James Holmes, remembered a lavish Christmas party for the estate children, with a huge tree, ice skating on the lake and his lordship arriving on a sleigh as Father Christmas. As Mayor of the City of Durham, the 7th Marquess carried on the tradition of providing entertainment for local children begun twenty five years earlier by his father during his own mayoralty of Durham. In July 1937, to celebrate the coronation of King George VI, nearly 3,000 pupils from Durham schools were invited to a treat in Wynyard Park.

A fleet of seventy five buses brought the children and their teachers to the grounds, where Punch and Judy, a coconut shy, roundabouts and swings known locally as shuggy boats provided great fun. The Durham Advertiser reported that fairground proprietor Sam Crowe made a

Lord Londonderry with children at a fairground, Wynyard Park, July 1937 (Photographic Library Beamish Museum Ltd)

good job of controlling the huge crowd. Lord and Lady Londonderry *'exercised endless patience and kindness'*, presenting each child with a commemorative tin of sweets before they left. A month earlier, in June 1937, a large group of members of Annfield Plain public library

Annfield Plain Public Library Outing, June 1937 (Photographic Library Beamish Museum Ltd)

travelled about twenty five miles to enjoy a summer outing at Wynyard. The following summer, in June 1938, appreciative crowds enjoyed traditional dances performed on the lawns in front of the Hall by members of the Durham County branch of the English Folk Dance and Song Society. In the 1950s, sports days for schoolchildren were held in the grounds of Wynyard Hall.

Country dancing in front of the Hall, June 1938 (Photographic Library Beamish Museum Ltd)

Requisitioned by the army during the war, Wynyard became a teacher training college from 1946-1960, but the family continued to live in part of the Hall. In 1947, students in the balcony above the statue gallery were able to catch a glimpse of the future monarch, when Princess Elizabeth stayed at Wynyard while visiting Durham City to lay the foundation stone of St. Mary's College. Many former residents of Wynyard village have fond memories of their own weddings, hosted at the Hall and its chapel by the 8th and the 9th Marquess, the last of his line to live at Wynyard Hall. Now a beautiful country house hotel, the hall continues the tradition, established at Wynyard by so many of the Londonderry family over hundreds of years, of offering a hospitable welcome which may still be described as entertaining royally.

CHAPTER 20

UPSTAIRS, DOWNSTAIRS

Throughout the 19th and 20th centuries, the smooth running of Wynyard was ensured by an army of servants and estate workers, housed in a network of basement rooms, unobtrusively catering for the needs of the people upstairs. In the original plans, bedrooms for the the 3rd Marquess and his wife were on the ground floor, to the left of the library, separated by a small room for their maids and valets. Alterations have occurred over the years and architects plans hanging in the private quarters of the Hall open a window on the lives of the hundreds of people who, over many years, have worked below stairs at Wynyard. While we cannot be certain that these plans were carried out in their entirety, their mere existence offers a fascinating insight into life at Wynyard beneath the splendour on show.

Life downstairs

Plans drawn up by architect Arthur Harrison of Stockton-on-Tees, in about 1910, the time of the 6th Marquess, show extensive cellars with particular rooms for storing confectionery, jam, ice and lumber plus large and small wine stores, as well as cellars devoted to beer, wood, coal and coke. A laundry, ironing room and drying room were adjacent to each other and a gun room, boot room, brushing room and a room for cleaning riding breeches catered for the needs of hunting and shooting parties. The butler's pantry would have been used for storage, cleaning and counting of silver and possibly for safe storage of the wine log and merchants' account books. Other important documents would have been kept in the deed room, while afternoon tea trays would be prepared in the still room, also used for making drinks and jams.

As well as a spacious servants' hall, rooms were provided for various members of the household, including the housekeeper, butler, valet, footman, carpenter and chaplain. The housemaids and kitchen maids were allocated small bedrooms, often in between storage areas or tacked on to the bedroom of a more senior member of staff. The steward was allowed his own sitting room as well as a bedroom, while personal rooms for the governess were situated on the first floor, near the school room and nurseries. On the same floor, ladies' maids were provided with rooms adjacent to the ladies they attended.

Faithful servants recognised

The Londonderrys appreciated their servants and estate workers, many of whom, like the Scotsons of Wolviston, served the family for generations. In the early 1800s, Thomas Scotson created Wynyard's marble pillars for the 3rd Marquess and his wife. In 1903, his descendant Thomas William Scotson began working at Wynyard, rising to the position of head carpenter. He is seen on the far left of the photograph, taken with other members of staff on the terrace at Wynyard. In 1932, his son, of the same name, received a glowing reference from Neville Wilthew, agent to the 7th Marquess, stating that the family had been employed at Wynyard for over 120 years without a break. Changing times meant that fewer staff were now required, otherwise the family service to Wynyard would have continued. On the death of the 6th Marquess in 1915, Thomas, along with all staff employed at Wynyard for ten years or more, received a sum of

Coat of Arms of Raymond Wood, Lord Seaham

Some estate workers on the terrace (With permission of Lillian Benson)

money to recognise their faithful service. When Thomas William Scotson died in 1958, a telegram conveyed Lord Londonderry's sympathy to his family.

Recognition of loyal service continued even after the sale of the ancestral home. In 1987, Raymond Wood, Lord Londonderry's agent and right hand man since 1956, joined his employer in moving to Dorset, in order to continue looking after the family's interests. On his retirement in 1999, twelve years after leaving Wynyard, Raymond was presented with a silver plaque originally given to Theresa, Marchioness of Londonderry when she cut the first sod for Dawdon Colliery in 1899. Suitably re-

engraved, the plaque records the gratitude of the 9th Marquess and his children *'for incomparable service, friendship and entertainment over a period of fifty years'*. In a further gesture of thanks and recognition, Lord Londonderry bestowed upon Raymond the Lordship of the Manor of Seaham, a title held by the Londonderry family since 1821. The coat of arms specifically designed for the new incumbent, incorporates the Stewart dragon holding the quill of the administrator, masonic symbols, the Christian fish, St. Cuthbert's cross, the anchor of Seaham, Raymond's home town, and the motto *'Ad Finem Fidelis'*, *'Faithful to the end.'*

CHAPTER 21

WYNYARD HALL TRAINING COLLEGE

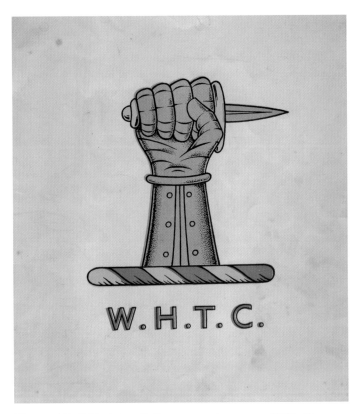

*Wynyard Hall Training College magazine cover, 1946-47
(With permission of Margaret Shepherd)*

*WHTC staff-Left to right, back row:- Miss Greener, Miss Soper,
Miss Young, Miss Whitworth, Miss Swaby, Miss Bunn
(Secretary), Miss Haytor. Front row:-Miss Cardno, Miss Brady,
Miss Cohen (Vice Principal), Miss Bertie (Principal), Miss
Miller, Miss Robinson, Miss Robson (With permission of
Margaret Shepherd)*

In 1946, under the Emergency Training Scheme instigated after the war, Wynyard Hall became a Training College. New shortened courses were designed to provide teachers urgently needed after the war had taken its toll. The post-war baby boom also saw a dramatic increase in the birth rate, classes averaging 40-50 pupils. The 7th Marquess, the original host, was followed in 1949 by his son Robin, whose wife and children were often seen around the grounds, the youngest, Alastair, succeeding to the Marquessate aged eighteen in 1955, a few years before the college closed in 1961.

Very soon extended to two years, later to three, the original course lasted just one year, with thirty six weeks of study, twelve weeks of teaching practice and only four weeks holiday. In the first college newsletter of April 1947, Wynyard principal Miss Sophie C. Bertie commended her students for helping to break down initial opposition to the Emergency Training Scheme. A team of exclusively female staff, seconded from universities and colleges around the country, provided courses in the education of nursery, infant and junior age children, later extended to include 'Sec Mod' and sixth form teaching. Specialised subjects including history, geography, biology, art, music, English, arithmetic, needlework, craft, drama, PE and health. Students also made teaching aids, toys and classroom equipment, as well as working in the college gardens, gaining skills and knowledge to help them set up gardens in schools.

*Some students 1950   (With permission of Olwyn Bragg,
pictured front row, second left)*

Transforming the Hall

Wynyard Hall was leased to the college for an annual rent of £500, but Miss Bertie insisted that Lord Londonderry retain responsibility for maintenance of the roof and guttering, repairing any damage caused by leaks. Having been occupied by the army during the war, the Hall looked somewhat neglected, *'like a badly battered barracks'*. After the army left in 1945, dilapidations included damage to a full size plaster female statue of a female, her hand broken off and a hole in her body. Some of the elaborate bronze ornaments had been ripped from the red marble mantel of the breakfast room fireplace, others damaged beyond repair.

Tutorial and domestic staff were engaged to prepare Wynyard for its new role, cleaning, polishing and unpacking parcels of bedding, crockery, pots and pans, books and other equipment. In the library, the magnificent buhl panelled bookcases and their contents were encased in hardboard, simple modern book shelves

Library bookcases boxed in for protection during Wynyard's time as a teacher training college (With permission of Margaret Shepherd)

placed in front of them. In the entrance hall, magnificently bound volumes detailing the history of Wynyard Hall were also covered. Lino protected the ornately patterned wooden floors. Otherwise, the building was little changed. Immense family portraits continued to look down from the walls, statues remained in the gallery, along with the Londonderry coronation coach. Fourteen carriages originally owned by the 7th Marquess, with the advent of

the motor car, became obsolete and were disposed of, their former shelter, the coach houses, used to accommodate students.

Many of the 120 students, all female, were allocated bedrooms in the Hall, while others occupied rooms in the stable block and houses around the grounds. Areas of the Hall were divided into twelve houses, some given names with historical Wynyard connections, such as Castlereagh, Mount Stewart, Vane Tempest, Wellington, Waterloo and Hambletonian, others according to locations, such as Gatehouse, Lakeside and Stone Steps. Most students were allocated a single room, measuring eight feet wide by six feet, sparsely furnished, with lino on the floor. Each corridor had just one bathroom, plus an ironing board, iron, kettle and toaster. Since the Hall generated its own electricity, luxuries like hairdryers and radios were not allowed. And, of course, there was no central heating.

Miss Bertie

The dining room next to the conservatory, now known as the ballroom, became the gym and the assembly hall, the

Miss Bertie, Principal (With permission of Margaret Shepherd)

stage also being used for dramatic presentations, continuing the Londonderry family tradition. Many of the college productions, including Peer Gynt in the late 1940s, involved music, encouraged by principal Miss Bertie. She also welcomed estate workers and villagers in to the college to enjoy the music and drama missing from the Hall during the war years. An accomplished contralto, she trained with one of Britain's foremost sopranos, Dame Isobel Baillie, and had performed with Sir Malcolm Sargent and Sir John Barbirolli. Her room, located behind the present day reception desk, contained a grand piano.

Having achieved her first school headship at the unprecedented age of twenty eight, on her appointment as principal of Wynyard in 1945, Miss Bertie insisted that the college be affiliated to Durham University. In 1950, taking a year's sabbatical, she travelled the world as vice president of the National Union of Teachers. Durham University later awarded her an honorary M.Ed. for exceptional services to education. Clearly proud of the achievement of setting up a college at Wynyard, she wrote to her students in the newsletter of April 1947. *'The happiness of friendship, the joy of watching the seasonal changes in this lovely parkland, the satisfaction of creative work, the pleasure derived from reading: these are some of the things you will always associate with life at Wynyard.'*

Social life

Despite being relatively isolated, the Wynyard students had a lively social life, with clubs for music, drama, folk singing, debating, poetry as well as more unusual interests, like bee-keeping. Local children, friends from Wynyard Estate and visitors from neighbouring army camps and RAF stations were invited to regular concerts and parties. The girls of Wynyard organised joint events with male students at a similar college based in Alnwick Castle, home to the Duke of Northumberland. Every year, a dance was held at both grand houses, half the girls travelling to Alnwick and half the men to Wynyard. At Christmas 1946, the students were disappointed when flying conditions prevented the planned visit of Lord Londonderry, the 7th Marquess, a keen aviator, often landing his bi-plane in fields in front of the kennels.

In those days when people relied more heavily on public transport, bus services from Wynyard to the nearest town, Stockton-on-Tees, were limited. A utility bus with wooden seats ran twice a week and would arrive back at college so loaded with students that, according to Margaret Shepherd (nee Adamson), the college's young secretary, *'it was a miracle it made it up Bottle Hill Bank'*. Girls were allowed to cycle in to town or take a taxi, using a designated driver from Thorpe Thewles, but had to obey a strict curfew. The atmosphere was rather like that of a girls' boarding school, even though most of the students were well past school-leaving age and many had served in the armed forces and other responsible positions before coming to college.

Abiding memories

When closure came in 1961, the remaining students and staff, along with much of the equipment they had used at Wynyard, transferred to Neville's Cross College in Durham City. At a farewell concert, renowned classical pianist John Ogden performed on a Steinway grand piano, loaned for the occasion by Lord Londonderry. For over 60 years after the establishment of the college, former students and staff, members of Wynyard College Association, continued to share memories through an annual newsletter and reunion. The college song, set to the tune of The Londonderry Air (also known as Danny Boy), conveys their depth of feeling for Wynyard and its history, coupled with gratitude for the opportunity to study alongside lifelong friends in wonderful surroundings.

In Wynyard Hall where scenes are changing ever
From ancient splendour, now a college new
Where we will strive with purpose and endeavour
To teach our flock and keep our promise true.
Let us go forth to face the years undaunted
Let Wynyard's name re-echo deeds of fame
In toil or trouble we will stand united
God grant we face the future in his name.

CHAPTER 22

WYNYARD GARDENS

Wynyard Park from the South West (George Nairn's Collection)

'Fruitfull of soile, and pleasant of situation, and soe bewtified and adorned with woodes and groves, as noe lands in that part of the contrie be comparable to them." In 1623, when this description was written, the original house and estate were owned by the Claxton family. The manors and land of Wynyard, Thorpe Thewles and Fulthorpe extended to 7,300 acres and were valued at £5,400. Fulthorpe Woods were worth a further £400. By 1633, the house had passed to the Davison family and in 1644, Richard Melsonby was appointed *'to preserve the woods of Lieutenant Colonel Thomas Davison at Wynyard and Fulthorpe' '* For centuries, the parks and gardens surrounding Wynyard Hall have provided a beautiful setting for the house.

DEVELOPMENTS IN 1819

There is, however, no evidence to indicate the shape of the park or gardens until the marriage, in 1819, of Charles Stewart and Frances Anne, heiress to Wynyard Hall

and Park. A document dated June 1819, headed *'Improvements and Alterations to be made at Wynyard'*, lists ambitious and detailed plans, including the creation of a flower garden and shrubbery. Planting was contracted to William Falla of Gateshead, owner of the largest nursery in Britain at that time, covering 500 acres.

Planting of trees and shrubs

First priority was given to the planting of shrubs and clumps of trees around the garden. The inventory for a tree nursery plantation established by Lord Stewart in 1822, shows a total of 340,200 seedling trees, comprising 18 different species, including 38,000 ash, 33,000 oak, 32,000 beech and 24,500 elm. A total of 12,000 coniferous plants included larch, Norway spruce and Scotch firs. Smaller numbers of mountain ash, horse chestnut, weeping birch and hazels were also grown.

In 1765, King George III had passed *'an act for the better preservation of timber trees and of woods and underwoods and for the further preservation of roots, shrubs and plants.'* Particularly keen to encourage the planting of *'oak, beech, chestnut, walnut, ash, elm, cedar, fir, asp, lime, sycamore and birch'*, many of which figured prominently in Wynyard Park, the King decreed the theft of young trees punishable by transportation to the colonies. The Bishop of Durham upheld similar sanctions with regard to woods and plantations under his protection, threatening whipping and hard labour as well as transportation.

Many of the trees grown at Wynyard had specific uses as well as providing scenic beauty. Oak provided a fine building material, chestnut trees were ideal for fencing, while ash was used to make cart wheels and the handles of tools. Larch plantations, installed between 1819 and 1824, proved an invaluable source of pit props, very useful to the burgeoning Londonderry colliery empire. Wynyard

sawmill, ideally situated within the woodland area, allowed continuous exploitation of the materials to hand.

Pleasure grounds

To the west of the Hall, the pleasure grounds are situated in the valley created by Brierley Beck, which was partially dammed to create the lake. In the 1819 plan, most of the pleasure ground walks, except the Grotto Walk, would be widened to twelve feet and new drives created. In Fanny's Glen, the drive around Salter Gill, the banks were to be planted with larches and silver firs. Another drive, Hardinge's View, may have been named after Henry Hardinge, who became brother-in-law to Charles Stewart in 1821 on his marriage to Lady Emily Jane, the seventh of Charles' sisters. The men had served together in the Peninsular War and, in later years, Hardinge, created 1st Viscount in 1846, took over as Commander-in-Chief of the British Army in 1852, after the death of the Duke of Wellington. As MP for Durham

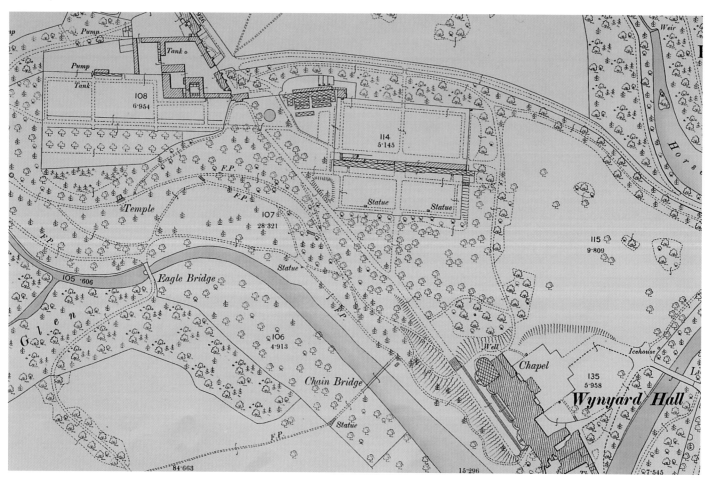

A map of the pleasure gardens from the 1856 Ordnance Survey

from 1820-1830, he served alongside Michael Angelo Taylor, husband of Frances Anne's aunt and guardian, so important in her young life.

Building and repairs

Lord Stewart and his wife insisted that *'the poor of the parish and neighbourhood should as far as possible be employed'* to carry out building and repair work. Old broken down fences were to be removed, gates painted dark green, the old railing outside the lodge to be replaced and neatly painted, paddock fences renewed and the line of the racecourse redefined. Apart from retaining and repairing fencing to keep animals in or out, the main intent was to take down enclosures wherever possible, in order to open up the parkland. Orders were placed for a large supply of lime for compost and gravel for walkways.

To make way for a summerhouse and dairy, the 1819 instructions ordered the removal of the existing gardener's house, along with the gardener himself. An additional note stated that *'in the event of a new gardener, the produce of the garden should be taken into consideration in the absence of the family.'*

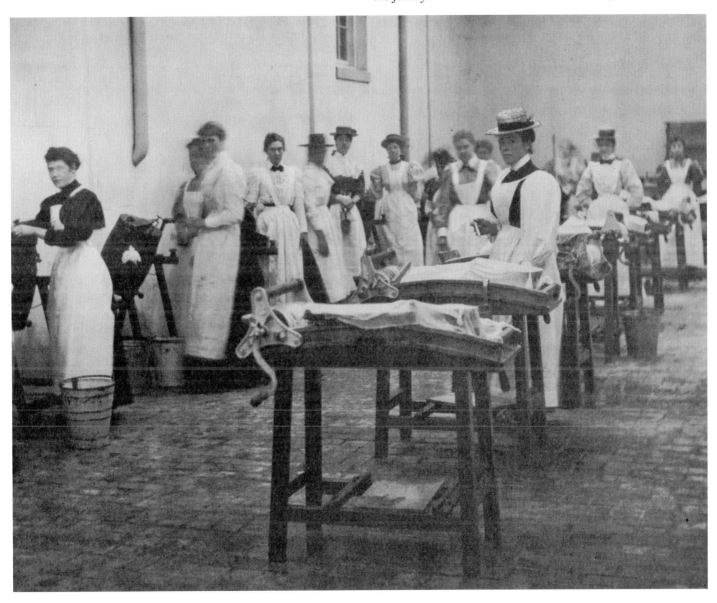

Not the laundry but the dairy, showing dairy-maids churning butter. Theresa and Lady Helen are in the group under the window. Photographed at Wynyard by Reginald c1890. From the Londonderry Album, with permission of Lord Londonderry

Front view of the Dairy
(Photographic Library Beamish Museum Ltd)

'A pre-1880 map shows the walled kitchen garden, rectangular and split into four quadrants, separated from the flower garden by a summer house and a row of sheds

and glasshouses. A further two summer houses face each other on opposite sides of the flower garden. Still standing beyond the walled garden, the dairy, at one time, employed up to thirteen dairy maids. Ellen Boyd, who died aged 73 on Easter Monday, 2 April 1877, worked for almost 30 years as a dairy maid to the Londonderry family. The front of the dairy, looking towards the Hall, boasted its own portico, a miniature replica of the entrance to the mansion, while the side facing away from the Hall was a simpler brick construction. Photographs from the 1890s show a very impressive head gardener's house, which still stands in the corner of the former kitchen garden.

According to the instructions drawn up in 1819, the melon ground was to be better enclosed, while hothouse plants and the green house were to be augmented. The fashion for hot houses full of exotics had become popular with the aristocracy since King George III began development of

The head gardener's house at Wynyard at the turn of the century. Photograph by Theresa. From the Londonderry Album, with permission of Lord Londonderry

the Royal Botanic Gardens at Kew in the late 1700s. Plant hunters such as botanist Joseph Banks (1743-1820), who sailed with Captain Cook, brought back a great variety of desirable plants from exotic locations around the world. Ownership of these exotic species and the glasshouses to protect them was a mark of social standing.

An integral part of the house, the Wynyard conservatory was filled with rare and costly flowers such as magnolia, camellias and orchids as well as choice exotic plants. A large Norfolk Island Pine, the first introduced into this country, took pride of place. Orange trees, formerly the property of the Empress Josephine, wife of Napoleon Bonaparte, arrived in 1829 at a cost of £1,250, but were lost in the fire of 1841. Situated at the western end of the mansion, overlooking the terrace, lake and pleasure grounds, the conservatory cost approximately £6,000 to build.

THE NEW HOUSE AND GARDEN 1822

In 1822, newly ennobled as Marquess and Marchioness of Londonderry, after commissioning the building of a grand new house at Wynyard, the couple embarked on ambitious landscaping plans, attributed to William Sawrey Gilpin (1762–1843). Originally a water colour painter, Gilpin worked for many years at the Royal Military College (Sandhurst), teaching cadets to draw accurate representations of landscapes and the lie of enemy positions. Made redundant at the age of sixty, he transferred his skills to landscape gardening. With no horticultural qualifications, but valuable experience in draughtsmanship and an undoubted artistic eye, he was entrusted with the design of hundreds of gardens, including those of Scotney Castle in Kent, Enniskillen Castle in Northern Ireland and a number of sites in Scotland, including Bowhill, Selkirk.

Landscaping by William Gilpin

Influenced by Humphry Repton (1752-1818), the last great garden designer of the 18th century, often regarded as the successor to Capability Brown, Gilpin favoured gently curved flowerbeds, raised terrace walks and irregularly shaped shrubberies with winding paths. His *'Practical Hints on Landscape Gardening'*, published in 1832, emphasised Gilpin's belief that planting should be on a grand scale, natural and irregular shapes providing pleasing images within the varied topography of the surrounding landscape. Gilpin's designs for Wynyard

included a Y shaped lake, with woodland along the main boundaries of the park, enclosing open parkland with scattered trees.

Mackenzie and Ross, writing in 1834, were clearly impressed by the natural effect achieved by Gilpin's design. In their view, the walks and pleasure grounds *'though not decorated with superb ornaments retain all the softer features of nature and are adorned with such embellishments as add to the native beauties of the place. A small rivulet runs from north to south through the Park forming a fine canal with gentle curvatures and margined with woods and shady walks.'* A small suspension bridge for foot passengers, added in 1831 at a cost of £314, was designed by Newcastle architect John Green and erected by Mr. R. Elliot also of Newcastle. Spanning 90 feet (27 metres), iron pillars supported chains and railings, beautifully ornamented in Grecian style with wrought and

A view with the old suspension bridge (Haydn Neal's Collection)

cast iron. The Chain Bridge, as it was known, spanned *'a ravine in these delightful grounds'* (Mackenzie and Ross) until its collapse in the 1950s.

The Lake

In 1794, Hutchinson's History of Durham described a fine canal stretching along the valley to the south of the mansion with easy curvature. In a memorandum from February 1821, instructions were given to increase the size of the lake and create an island for swans, a further memorandum the next year noting the importance of keeping the lake clean. In 1824, plans were made to remove earth from the south side, raise the bank and create a dam, thus widening the lake, which, by 1889, covered 10 acres. At the Eagle Bridge, Brierley Beck flows in to the lake to the west of the hall. Another beck flowing into the Horseshoe Pond, passes under the Lion Bridge, joining the pond at the eastern end, creating the Y shaped mound where the house stands. The lower part of the lake is dammed by the Dog Bridge.

Critical acclaim

An artistic and horticultural triumph, the description written by Durham historian William Fordyce in 1857 paints a clear picture. *'From the mansion, a broad terraced walk conducts to the gardens, which cover many acres of ground. The front or flower garden is flanked in its whole length with an extensive range of glass houses, containing pines, grapes, figs, peaches and many other fruits and rare and exotic flowers. A broad gravel walk or drive, arched over with trellised wire, and clustered with roses, jessamines and other flowers, leads from the gardens to the orchard, and to the dairy - a pretty rustic building. To the south of the gardens, and sloping down towards the lake, are the extensive pleasure-grounds, which are intersected with numerous gravel drives, and contain an aviary and a pretty Grecian temple. The park also contains grass rides several miles in extent.'*

Writing in 1861, historian and friend, Sir Archibald Alison, Bart., commended the systematic approach of the 3rd Marquess, who began by improving the drainage of the heavy clay soil, before going on to create broad circular plantations and undulating surfaces, intersected by wooded dells and green rides, allowing clear and changing views of a series of picturesque scenes. Landscaping and creating the pleasure grounds had cost the 3rd Marquess and his wife a total of £18,000.

Wynyard Hall and Park at the time of the 3rd Marquess

A view across the lake and park taken at a Forester's Fete 1865
(A carte de visite from George Nairn's collection)

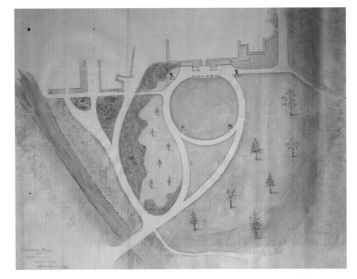

Additional landscaping plans by Edward Kemp from 1857,
not completely implemented (Reproduced by permission of Lord
Londonderry and Durham Record Office – DRO D/Lo/PO283a)

Proposals from Edward Kemp

Development of the gardens continued throughout the 19th century, additional landscaping plans being drawn up in 1857, three years after the death of the 3rd Marquess. Edward Kemp (1817-1891), a protégé of the great garden designer Joseph Paxton, suggested rearranging the approach to the mansion, instating a curved drive sweeping around extensive lawns, replacing the gravelled forecourt and removing the gates which originally stood in front of the Hall. An influential writer on gardening style, his articles featuring regularly in the Gardening Journal, Kemp proposed planting groups of evergreens to screen the view of the stables and to clothe the bare bank at the opposite side of the drive. He also suggested a small temple in the pleasure grounds, paths leading to it to be brought to a uniform width, narrowing the broader walk and giving greater length to the vista. He recommended a flight of steps to replace the slope leading from the terrace beyond the conservatory.

There is no evidence to suggest the extent to which Kemp's proposals were implemented. However, garden bills for 1858, including items such as cement, paint, ironmongery, garden pots, chairs and seats from the Ebbw Vale Iron Company, as well as shrubs and plants, amounted to a total cost of £266. This seems to indicate that some of his proposals were effected, although they made have been held in abeyance for a while. The gates in front of the house, still in place on a *carte de visite*

photograph of 1865, the year of Frances Anne's death, were removed at some stage. The Golden Gates, a different design from those shown on the *carte de visite*, have occupied their present position at the entrance to Wynyard since at least 1857, as shown on a map of that date.

An 1865 Carte de Visite shows the front entrance gated
(George Nairn's collection)

The flight of steps suggested by Kemp is shown on a line drawing from the visit of the Prince and Princess of Wales in 1884. The circular Roman temple still standing in the pleasure grounds bears a plaque with a poetic inscription to John Manners, 5th Duke of Rutland, who died in 1857, the date of Kemp's proposed temple.

LISTED FEATURES

The garden's many listed features add greatly to the character of the parkland. The Lion Bridge, the Wellington Obelisk, the Golden Gates and their accompanying features are Grade II*, while the Greek and Roman Temples, in a poorer state of repair and not easily accessible from the Hall, are accorded Grade II.

The Temples

The fashion for garden follies prevalent in 18th and 19th century England is still evident in parks attached to great houses such as Painshill Park in Surrey and Stourhead in Wiltshire, as well as at Wynyard. Primarily for decoration, follies in the guise of Greek and Roman temples were particularly popular, symbolising classical virtues or ideals. To the west of the conservatory, stone steps, formerly situated at the end of the terrace, led to a path through the valley and pleasure gardens, where the Wynyard temples still stand, their former glory somewhat diminished. Both are attributed to Benjamin Wyatt, commissioned to produce the 1822 designs for the house.

The Greek temple, to the north-west of the hall, may date from the early to mid 18th century, when John Tempest and his son John resided at Wynyard. Described as tetrastyle, i.e a building or portico with four columns in front, the folly is made of ashlar, an expensive decorative stone, with rendered brick for the back and side walls. A podium of five stone steps leads to the Doric portico with its fluted columns, entablature and pediment, but a group of plaster cast statues originally placed on a pedestal against the back wall are no more.

The Grecian Temple 2011

The circular Roman Temple, erected in the first half of the 19th century, also ashlar built, has suffered less from the effects of weathering. Four Roman Doric fluted columns, two attached to the curved wall, support a saucer dome

The Grecian Temple 1912 (from the garden album of Theresa, Lady Londonderry, 1912, with permission of Lady Rose Lauritzen)

The Roman Temple photographed 2011

topped with a pine cone finial. On the back wall, a plaque with a poetic inscription dedicated by F.A.V.L (Frances Anne Vane Londonderry) in memory of the 5th Duke of Rutland, a family friend and visitor to Wynyard reads :-

Oh sainted shade,
Those touching words which gave
A last sad proof of friendship from the grave
When death from earthly honours bade thee part
Have found an echo in this grateful heart
Which, mourning still, asserts this mourner's claim
To raise her monument to Rutland's name.

The Lion Bridge

Possibly designed by Benjamin Dean Wyatt, the 19th century Lion Bridge is one of the few features remaining from the time of Henry Vane Tempest, father of Frances Anne, Marchioness of Londonderry. The bridge provides a crossing point for the eastern side of the ornamental lake, itself an important aesthetic element in Wynyard Park, a reflective foil to the magnificent Hall. Guarded by lions couchant on pedestals at either end, the deep

The Lion Bridge photographed 2010

segmental arch of the bridge is decorated on the underside with an ornamental moulding known as *archivolt*. The *spandrels*, or spaces either side of the arch, bear *paterae*, motifs in the form of rosettes. The lions' pedestals are similarly carved, with additional relief swags. Built in ashlar, the bridge is topped by an attractive balustrade parapet above a frieze and cornice. Paired Doric pilasters at either end complete the imposing structure, which was granted II* listing in 1967. During the 1960s, the Lion Bridge was said to be haunted by the ghost of a young housemaid who, in the late 19th century, suffering from unrequited love, threw herself into the water beneath the

The Lion Bridge photographed 2010

bridge. The cloaked spectre of a grey lady, suspended a few feet above the ground, is also said to frequent the grounds and the Hall.

The Wellington Obelisk

After outstanding success in the campaigns of the Peninsular War, the Duke of Wellington became Commander in Chief of the British Army in 1827. In September of that year, during a triumphal tour of the North, the Duke stayed at Wynyard with his old comrade in arms Charles Stewart, 3rd Marquess of Londonderry. During his visit, Wellington laid the foundation stone of

The Wellington obelisk

a planned memorial arch, later changed to the obelisk, 127 feet high, still standing in Wynyard Park. The 3rd Marquess was disappointed not to be given a cabinet seat when Wellington became Prime Minister in 1828 and the original plaque inscribed 'Friend of Londonderry' was later replaced by the simple 'Wellington'.

The Golden Gates

The Golden Gates (George Nairn's collection)

An 1856 map of Wynyard shows the Golden Gates in their present position on the southern edge of the parkland, about a mile from the house. The *'wrought iron gates, gilded with spearhead standards'* were granted Grade II* listing in 1967, along with the gate piers, screen railings and lodges. The twin lodges are built of ashlar, decorative stone used throughout Wynyard, with Welsh slate roofs. One storey high, with pedimented ends and prostyle porches, the lodges have sash windows with glazing bars in architraves. In the early 1900s, Robinson Walker, a stonemason at Wynyard, and his wife Jane Anne lived in one of the lodges, now available to rent as holiday cottages. Another resident of the lodges, James Holmes, who died in 1934, was also a mason for the estate. His daughter Edith, worked at the Hall as a maid and later became gate keeper. She died at Golden Gates in 1971.

Ice Houses

Not listed, but nevertheless interesting, Wynyard possesses two ice houses, the forerunners of refrigeration. One, still visible, is set into the slope of the river bank near the Lion Bridge, its wooden door now securely locked. A second, no longer evident, was constructed a little further along the bank.

The Golden Gates photographed 2011

Introduced to Britain around 1660, by the eighteenth century ice houses had become increasingly fashionable amongst owners of major houses like Wynyard. Not normally used for the storage of food, ice was used in cooling drinks and for making cold confections in the kitchens. Usually brick built, domed structures, with most of their volume underground, ice houses were mainly conical or rounded at the bottom to hold melted ice, with a drain to take away any water.

A flight of steps leads down into the rectangular chamber, built into a bank so that the entrance passage is horizontal, straw providing additional insulation. Ice houses were often covered with a thick layer of earth and surrounded by trees to provide additional shade. Supported on some form of racking, thick slabs of ice could be stored for over a year. Ice may have been collected from the river and lake or could have been replenished every few weeks from commercial sources, such as the Kent & Sussex Pure Ice Company, who advertised daily delivery of ice in 1879. The use of ice houses declined with the advent of mechanical refrigerators from 1900 onwards.

DEVELOPMENT OF THE GARDENS 1884-1915

Succeeding to the title in 1884, during their stays at Wynyard, the 6th Marquess and his wife drove through the grounds together every day, their tenants very grateful to see the estate brought back to life after a period of decay and neglect. *'Theresa, Lady Londonderry knew every blade of grass,'* one of them reported, *'It was she who made Wynyard.'* Developments in the design of the garden attracted national interest almost immediately. According to an article in the Journal of Horticulture and Cottage Gardener of March 1889, the couple were *'evidently proud of their noble demesne and have spared no expense to improve its natural advantages'*. The writer, L. Castle, described 2000 acres of gently undulating park land, affording pleasant views of the Cleveland Hills. Magnificent beech trees, their *'massive boles and widely spreading branches',* produced a memorable effect alongside large numbers of oak and elm trees. The pleasure grounds covered sixty five acres, the lake *'imparting much character to the scenery'*. Handsome Cedars of Lebanon, English and Irish Yews and other pine trees thrived.

Massive sequoias, or giant redwoods, so popular with the Victorians, were particularly apt in the Wynyard garden,

named as they are Wellingtonia gigantea, after the Iron Duke himself. Known in the United States as Washingtonia, the tree can reach heights of over 100 feet and was officially renamed in 1939, to clear up the confusion, *sequoiadendrum giganteum*. At Wynyard, the tree's original name honours the friendship forged during the Peninsular Wars between the 3rd Marquess and his commanding officer. The Wellington obelisk still standing in the grounds commemorates the Duke's visit to Wynyard in 1827.

While the influence of the 3rd Marquess and his wife Frances Anne is evident in the impressive parklands and pleasure grounds at Wynyard, the 6th Marquess and, in particular, his wife Theresa brought creative energy and vision to the development of the formal gardens. A garden album, created by Theresa, Lady Londonderry in 1912, records in affectionate detail the gardens she created and adored. Produced shortly after the death of her mother at the age of 76 and rediscovered only recently at Mount Stewart, the Londonderry's Irish home, Theresa's album offers a fascinating insight into the design and planting of the formal gardens at Wynyard. Details provided by horticultural journalists of that earlier era also help the modern visitor to visualise the splendour of the formal gardens developed at the turn of the 20th century. Many of the original features have now gone, but clues left in the landscape allow the imagination to recreate the planned designs, while Theresa's photographs bring back to life the glory of the gardens, so much enjoyed by her family, friends, eminent visitors and Theresa herself.

More detailed description of the formal gardens in their heyday follows this introduction.

A walk through the formal gardens

Steps leading from the terrace (from the garden album of Theresa, Lady Londonderry, 1912, with permission of Lady Rose Lauritzen)

A pleasant walk, either on foot or in the mind's eye, leads the visitor through the present day grounds, now mostly laid to lawns and shrubbery, with vibrant carpets of daffodils in springtime. To the right of the terrace, on the south side of the house, a flight of stone steps, clearly visible in Theresa's 1912 photograph, is now replaced by a grass bank. From the top, a long straight walk heads north westwards to a classical porticoed building in the distance. After a few metres, the path divides, the right fork leading uphill to the former Italian Garden. Two large stone gate posts indicate the original boundary, while a

Site of the flower garden showing the stone posts which formerly supported the Ratisbon Gates

The walk from the Hall to the Dairy

pair of identical plinths, now devoid of statues, would have been situated within the garden. Through the green gate, beyond the Italian Garden, the present Walled Garden formerly used for growing fruit and vegetables, is destined to become Sir John Hall's Rose Garden.

Returning to the fork and continuing along the main route, the path passes a large mound marking the grave of the race horse Hambletonian. The classical building close by is the old dairy, its ornate frontage a miniature version of

the Hall. The rear of the building, a much simpler brick construction, originally adjoined a group of utility buildings, including stables. A large private house, converted from the original red roofed barn, looks on to land formerly devoted to a series of ornamental gardens, including the Rose Garden, planted by Theresa, Marchioness of Londonderry. Beyond, an extensive lily garden incorporated impressive plant-covered walkways, a garden house and a thyme walk linking to the wild garden and herbaceous border.

Large ornamental gates, still standing, led to a broad herbaceous border, parallel to the extensive Wild Garden, whence a flight of steps led to the lakeside footpaths,

Gates leading to the broadwalk of herbaceous planting

Steps from the Wild Garden to the woodland footpaths and temples

where Greek and Roman Temples still stand. In the bottom of the valley, a dam on the beck at the Eagle Bridge marks the commencement of the lake. Towards the Hall, two ornate metal columns mark the site of the Suspension or Chain Bridge which spanned the lake for over 100 years.

The Italian Garden

In 1889, according to the Journal of Horticulture and Cottage Gardener, the Italian garden covered two and a half acres. *'Situated some distance from the mansion in front of the range of fruit houses and entered by some elaborate and very handsome gates, the beds are large and simple in design.'* The wrought iron gates, brought to Wynyard by Frances Anne, Marchioness of Londonderry, came from the cathedral at Ratisbon in Bavaria.

The Eagle Bridge photographed 2011

Italian gardens showing the Ratisbon Gates (from the garden album of Theresa, Lady Londonderry, 1912, with permission of Lady Rose Lauritzen)

Now known as Regensburg, the town was the site of a major battle in 1809, followed by widespread looting. A central boss bears, in Roman numerals, the date 1648 and the coat of arms of Albert IV von Toerring-Stein, Bishop of Ratisbon from 1613 to 1649. The five gates, each one 10 feet 5 inches high and 7 feet 3 inches wide (over 3 x 2 metres), formed an impressive screen between two stone gateposts and were never opened. A smaller gate to the right allowed access to the Italian Garden. A bell, the remains of which are still visible at the top of the right hand gate post, rang to announce the arrival of Lord and Lady Londonderry, warning the gardeners to make themselves scarce.

A grass walk divided the garden in to two equal parts, a series of scroll beds creating the effect of an intricately patterned carpet. Planted to a colour scheme of yellow, pink and white, each bed was edged by slow growing evergreen box *(buxus sempervirens)* and a path of decorative spar stone. Arranged in bold masses to stunning effect, the brilliant colours of tender plants such as pelargonium, calceolaria, violas and mimulus were muted by the interplanting of foliage and neutral tints. Beds also included alyssum, dahlias and a great many begonias, bred at Wynyard by head gardener Mr. E.H. Gribble. Lush turf lawns surrounding the scroll beds were filled with more beds of colourful annuals. Blue borders completed each end of the garden, delphinium Carter's Butterfly proving particularly effective. George Gordon, writing in The Gardener's Magazine of January 1907, was just as

The Flower Garden (George Nairn's collection)

impressed as his 1889 colleague to see *'the art and practice of gardening attained to a high degree of development'*.

Theresa's album records that the beds were laid out with different designs each year. In 1911, to mark the coronation of King George V, *'the left hand border was planted with scarlet and crimson geraniums, with white and yellow in front ... making a brilliant blaze of colour.'* In 1912, the lower borders were planted with shaded blue violas, the pyramids filled with Madame Kraus ivy leafed pink geraniums. Four central beds were planted with Paul Crampel geraniums, a vibrant scarlet, also used for many years outside Buckingham Palace to match the tunics of the guards. On one side, the garden was bordered by vineries, grown against the brick wall still standing today. Opposite, yew hedges, rather than walls, flanked the Ratisbon Gates, which, in 1912, were bordered by pale pink China roses and, representing Lord Londonderry's racing colours, orange and purple violas, the black cap suggested by *perilla* or purple mint. Two large stone plinths bore beautiful bronze statues, one of Achilles, the other Ajax defying the lightning.

Towards the wild garden, the complex design was completed by a hedge of golden privet, roses and further ornate carpet bedding. 75,000 plants were used to create the stunning effects achieved in the various Wynyard gardens. At the western end, a raised mound with seats gave a wonderful bird's eye view of the planting, allowing visitors to appreciate the true glory of the intricate design. According to Theresa, *'to sit on the seat under the oak on the rising ground and to look at the brilliant colours displayed in this garden is most satisfying to the eye.'* Nearby, she describes *'a beautiful Louis XVI basket lying on the grass, the basket made of echeverria and sedum glaucum (succulent plants), the contents double crimson Lafayette begonias.'*

The Dairy

Just beyond the Italian garden, the dairy, described by Theresa as *'a facsimile of the house itself, with its miniature Corinthian pillars'*, still stands today, its classical design visible even at a distance. In 1912, the main building was almost covered with ivy, its pillars entwined with more ivy, clematis and hops, beds of roses

The dairy (from the garden album of Theresa, Lady Londonderry, 1912, with permission of Lady Rose Lauritzen)

completing the picturesque effect. To the left, graves of pet dogs, their likenesses carved in stone, commemorated Lina, a real friend 1880-1894, and deerhounds Sulky (1885-1895) and Langwell (1897-191), faithful companions for a total of 26 years. Also buried close by, Sir Henry Vane's famous racehorse Hambletonian and the pet dog beloved of his little daughter Frances Anne, later wife to the 3rd Marquess of Londonderry. Although the only remaining trace of these burial places is the mound marking the last resting place of Hambletonian, the family's enduring attachment to animals is clear in a stone inscription recorded in Theresa's 1912 album.

'There are men both good and wise
Who hold that in a future state
Dumb creatures we have cherished here below
Shall give us joyous greeting
When we pass the Golden Gate
Is it folly that I hope it may be so ?'

Ornamental trees

From the western end of the flower garden, George Gordon, writing in The Gardener's Magazine of 1907, described a broad walk wandering through ornamental trees and conifers including silver firs, such as *abies pungens glauca*. Numerous weeping trees included the pendent form of *Ulmus Montana* (the Scotch or Wych Elm). Masses of flowering and ornamental-leaved shrubs were planted to great effect, particularly noticeable in the association planting of the purple foliage of *prunus pissardii* with the golden *spiraea opulifolia aurea*. Theresa planted copper beech and lime trees amongst the older specimens, intending to preserve and develop the woodlands for the benefit of her grandchildren and great-grandchildren *'if the Radical Party have not taken all their property away from them.'*

Theresa's Rose Garden

At the turn of the 20th century, Theresa, Lady Londonderry, created a magnificent rose garden, possibly as a tribute to her son Reginald, who, after a lifetime of ill health, died in 1899, at the age of nineteen. Another young relative, Charles Henry, only son of Ernest Vane-Tempest, son of the 3rd Marquess and Frances Anne, died the same year, aged 27. Although the roses are long gone, pink decorative stones set around a drinking fountain in the north wall remain, but are not accessible to the public.

Plaques in the rose garden planted by Theresa, Lady Londonderry 1899

A date stone inscribed 1899 and 1900 records that *'This garden was planted in one century and flowered in the next'*. Alongside, the simple sentiment, *'A rose garden is no place for grief.'* A familiar quote from Shakespeare's Romeo and Juliet is particularly apt.

'What's in a name ? That which we call a rose
by another name would smell as sweet.'

In a longer quote, Shakespeare's Othello, almost halted in his jealous determination to kill his innocent wife Desdemona, compares her to a beautiful flower blooming in a garden.

'When I have plucked thy rose
I cannot give it vital growth again,
It must needs wither. I'll smell thee on the tree.
Oh, balmy breath, that dost almost persuade
justice to break her sword!'

*Plaque in the rose garden planted by Theresa,
Lady Londonderry 1899*

Theresa also selected quotes from the 11th century Persian poem, the Rubaiyat of Omar Khayyam, translated into English by Edward Fitzgerald in 1859. One stanza continues the floral theme.

*'Look to the Rose that blows about us – 'Lo,
Laughing,' she says, 'into the World I blow:
At once the silken Tassel of my Purse
Tear, and its Treasure on the Garden throw.'*

Another poignantly presages the future, the garden continuing to bloom without its creator.

*'Ah, Moon of my Delight who knowst no wane,
The Moon of Heav'n is rising once again:
How oft hereafter rising shall she look
Through this same Garden after me, in vain!'*

*Plaque in the rose garden planted by Theresa,
Lady Londonderry 1899*

Lines from Victorian poet Robert Browning reiterate the transitory nature of the rose.

'I pluck the rose and love it more than tongue can speak
Then the good minute goes
Already how am I so far
Out of that minute?'

Plaque in the rose garden planted by Theresa,
Lady Londonderry 1899

The garden had become well established by 1907, when George Gordon of The Gardener's Magazine admired climbing and rambling roses grown over pillars and arches. Dwarf roses filled great beds, each devoted to a single variety. Hybrid tea roses, many chosen for their suitability to the local climate, included Maman Cochet, Betty, Lady Ashtown, La France, Liberty, Corallina and Killarney. In her 1912 album, Theresa mentions other favourite roses, such as Richmond, Madame Ravary, the Belle Sebright, Hugh Dickson and Madame Lambard, *'showing up quite gloriously against the red brick dust paths.'*

A stone inscribed in French describes the blue sky and sunshine of this beautiful place changing all too quickly to sorrow and rain.

'Gai endroit ton soleil luit
Le ciel est bleu,
L'heure ne passe que trop tôt,
Et demain, il pleuvra peut-être.'

Another exhorts us to suffer the thorns while hoping for the roses.

'Souffrons les épines
En espèrant les roses.'

Theresa recorded all the inscriptions in her 1912 album, including two recent additions, carved in 1911, on to stone shields, engraved with roses. Lines from Robert Browning suggest that blooms should be allowed to flourish untouched.

'Then how grace a rose? I know a way!
Leave it, rather.
Must you gather?
Smell, kiss, wear it - at last, throw away!'

Another recalls the loss which may have inspired the creation of Theresa's beautiful rose garden, for her, *'a blessed retreat'.*

'The thorn of parting, red and keen,
Though it be hidden, grows
Neath the inner heart
Of hearts of every summer rose.'

Theresa recorded planting all the first roses in 1899 *'with my own hands.'* As she wrote her album in August 1912, the garden displayed *'a wealth of blossom and surrounded as it is by trees, it has a delightful sense of seclusion.'* The garden gave pleasure all year round. *'Even in December, the yew trees round it and the green rose leaves, with here and there a crimson blossom, make it a lovely and peaceful retreat and the smell of sweet briar in the spring and summer is absolutely intoxicating.'* Opposite the wall of poetic inscriptions stood *'a little beehive of a summer house'*, where the joys of the rose garden could be savoured.

The Stone Garden

Leading from the rose garden, a handsome pergola, replicating the rose pergola at Alton Towers, Theresa's

The Stone Garden (from the garden album of Theresa, Lady Londonderry, 1912, with permission of Lady Rose Lauritzen)

ancestral home, supported elegant swathes of crimson ramblers, clematis and variegated hops. This led into the Stone Garden, with its manicured lawns, central sun dial and two beautiful stone seats, facing each other and backed by yew hedges. Against the old garden wall, two rows of tall sunflowers formed a stunning backdrop to a colourful border, filled, in 1912, with begonias, heliotropes, pink mallows and blue asters.

The Water Lily Tank

Beyond the Stone Garden, referred to by a friend of Theresa's as the College Garden, three steps led down to the Water Lily Tank, set into a series of formal lawns. An elevated stone seat in the corner allowed an excellent view of the white, crimson and yellow water lilies. Alongside, a parterre of white, yellow and mauve violas beneath white and golden poplar trees, planted to disguise the barn, only its red roof showing. Completing the scene, a flower-filled stone jardinière, and, on the wall, three small lead figures – Cupid in the centre, flanked by two small children, a boy who has taken a bird from its nest, a girl left holding the nest with four eggs inside.

The barn with its red roof (from the garden album of Theresa, Lady Londonderry, 1912, with permission of Lady Rose Lauritzen)

The Lily Garden

Two steps led down to a walkway of arches clothed in ivy and Virginia creeper, yew hedges either side and a border of white and yellow. Alongside, the lily garden, its grass close cropped, looked back towards a high yew hedge enclosing the long herbaceous border. Here and there, marble fonts, stone tanks and baskets, all filled with lilies, mingled with stately conifers and elegant flowerbeds. A keen sailor, Theresa also included in the lily garden, *'an amusing remembrance of yacht racing in topiary'*, two boats in full sail formed from yew, with a steamer created

La Paz (from the garden album of Theresa, Lady Londonderry, 1912, with permission of Lady Rose Lauritzen)

Lily Garden (from the garden album of Theresa, Lady Londonderry, 1912, with permission of Lady Rose Lauritzen)

from box, *'waiting to bring them home should the wind fail.'* A gift from her mother, two beautiful Siberian crab trees, crimson fruits vivid against their green leaves, stood even taller than the yew hedge. Nearby, surrounding another magnificent tree, a seat where the peace and harmony of the garden could be enjoyed.

The Garden House

Beyond the lily garden, and running north-south parallel to it, a long rustic pergola covered in climbers, led to Theresa's *'blessed retreat'*, the garden house, still standing, in a private part of the garden. New in 1912, stone built, with glass windows and doors, and fitted with electric lighting, the garden house was named 'La Paz', Spanish for 'peace'. Beautifully furnished with comfortable chairs, tables of Frosterley marble and a cabinet filled with fine old china and cut glass, the house provided the perfect spot for the garden designer. A mahogany bureau, complete with writing desk, book cases crammed with reading matter, including gardening books and two gilt framed mirrors, their tops decorated with

The writing table (from the garden album of Theresa, Lady Londonderry, 1912, with permission of Lady Rose Lauritzen)

carved gardening implements, completed the fine interior. Leaving the garden house and walking beneath the pergola, Theresa would come, at the end of the walkway, to a gift from her daughter Helen, known as Birdie, a stone statue of Cupid playing a harp.

The Herbaceous Border

Beyond the statue, a high yew hedge marked the boundary of a wide herbaceous border, concluding at either end with ornate wrought iron gates, still in situ, although now a little rusty. According to Theresa's 1912 album, the border, 270 yards long, was planted between 1886 and 1889, the gates made in Glasgow, a copy of the Ratisbon Gates in the Italian Garden. A broad central walk, edged with grass verges, allowed the visitor to view, on either side, collections of beautiful plants tastefully arranged in sumptuous wide borders. Four hundred species or varieties of hardy plants were screened from the wind by yew hedges, always pruned by knife, rather than shears. They had reached eleven to twelve feet in height by 1912, when Theresa recorded in her album a list of the plants arrayed on either side of the walk – *'purple, blue, red and rose coloured flox, lupins, daisies, hollyhocks, acanthus, 'love in a mist', statice and innumerable flowers and plants.'* At the western end of the border, a plaque on the boundary wall reads *'1886 -1915 These gardens were made and tended by Theresa, Marchioness of Londonderry.'*

Plaque mounted on the gate post at the end of the broad walk

The Thyme Walk

Towards the boundary wall bearing the commemorative plaque, running north-south and dissecting the herbaceous border, a thyme walk ran from the wild garden towards the lily garden. Beneath arches covered with Dorothy Perkins rambler roses, *' just a mass of pink blossom'*, diamonds of thyme set in to the grass path led to seats and sundials situated at either end of the walk way. Theresa describes the thyme walk *'fringed with heliotrope, pink and white sweet peas, pale grey and rose asters.'* Lavender and roses completed the fragrant display. The luxuriant growth of climbing plants and foliage meant that, from the seats, the herbaceous border, so close by, could not be seen. The sun dials bore poetic inscriptions,

Thyme Walk and sun dial (from the garden album of Theresa, Lady Londonderry, 1912, with permission of Lady Rose Lauritzen)

some in Latin, Italian and French, all reflecting on the passage of time. On the south sun dial, quotes from the Persian Rubaiyat of Omar Khayyam.

'Come fill the cup and in the fire of Spring
The Winter garment of repentance fling
The bird of time has but a little way to fly
And, lo, the bird is on the wing.'

'The moving finger writes and
Having writ, moves on,
Nor all your piety nor wit
Shall lure it back to cancel half a line
Nor all your tears wash out a word of it.'

'What boots it to repeat
How time is slipping underneath our feet –
Unborn tomorrow and dead yesterday
Why fret about them
If today be sweet.'

The north sun dial, in similar vein, quotes from 'Katrina's Sundial', a poem created by American author and clergyman Henry van Dyke (1852-1933). He wrote the lines for his friends Spencer and Katrina Trask, who, in 1899 in New York State, created a garden to honour their love and in memory of their four children, who all died young.

'Time is too slow for those who wait
Too swift for those who fear
Too long for those who grieve
Too short for those who rejoice
But for those who love, time is eternity.'

'Hours fly, flowers die
New days, new ways
Pass by, love stays.'

At the lower end of the thyme walk, a stone water lily tank, surrounded by yews and fringed with lavender, contained a fountain, water spouting from the mouth of a dolphin held by Cupid. On the opposite side, a Christmas gift from Theresa's daughter Helen, a stone seat flanked by *'a wealth of lilies'*. Leaving the thyme walk at the lower end, the visitor would step in to the Wild Garden.

The Wild Garden

On the southern edge of the herbaceous border with its carefully arranged beds, the wild garden presented a range of plants in a natural setting. Hardy shrubs and plants, placed in large groups for effect, took their place alongside bulbs, allowed to colonise naturally. Grass paths, known as *'the garden river'* cut through the meadow to allow access to visitors without spoiling the natural effect. The design of the garden may have been influenced by William Robinson, whose best selling 'The Wild Garden', published in 1870, advocated a move away from the formal beds of Italianate gardens, popular in the Victorian era, to a more natural approach, featuring native species in a more relaxed setting.

A present from Theresa's brother Charles, two stone posts surmounted by fruit baskets, still stand at one of the entrances to the wild garden, unlike another gift, a stone pagoda, brought from Japan in 1903 by Theresa's son Charley and his wife Edith. The wild garden also contained stone vases and fonts, bronze birds and Japanese lanterns, where Theresa would often place a

Fruit baskets and broad green path (from the garden album of Theresa, Lady Londonderry, 1912, with permission of Lady Rose Lauritzen)

Pandora and the praying boy (from the garden album of Theresa, Lady Londonderry, 1912, with permission of Lady Rose Lauritzen)

light – *'in hopes that one's most and ardent and heart-felt wishes might be granted.'* Green and variegated shrubs, including holly, *griselinia litoralis*, flowering privet and golden poplar mingled with other flowering shrubs, including purple plum, lilacs, spiraeas and *pavia macrostachya*, a deciduous shrub with white flowering panicles resembling a bottle brush, hence its popular name. A splendid statue of Venus originally stood at the entrance to the wild garden, where an ancient apple orchard, carpeted with daffodils in the spring, followed by lilies and montbretia, is, sadly, no more.

Close to Venus, old fashioned pink blush roses recalled Theresa's childhood days at Alton Towers. Nearby, a mass of Dorothy Perkins, a rose featured throughout the garden. Only introduced to Great Britain from the USA in 1901,

named after the granddaughter of Charles Perkins who helped to develop it, the rose won top honours in 1908 and began the tradition of naming roses after people. The chain of ladies' clothes shops took its name from the rose in 1909. As Dorothy Perkins was already flowering away at Wynyard in 1907, when the Gardener Magazine visited, Theresa appears to have been at the forefront of garden design. Another innovation, *'Gruss an Teplitz'*, a dark red hybrid China rose, introduced in 1896 and now considered an old historic rose, covered a stone tank full of water lilies. A bronze stork stood to one side, apparently waiting for the winged lead figure in the tank to catch a fish. Pergolas festooned with crimson roses and with pink Dorothy Perkins, led to a rustic arbour covered with honeysuckle, crimson ramblers, hops and passion flowers.

Old fashioned stone cisterns and drinking troughs were filled with plants such as sweet-scented verbena, chosen for their fragrance. Sweet peas, pelargoniums with scented foliage and *nicotiana,* the sweet-scented tobacco plant, mingled their fragrances with the vanilla flavour of purple *heliotropums.* Sometimes called cherry pie, the purple flowering plant, very popular in the Victorian era, included a variety named Florence Nightingale. In her 1912 album, Theresa described *'a little delicious scented garden, backed by crimson and dark red dahlias against the yew hedge, a sweet pea hedge and sweet scented briar, southernwood, evening stocks and mignonette, sweet scented geranium and white tobacco plant ... a rare mixture of scents ... which brings back multitudes of remembrances, sentiments and places, as if it were a key unlocking rooms in one's heart and brain.'*

At the far end of the wild garden, a little open summer house looked on to a marble font, another gift from Theresa's *'dearest mother'.* Filled with lilies, the font stood in a bed of African rock roses and golden yellow *Canarienvogel,* a dwarf polyanthus rose, also known as canary bird. *Rosa wichuriana,* a semi-evergreen China rose with white petals and a yellow centre, spread along the ground above a weeping ash tree. Purple gladioli, yellow nemesia, pale mauve and yellow dahlias provided *'a brilliant blaze of colours',* further enhanced by purple passion flower and pink blush roses climbing up stone columns topped by balls. Between the columns, which divided the wild garden, beds of orange lilies completed the vibrant show. Apple trees sheltered the path on either side.

Scotch firs, tall and meeting overhead, turned the grass paths into *'church-like aisles',* brightened by a fuchsia hedge and a mass of crimson monarda. Towards the centre of the wild garden, a seat beneath a beautiful beech tree looked on to the rock garden, newly created in 1912. Hedges of *rosa rugosa* lined a path leading towards steps at the furthest edge of the wild garden. In those days, from this elevated position, as well as a clear view of the house and lake, the visitor could enjoy the distant panorama of Bilsdale, Baydale and the Cleveland and Hambleton Hills. Still in situ, although now rather worn, stone steps edged by elegant stone vases led down to the valley, taking the visitor back to the Hall. Theresa's 1912 album records that the steps, brought from Seaham, were crowned by pillars bearing graceful figures made from French metal. Believed to have been bought by Frances Anne, wife of

the 3rd Marquess of Londonderry, the statues, portraying Pandora and a praying boy, are no longer present, but, half way down the steps, a pair of low ornamental gates of Italian iron work still survive.

At the foot of the steps, surrounded by golden privet, *'a delightful seat for thought and meditation'* provided the ideal spot to admire the house and lake, as well as the *'variegated poplars, yews, beeches, copper beeches and purple planes which fill up the valley'.* A left turn leads towards the house along the Goshawk Walk, named after one of the pets so beloved of Frances Anne. Stone memorials, said to have been created by Lord Ravensworth, architect of the memorial room to the 3rd Marquess, bear inscriptions conveying the depth of affection Frances Anne felt for her departed pets.

A Goshawk by name, though a greyhound by race
I rivalled a Goshawk in fleetness and grace
Forsaking the hills where I sported in youth
My mistress I served with devotion and truth
And though on her wrist I could not take my stand

The Goshawk memorial

I couched on her lap and I fed from her hand
Dear mistress, farewell, when I drew my last breath
The pang of our parting was sharper than death.'

Now badly weathered, the statue was originally protected by an ivy covered arbour which, containing a seat, also offered a resting place and shelter for visitors to the garden. In her 1912 album, Theresa wondered, *'how many vows have been exchanged, how many plans made, how many aspirations dreamt of'* by generations of people walking along this, one of the oldest walks in the garden. Further along, another of Frances Anne's pets acquires immortality in stone.

'Tiny was small in stature, but we find
His little body held a mighty mind
And tiny caskets oft enclose a gem
Of lustrement for Sultan's diadem.'

Simpler pet memorials of more recent date were erected in the Wild Garden, the favourite part of the garden and final resting place of Robin, 8th Marquess of Londonderry and his wife, Romaine, reinterred in the family vault at Long Newton after the sale of Wynyard in 1987. The wild garden clearly meant a great deal to Theresa, too, as the final words of her journal demonstrate.

'Wild garden, grow !
To me your paths are memories
And every flower a friend.'

The border in front of the house

Running alongside the conservatory and along the terrace on the south side of the house, in 1907, *'a spacious flower border ... resplendent with colour'* contained blue lobelia, a variegated pelargonium Madame de Salleri and crimson seedling begonias, the plants arranged in bands of colour, enhanced by vases of flowers placed at intervals and a striking border of rich golden conifers. In her 1912 album, Theresa explained that the planting scheme never changed, representing as it did the colours of the Household Brigade. Both her father and husband served with the Life Guards, a senior regiment of the British Army, which, along with the Blues and Royals, make up the Household Cavalry. The border offered a constant reminder *'of the splendid array of battles in which the Life Guards and Foot Guards took part.'*

Theresa's album leaves us in no doubt of her commitment and devotion to vast areas of Wynyard gardens, outstanding in their time. *'The intense pleasure which this garden has given me, I cannot put in words. I have designed the whole of it ... the herbaceous border, the thyme walk, the rose garden and the wild part.'* Concluding her album on 2 October 1912, her 37th wedding anniversary, she confided that *'every plant, flower, stone and path'* evoked memories, adding *'I look back through the long vista of years and I must say with absolute truth that my happiest days at Wynyard have been spent in the planning, planting and now in the enjoying of this garden.'* Theresa had to leave her beloved garden in 1915, on the death of her husband, the 6th Marquess. She died just four years later. The Wynyard garden album dedicated to her son Charley, later the 7th Marquess, and his wife Edith went with them to the Londonderry's Irish home, Mount Stewart, where Edith created another wonderful garden, now owned by the National Trust.

Kitchen Gardens

Much of the kitchen garden was situated in the area now known as the Walled Garden, the planned site for Sir John Hall's Rose Garden. The Head Gardener's Cottage still stands in the corner of the walled garden, which, in living memory, was divided into beds edged with box hedges and accessed by gravel paths. The beds were used for the cultivation of apple trees and vegetables, fruit trees were trained on the walls and soft fruits, including vines, peaches and figs, grown in glasshouses on the wall opposite the Head Gardener's cottage. He marked the beginning and end of the gardeners' working day by ringing the bell, which still hangs at a central point high up on the wall adjoining his house.

The 1889 Journal of Horticulture described the kitchen and fruit gardens covering eleven acres, the soil mainly a good loam, but heavier in parts, with a clay sub-soil. Several varieties of pear, including Williams' Bon Chretien, Doyenne de Comice, Napoleon, Pitmaston Duchess and Louise Bonne of Jersey were grown as cordons or against walls, one magnificent specimen of Marie-Louise growing to 11 feet high and extending over 50 feet horizontally. Bush varieties of apple trees were allowed a space of 18 feet square to each tree, every row consisting of a single variety. Prince Albert, Blenheim

The head gardener's cottage in the corner of the walled garden (Courtesy of FPDSavills)

Cyril, son of Head Gardener Joseph Henry Yarrow, in front of the glass houses (with permission of Elizabeth Calvert and Valerie McLeod)

Pippin, Tower of Glamis, Keswick Codlin, Adams' Pearmain, Scarlet Nonpareil – just a few of the choice fruits grown by the Wynyard gardeners of the time. Apricots, peaches and Morello cherries also did well growing on walls and in the open, while vegetable crops were grown in abundance.

In later years, the 8th Marquess sent to France for apple trees, which were grown in pots within the glasshouses and carried outside in the summer.

Tender fruits under glass

The 1889 Journal reported that more tender fruits were grown in the Fruit House, 315 feet long and consisting of ten divisions, seven being vineries, two peach houses and one devoted to camellias. In another part of the garden, cucumbers, melons, figs and late peaches were also grown under glass. According to The Gardener's Magazine of January 1907, melons were still growing on cordons, long

The gardeners' bell

after they had disappeared from the dessert menus of most establishments. The glass houses continued to produce early, mid-season and late fruits, such as peaches, nectarines and grapes.

Late varieties still on the vine included Muscat of Alexandria, Alnwick Seedling, Alicante, Lady Downes and Wynyard Honapoot, a new red muscat variety of great promise. Brought by Lady Londonderry from Constantia, Cape Town in South Africa, the vine produced long, handsome bunches of large berries, bright red and full of flavour. In 1918, the vinery was increased by the addition of Bailleul grapes, brought back as cuttings from the battlefields of France by James de Rothschild, a brother officer of the 7th Marquess.

Glasshouses for exotic flowers

Reported in the Cottage Gardener Magazine of 1889, an additional plant house, 222 feet long and 18 feet wide, had been erected three years earlier by Messrs. Richardson of Darlington. Later known as Amdega, the company provided glasshouses for many fine houses like Wynyard. Made up of six sections, the east end of the plant house contained 50 different varieties of tea rose, favourites including Grace Darling, Princess of Wales, The Bride and Lady Castlereagh, one of the varieties from Newtownards on the family's Irish estates. Other divisions were devoted to orchids, gardenias, dipladenias, crotons and dracaenas. A further greenhouse held a collection of fragrant flowering plants, scented rhododendrons being particularly favoured.

The Gardener's Magazine of 1907 reported numerous plant houses, many devoted to orchids, indicating the huge demand for cut flowers and decorative plants for the mansion. An average of 600 plants of the begonia Gloire de Lorraine were grown annually. In one house, gardenias and stephanotis filled the air with fragrance, while another blossomed with the pure white of the Amazon Lily, *Eucharis grandiflora*, a beautiful shade loving plant, originally found in South America.

Three more houses were taken up with Malmaison carnations, scented of cloves, and named after the Paris house and garden of the Empress Josephine, wife of Napoleon Bonaparte. Twenty five remarkably fine orange trees, said to have come from Malmaison, took pride of place in the original conservatory until they were destroyed in the devastating fire of 1841. One of the cult flowers of the turn of the last century, the Malmaison carnation, now rare, is still used in producing fragrant soaps and bath oils by the company Floris, perfumers to Her Majesty the Queen.

The Conservatory

Adjoining the mansion, the conservatory, an elaborate structure 77 feet long and 27 feet high, provided the perfect setting for palms, tree ferns and other permanent occupants. In 1907, the gardening journalist described *'a spacious winter garden with a roof of three spans and a style of architecture in agreement with that of the mansion.'* An abundance of flowers *'in the most robust state of health'* included *begonia rex*, maidenhair fern (*adiantum cuneatum*) and *ficus repens*, a creeping fig. From the roof, *bougainvillea glabra* descended in clouds of mauve, while the pillars were clothed with *cobaea scandens variegata*, a woody evergreen perennial climber, native to Mexico. Over the pathway, the slender branches and pungent leaves of the elegant *asparagus deflexus* from tropical Africa trailed from hanging baskets. From Guatemala, fine specimens of the blue, rose and white forms of *achimenes longiflora*, similar to the climber Morning Glory, were especially noteworthy. Palms, ferns and other fine foliage plants completed the luxuriant effect.

Visitors

Thousands of visitors flocked to Wynyard annually at the turn of the 20th century, when the gardens were open to the public three days a week for a considerable part of the year. As early as 1888, the 6th Marquess advertised the grounds open to the public on Saturdays from 2pm to 7pm. People came from a radius of twenty miles, presumably by pony and trap, charabanc or even on foot. King and Boast ran a charabanc and brakes service from the Oddfellows Hall in West Hartlepool, the price of a return ticket 1/6, access through the Golden Gates.

The gardeners

Gardeners at Wynyard during the time of the 3rd Marquess and his wife included George and John Dalziel, both of whom had children baptised at the church of St. Thomas of Canterbury, Grindon in the early 1830s. An even earlier Wynyard gardener, James Davison, must have worked at Wynyard for Sir Henry Vane Tempest, as the baptisms of his sons, Charles and George, are listed in Grindon parish records for 1814 and 1817, before the marriage of Frances Anne and Charles Stewart.

In March 1875, during the time of the 5th Marquess, Mr Jones of Wynyard Gardens paid over £47 to more than twenty local and national suppliers, including £8 to Coxhoe Lime Company. However, the efforts of the gardeners resulted not only in beautiful surroundings for the Hall, but also valuable income. A list of produce sold from Wynyard Gardens in 1874 included cut flowers and eighteen dozen bedding plants. The gardens at that time could well be described as fruitful, producing for sale 158 pounds of grapes, 122 quarts of strawberries, 62 pounds of pineapples, 24 pounds of redcurrants, 20 melons, 282 peaches, 96 nectarines and three stone of pears. Also sold from the garden were 700 lettuce, eleven dozen cucumber, three dozen cauliflower, four dozen artichokes, five stone of onions, four pecks of peas and five pecks of beans. Each artichoke cost just one old penny, a peck of peas or beans one shilling, the equivalent of five pence today. A

peck equals 16 pints or 8 litres, so you got a lot for your money. The grand total for produce sold from the Wynyard Garden in 1874 was £65/2/6.

In 1907, commending the *'artistic perceptions'* of the 6th Marquess and his wife, Theresa, George Gordon of the Gardener's Magazine also praised head gardener Mr H.E. Gribble, *'who has long enjoyed the reputation of being one of the foremost gardeners of the day'*. As well as tending to glasshouses, formal parterres and trimly kept lawns, in order to create gloriously effective gardens, Wynyard gardeners, at that time, produced 75,000 plants annually. A great deal of work was required in the fruit and vegetable gardens, which were ornamental as well as productive. By 1907, quantities of sweet peas were growing up new fangled wire supports, rather than old-fashioned pea sticks.

Joseph Henry Yarrow, head gardener at Wynyard from 1926 until 1948, took particular charge of the palms and ferns in the conservatory, and is also remembered for his greenhouse work, growing grapes, figs, nectarines and peaches. Slipper orchids were used in corsages for the ladies of the house and for bridal bouquets, which also incorporated orange blossom from the trees grown in the greenhouse. Baskets of fruit from the gardens were sent to Mount Stewart, the Londonderry's home in Ireland. Before coming to Wynyard as Head Gardener in 1926, Mr Yarrow worked for the Londonderrys at their hunting lodge near Oakham in Rutland, where they rode with the Cottesmore Hunt, a particular favourite of Henry Chaplin, father of Edith, 7th Marquess of Londonderry.

Joseph Henry Yarrow (Head Gardener 1926-1949) and family in front of the old orchard (with permission of Elizabeth Calvert & Valerie McLeod)

Up to the outbreak of war in 1939, more than two dozen garden workers were employed at Wynyard. Often single men from local villages, many of the gardeners and gamekeepers lived in very basic accommodation provided on the estate. Bill Aitchison, legendary head gardener in recent years, recalled moving in to the bothy as a young lad. Each worker had a small room with a bed and chest of drawers and, at the end of the corridor, a single sink with a cold tap.

The 1960s

Although the beautiful formal gardens of earlier days are now a distant memory, in more recent times, the 9th Marquess did much to resurrect the hall and grounds after years of neglect. Completed in 1963, extensive renovations, including the demolition of the stables and servants' quarters, opened up views looking towards and from the house. New landscaping of the grounds between the house and the lake restored the graceful beauty of the south front of the hall, revealing the classical lines envisaged by the original architect. 20,000 tons of earth brought on to the site helped to create this impressive new landscape. The 9th Marquess also instigated work to restore the lake, removing silt which had accumulated over decades.

The 1960s also found the conservatory in a sad state of disrepair, its roof having fallen in years earlier, victim of a wartime bomb. As part of his plan for adapting the Hall to suit the needs of a young modern family, the 9th Marquess removed the roof completely and, using deep blue mosaic tiles imported from Italy to cover the floor, converted the conservatory into *'the best designed swimming pool that any stately home in the country possesses.'*
(Daily Telegraph June 1964)

The Conservatory in the 1960s (with permission of Margaret Shepherd)

Looking to the future

The sale of Wynyard to Sir John Hall in 1987 marked another milestone in the development of this beautiful place. As well as embarking on major restoration work in the house, Sir John turned his attention to the grounds, engaging consultants to provide a landscape management plan for the parkland and gardens. A tree survey in January 2000 proved the expertise of those 19th century gardeners in selecting trees with a long life span. 168 oak trees were found to be in good condition, along with 46 horse chestnut and nineteen beech trees. Other species, including ash, sycamore, lime, cherry, Scots pine and larch had also survived well in smaller numbers. The consultants observed that *'the mature mixed woodland belt, distribution of copses, tree groups and individual scattered specimen trees'* contribute significantly to the picturesque character of the park. Additional tree groups or specimens will adhere to the historic plans, respecting the original intentions and retaining attractive vistas. The team also suggested that, to ensure practicality of use and maintenance, the Walled Garden and Italianate Gardens be restored and enhanced using plans originally drawn up for other parts of the garden.

The New Rose Garden

In common with the rose garden of Theresa, Marchioness of Londonderry, planted in one century to flower in the next, Sir John Hall's 21st century rose garden aims to acknowledge the powerful spirit of the past whilst creating for the future a legacy to his ownership of Wynyard. Inspired by Sir John's love of growing roses at his childhood home at Ashington in Northumberland, the spectacular garden will contain an impressive collection of roses, many rare and exotic.

Michael Marriot, technical director of David Austin roses, recently commissioned to replant the roses at London's Kew Gardens, worked in partnership with acclaimed garden designer Simon Dorrell, famed for his Arts and Crafts style gardens at Hampton Court in Hertfordshire and at Bryan's Ground, his home on the Welsh Borders. Together, they created a design combining a classic 19th approach with a contemporary eye for form, colour and composition. A series of interconnecting garden spaces or rooms, intimate in scale, both formal and informal in style, will allow the gardens to illustrate the versatility of the rose in all its fragrant glory. Quieter, contemplative green spaces and water features will provide a gentle contrast with the riotous colours of the roses, giving each part of the garden its own distinctive atmosphere.

Romantic, highly scented and flower-filled, the rose garden, containing almost 10,000 plants, will cover four acres. Climbing and rambling roses will grow on walls, pergolas and obelisks, clamber over buildings, through trees and, to stunning effect, over a multitude of arches in the Mezquita garden, modelled on the breathtaking Moorish mosque in Cordoba. Formal plantings of hybrid teas, floribundas and English roses, known for their repeat flowering and wonderful scents, will flow into informal gardens combining roses with perennials and flowering shrubs. Old roses, such as gallicas, damasks and albas, will feature, with gentle underplanting, carefully selected to enhance and complement the main attraction, the wonderful collection of roses.

Incorporating Sir John's collection of statuary and garden artefacts, the garden will become a haven for wild life, rich in fruits and seeds, as well as still and running water, complementing the diverse habitats already available in the parkland and garden. Strategically placed seats will allow visitors plenty of opportunity to admire the gardens at their leisure, relishing the intoxicating scents and sights, flowers and fragrance abundant all year round.

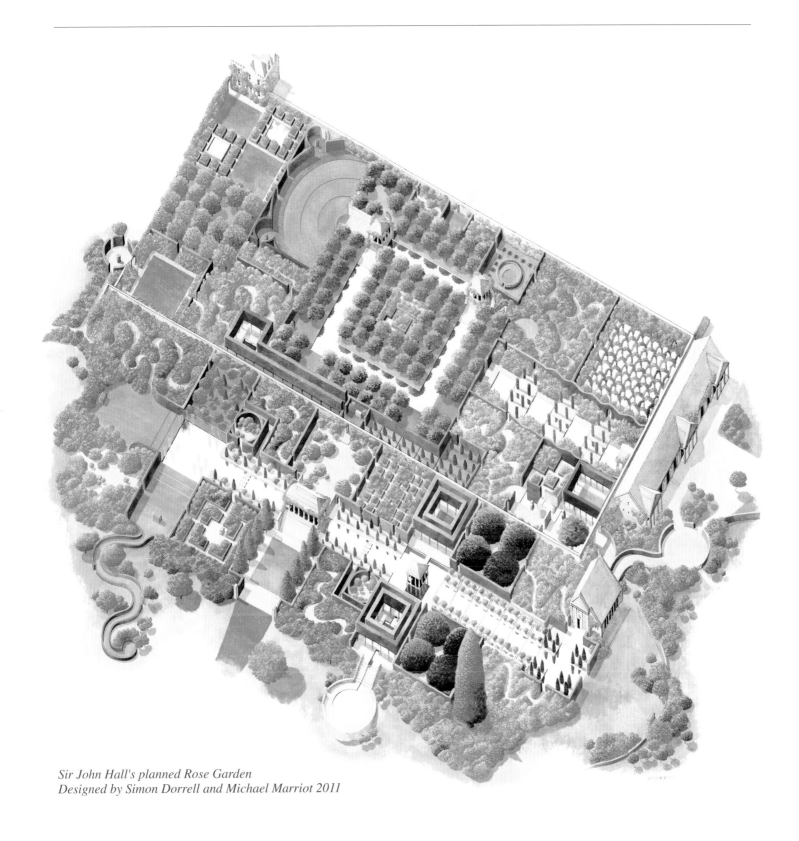

Sir John Hall's planned Rose Garden
Designed by Simon Dorrell and Michael Marriot 2011

CHAPTER 23

WYNYARD PARK

In 1344, Bishop Bury gave Henry de Langton and his son William a grant of free warren, which allowed them to hunt game, including hare, fox, wild cat, pheasant, partridge, woodcock, plover and lark. Thus began a long history of rural pursuits at Wynyard. Sir Henry Vane Tempest, father of Frances Anne, Marchioness of Londonderry, a great lover of horses and racing, kept racehorses at his stables at his home in Long Newton. At Wynyard, he created in the grounds his own racecourse, one mile long and complete

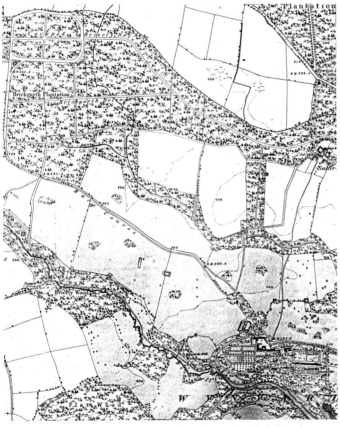

Map showing the Racecourse and Cock Pit (top left-hand corner) from 1856 Ordnance Survey

with horse boxes and stables. In 1819, within their ambitious plans for the grounds, his daughter Frances Anne and her husband Charles Stewart, as well as putting the brewery in order, restoring the poultry yard and repairing the butcher's shop, also intended to improve provision for horses, creating a second stable yard and additional stables.

Rural pursuits

A born gambler, Sir Harry loved betting on cockfighting as well as horse racing, his cockpit in the grounds at Wynyard said to be 'very commodious' with tiered seating all around. Many of his cocking matches reported in the 'Sporting Magazine', 'Sir Harry's Greys' award-winning birds were famous throughout the north. Although the baiting of bulls and bears generally fell into disuse by the end of the 18th century, the bear garden installed by her father was still in use in Frances Anne's day. A stone cage surmounted by an eagle, the bear pit, surrounded by monkeys in wire cages, stood in 'The Pleasure Park', where the Eagle Bridge crossed Fulthorpe Beck. In a letter of August 1848, Disraeli, concerned by Frances Anne's tendency to seek out danger, including keeping a bear, warned, *'When the latter ceases to kiss your fair hand and begins to lick his own paw, he is getting dangerous.'*

Foxhunting

The 3rd Marquess and his wife also continued Sir Henry Vane's practice of keeping horses and hounds for hunting at Wynyard Park, a dog boy specifically employed to help superintend the hounds. Grindon parish church records of 1835 show John Stevenson employed as huntsman to the Marquess of Londonderry, his daughter Hannah being baptised on December 1. The York Herald of 19 December 1840 carried notification that the Wynyard foxhounds would meet at 10.30 a.m. on Monday December 21 at the Two Mile House and again on Christmas Eve at the Wynyard Park kennels, situated near the gamekeeper's cottage. The Morning Post of 10 October 1842 reports *'a grand field day at Wynyard with the splendid pack of hounds belonging to the Marquess of Londonderry.'*

Upwards of 100 horsemen including the Duke of Rutland, the Duke of Leeds, the Marquis of Blandford, Lord Ravensworth and HRH the Duke of Cambridge, grandson of George III, took part in the hunt. The royal visitor, very impressed by the beauty of the surrounding countryside and extensive views, *' appeared in excellent spirits and was extremely affable during the day, often stopping to chat when he had an opportunity with the old farmers he met on*

The kennels photographed 2011

his way.' The ladies took carriages from the Hall to join the menfolk at the end of a remarkably fine day's hunting.

A later hunt, in November the same year, did not have such a happy outcome. The Freeman's Journal and Daily Commercial Advertiser of 1842 records an accident at the Two Mile House near Stockton, when the Marquess broke his right arm in a fall from his horse and had to be rushed back to Wynyard for surgical attention. Now the site of a public house, 'The Horse and Jockey' on the A177 Stockton to Sedgefield Road is still known locally as the Two Mile House.

Shooting

Shooting parties took place at Wynyard for centuries, so the need for good breeding and management of game birds was essential. Ideal locations for roosting were found at Close Wood and Fanny's Glen, presumably so-called after the familiar name for Frances Anne. Land was

planted up with beans and buckwheat especially for pheasants and partridges, 386 of which were reported killed in the autumn of 1821. A 1923 map of Wynyard Park shows a pheasantry to the east of the Lion Bridge. Poaching was a problem from the outset. In 1830, gamekeepers apprehended three poachers, one from as far away as Yorkshire. The same year, a neighbour of Lord Londonderry shot pheasants in their roosts, four nights running, later claiming the intended targets were wood pigeon. Lord Londonderry's 1848 Orders for Gamekeepers, amongst other directives, state that *'a reward of £1 will be given to any keeper who apprehends a poacher. If two keepers apprehend one, 10s. a piece.'* A rabbit catcher was employed and instructions given to *'destroy the rabbits by every means except snares, that being dangerous for hares.'*

At home for Christmas at Wynyard in 1845, two of the Londonderry sons, Lord Seaham, and Adolphus Vane,

Group taken during a shooting party.
Back row: The Hon. James Lowther (left), Viscount Coke (3rd from left), Lord Henry Vane Tempest (5th from right), Viscount Chaplin next to him, Lord Ormonde and N. W.

Apperley on extreme right.
Front row: Lord Londonderry (left), Lady Randolph Churchill (next to him), Viscountess Coke (2nd from right). Photograph by Reginald or Theresa *c*1890.

From the Londonderry Album, with permission of Lord Londonderry

aged 24 and 20 respectively, arranged a shoot, bagging a daily average of 200-300 birds. In 1852, when the family were at Wynyard principally to celebrate Frances Anne's birthday on January 17, her eldest son Viscount Seaham, led a shooting party of six guns, which bagged about 340 head of game in three hours, mainly hares, pheasant and a few woodcock. In December 1883, the Prince and Princess of Wales, while on a royal visit to Stockton-on-Tees, stayed at Wynyard as guests of the 5th Marquess, as Seaham had now become. A party including the Prince of Wales, the Earl of Fife, the Duke of Sutherland and Count

Herbert von Bismarck, German Foreign Secretary, enjoyed three days shooting at covers at Newton Hanzard, the Home and Bottle Hill. Farm tenants, labourers and estate workers were employed as beaters. The ladies, including the Princess of Wales, joined the gentlemen for lunch in a tent.

The passion for shooting reappeared during the time of the 6th Marquess, who held the title from 1884 to 1915. He employed a falconer and, in order to maintain the number of pheasants, eighteen permanent gamekeepers.

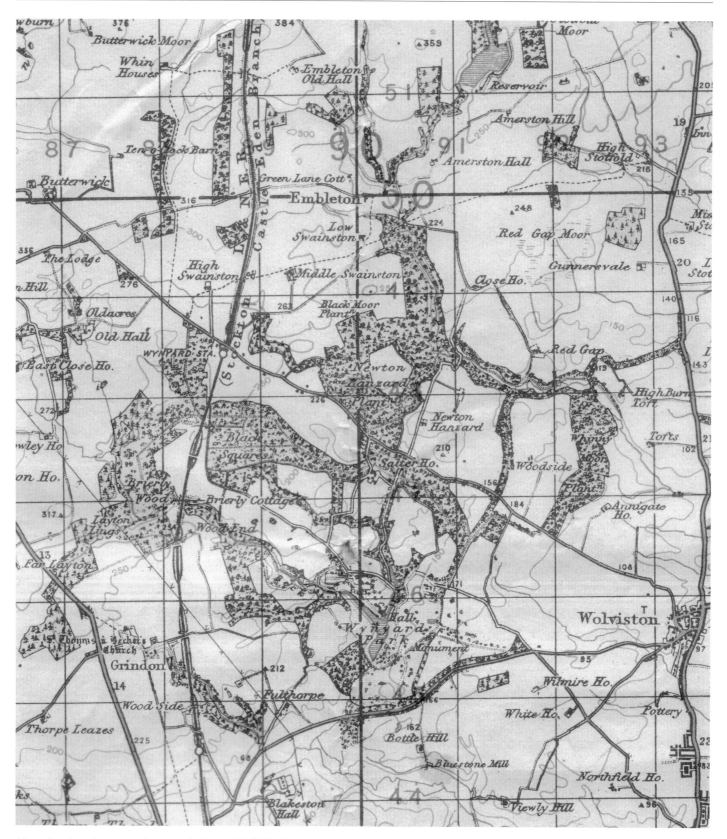

Map showing the estate farms and shoots, 1943 Ordnance Survey

In addition to over sixty staff, extra beaters were employed part-time. On a good day, up to 4,000 peasants would be shot. As well as small shoots for friends and tenants, throughout the 1890s, grander shoots were organised for visiting dignitaries including Lady Randolph Churchill and the Prince of Wales, future King Edward VII, who wrote in November 1890, *'In the two days shooting at Wynyard, we killed 7,843 head, out of which 5,817 were rabbits and 1,973 pheasants.'* Much of the game bagged was handed on to other people, either as gifts or for sale. The Wynyard game book commencing in 1913 records a gift of four pheasants each to Sergeant Dadds in Sedgefield and Superintendent James, possibly from Stockton. In January 1914, one Sergeant Savage also received a brace of pheasant. On 16 December 1913, 1196 pheasant were despatched to Wm. Scholes and Son of Stockton, presumably game dealers.

Shoots listed in Londonderry records for 1913-14 include Old Redgap, Whinnie Moor, Newton Hanzard, Bottle Hill, Home Beat, Old Warren, Long Newton, Black Squares and Old Acres. Important visitors whose names appear in the game book around this time include the Spanish Ambassador, the Earl of Enniskillen and Prince Lichnowsky, German Ambassador to London from 1912-1914. Sent to repair relations between Britain and

Bronze sculpture of boar hunt

Germany, but distrusted by his own government and recalled at the outbreak of war, the prince was admired by Sir Edward Grey, British Foreign Minister at the time. Responsible for the prophetic statement ' *The lamps are going out all over Europe. We shall not see them lit again in our time'*, Grey believed that, *'Had Lichnowsky continued to be the trusted representative of his government, after the murder of the Archduke, war might have been avoided.'* Another pre-war visitor Henry Cust, editor of the fashionable Pall Mall Gazette, enjoyed passionate liaisons with several society ladies, including, allegedly, Theresa, Marchioness of Londonderry.

In December 1930, Colonel Omar Singh and Brigadier General Cameron accompanied the Indian prince, the Maharajah of Alwar in a shooting party. Another distinguished party, visiting in November 1936, managed to bag, in just two days, 420 pheasant, 29 duck, 13 rabbits, three woodcock and one hare. Back in 1812, James Westwick, keeper for Sir Henry Vane Tempest, under his

Bronze sculpture of deer hunt

master's orders, shot a hare spotted from the window of the gun room at a distance of 155 yards. The successful shooting party of November 1936 included Captain Lumley, Count Alvo, John Frederick Lambton, 5th Earl of Durham and Herr Joachim von Ribbentrop, German Ambassador to Britain, later to become Foreign Minister to Adolf Hitler. Numbers of game gradually decreased and an average daily bag of 500 pheasants reduced to about 1,500 in a full season after the war, when beaters were paid approximately £3 per week. The Glorious Twelfth of August marked the beginning of the grouse season, while shooting for partridge began on September 1 and pheasant on October 1. Both ended on February 1. There was no close season for hares, which abounded at Wynyard during the early 1900s.

Deer hunting

In the 1800s, herds of deer were a common sight on park lands. At Wynyard in 1819, to protect the new growth from deer, carpenters placed fencing around young trees in the newly planted woodland. Bronze statues in front of the Hall bear witness to the enthusiasm of the 3rd Marquess for hunting deer and wild boar during his time as ambassador to Vienna in the 1810s. At Wynyard, deer were bred for his table and gifts of venison were regularly sent to members of his family when visiting Ireland.

Records from 1831 show a herd of 456 deer kept at Salterhouse, Wynyard's home farm. An extensive deer park is indicated on a map of Wynyard in 1859, while an earlier map, from 1855, shows a deer shed, no longer in evidence by 1895. A squared C-shaped building approximately 8x4 metres with projecting arms of 11 metres at each end, the deer shed was situated between the Wellington Monument and an ornamental fishpond known as the Swancar.

The 6th Marquess had only recently acceded to the title when, in 1885, the pack of beagles from the Durham Hunt were brought to Wynyard for a deer hunt. According to an account in the Leeds Mercury at the time, *'the sport was most successful and enjoyable'*, consisting of two runs each lasting a couple of hours, with luncheon served in between. The hounds earned *'the warmest encomiums by the manner in which ... they held the line of each buck they chased, whilst the large mounted field uniformly followed as straight as an arrow.'*

The deer hunt of 1885 was attended by a large party of distinguished and aristocratic guests including the brothers of the 6th Marquess, Lord Henry and Lord Herbert Vane-Tempest and Mr R. Yeoman MP. The Honourable Captain William Dawnay of the Staffordshire Militia, son of the 1st Earl of Downe, was accompanied by his wife, Lady Adelaide, daughter of the 6th Earl of Macclesfield. The Earl of Zetland, Master of the Zetland Hunt based in Richmond, North Yorkshire, attended with his wife. Viscount Castlereagh and Lady Helen Vane-Tempest, children of the 6th Marquess, also took part, aged seven and nine respectively on the day of the hunt. Lord Londonderry's private secretary Captain Newton Wynne Apperley completed the party. Before moving to Wynyard, N.W. Apperley kept his own pack of hounds at Machynlleth in Wales, home to the 6th Marquess before his marriage. His father Charles James Apperley, known as Nimrod, (1778-1843), moved in the best social circles and was well-known in his day for lively accounts in The Sporting Magazine on fox hunting, horse racing, cock fighting and pheasant breeding.

A Changing World

Traditional rural pursuits continued at Wynyard even through the turmoil of two world wars. The 7th Marquess lived through both wars, succeeded by his son in 1949. During the second World War, furniture from Wynyard was sent to London to help out families who had lost everything in the Blitz. According to Miss J. Holmes, daughter of estate mason James Holmes, the Hall also provided brief respite for evacuees and 3,000 soldiers returning from Dunkirk. In 1942, the Ministry of Defence moved into Wynyard, transforming the Hall with reinforced dormitories, lecture rooms and an officers' mess.

In the grounds, an underground operational bunker, still in existence, was created for the use of a top secret Auxiliary Unit, the Wynyard group named the South Durham Maquis. Sometimes known as the British Resistance, these specially trained, highly secret units were set up by Winston Churchill in 1940 in order to resist an expected Nazi invasion. Operational patrols of four to eight men, often farmers or landowners, were recruited from the local Home Guard, then trained in unarmed combat, demolition and sabotage. The Royal Engineers built 400-500 Operational Bases (OBs), in local woodland with a camouflaged entrance and emergency escape tunnel. Stood down in

1944, members received a letter warning that, although their efforts would not be forgotten by their leaders, official recognition was not possible. The existence of the Auxiliary Units remained a secret until the 1990s. A mock aerodrome at Warren Farm and barrage balloons over the Wynyard estate were intended to alleviate the risk of bombing, while 'War Ag' workers, employed by the Ministry of Agriculture, cultivated the land in the absence of so many people called up to fight in the war.

From 1946-1961, while Wynyard was home to a teacher training college, the Londonderry family continued to live in part of the house, but maintenance of the grounds was not given a high priority. After the early deaths of the 8th Marquess and his wife, within just four years of each other,

the 9th Marquess inherited the title in 1955, aged 18. The last Londonderry to live at Wynyard, during his tenure shooting syndicates operated at Wynyard. At the beginning of the season, every tenant received a brace of pheasant, personally delivered by the Marquess. Local people have fond memories of working as beaters under the guidance of head gamekeeper, George Douglas and his deputy, Norman Daggett. The Wynyard estate continued to support shooting of a different kind in the second half of the 20th century, when, as well as pheasant shooting, estate workers established clubs for rifle and clay pigeon shooting. In the 1980s, Vaux Breweries donated a gold cup and £400 prize money for the national clay shooting championship. In 1984, Wynyard hosted the World Championship.

Clay pigeon shooting at Wynyard Country House Hotel (Photograph courtesy of Holden and Jones)

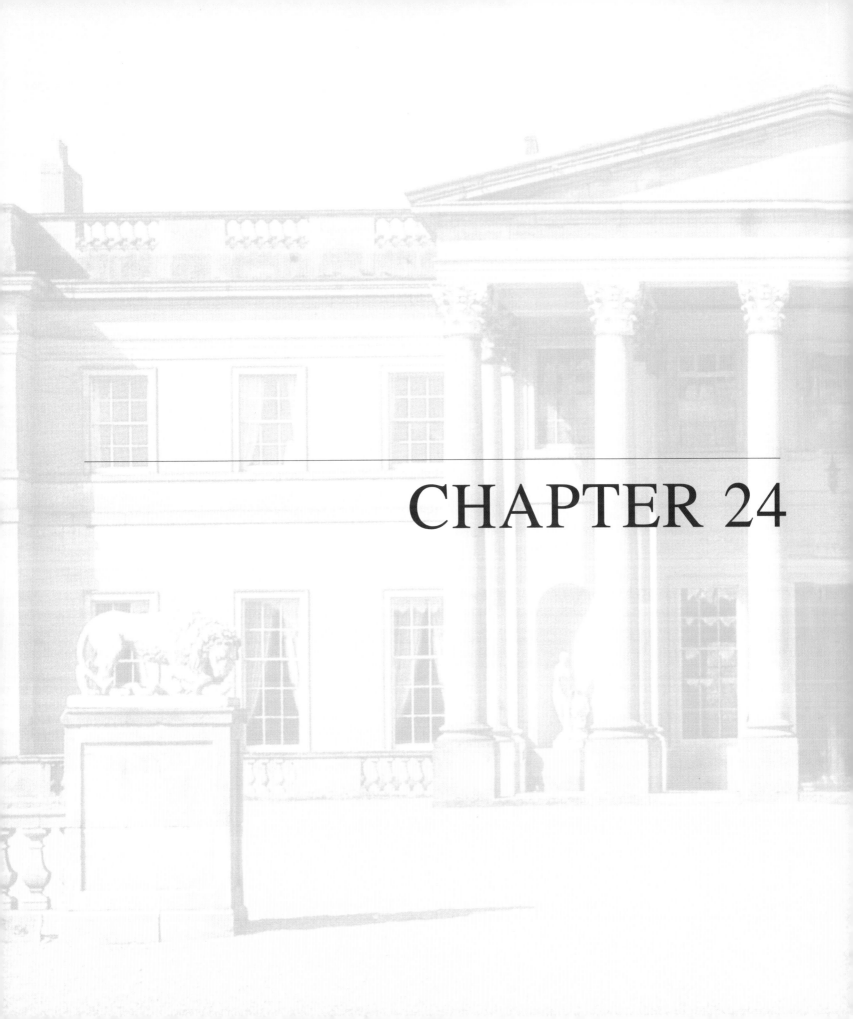

CHAPTER 24

WYNYARD ESTATE AND FARMS

Sir Henry Vane-Tempest's cattle painted by T F Wilson 1809 (Photographic Library Beamish Museum Ltd)

Sir Henry Vane Tempest

Painted by T F Wilson in July 1809, these magnificent beasts, bred by Sir Henry Vane Tempest, indicate the standard of livestock seen at Wynyard at the turn of the 19th century. On the left, a shorthorn cow, four feet nine inches in height from shoulder to ground, six feet ten inches in length from tail to horns. On the left, a shorthorn bull "Wynyard", calved 3 April 1806, sired by Favourite, his dam Phenomenon. Bigger in every dimension than the female, the bull measures five feet in height and seven feet four inches in length.

'To the day labourer, not having a cow, and who has been constantly employed by Sir H.V.Tempest and who has brought up and educated in the habits of Industry and Religion, the greatest number of Children born in Wedlock, without Parochial Assistance, FIVE GUINEAS.' Instituted by Sir Henry Vane Tempest in the early years of the 19th century, the recipient of this rather unusual award was required to provide character references and certificates from his master and from local clergyman the Rev. Robert Waugh of Bishop Middleham, near Sedgefield. As well as children, Sir Henry encouraged his tenants to breed their own livestock, awarding trophies for sheep, cattle and pigs, as well as for agricultural skills such as hedge cutting and ploughing. Tenant farmers were encouraged by awards of silver trophies, given for the farm in the best condition, the best crop of turnips, the cleanest crop of drilled beans and to the *'tenant who shall have most effectually under-drained the greatest number of roods on his farm since the 13th of May 1803.'*

Frances Anne and the 3rd Marquess

After marrying Frances Anne in 1819, Sir Henry's son-in-law, the future 3rd Marquess of Londonderry, continued this tradition of encouraging agricultural achievement, awarding prizes of cash and silverware for categories including *'best quantity of cattle for all purposes'*, *'best and most extensive dairy'*, *'the most improving and best cultivated farm'*, *'best, nicest and most productive garden.'* For every five acres, farmers hoping for an award were required to grow turnips in one rood (a quarter of an acre), at least double the proportion of winter green food. At the Rent Day held at Wynyard on 23 November 1828, Matthew Ryle of West Herrington was awarded the silver tankard for the farm in the best state of cultivation.

Situated near the North Lodge, in the 1830s, Salterhouse Farm, the largest on the Wynyard estate at approximately 350 hectares, supplied meat, milk and other provisions to the Hall. The home farm at Wynyard, Salterhouse led the way in introducing new crops and stock breeds, setting an

Salterhouse Farm (with permission of Tees Archaeology)

example for tenant farmers in the surrounding villages of Thorpe Thewles, Embleton, Redmarshall and Long Newton. The farm also produced hay, oats and beans to feed the numerous horses working on the estate, wheat for the pheasants and poultry, winter food for the deer and manure for the vegetable and rose gardens.

During the time of the 3rd Marquess, annual income from the Durham farms, which covered 5,000 hectares, amounted to £9,000, much of which he used to guarantee loans necessary for the development of the Londonderry pits. Determined to develop the quality of the Wynyard farmlands, at the 1846 annual meeting of his tenant farmers, the 3rd Marquess announced his intention to improve drainage of the entire estate at his own cost, charging five percent on the outlay of capital. The provision of cattle sheds and artificial fertilisers

encouraged farmers to move away from their traditional practice of growing large crops of wheat, a crop becoming less economical to grow as cheaper imports were causing local prices to fall. The 3rd Marquess also offered to help *'the poorer class of tenantry in carrying out an improved system of husbandry when their own means were insufficient.'*

In 1846, he also ordered renovation of cottages and out buildings, spending £50 to replace roof tiles and almost £110 on extensive work at Home Farm. A Mr. Hay charged £20 for preparatory work cutting, draining and gardening at Close Bank in readiness for a new drive installed between Salterhouse and Close Bridge, at a cost of £35. During the 1850s, general expenditure on the estate amounted to approximately £5,000 per annum, almost £1,000 devoted to game and deer.

A report compiled by Mr. A.B. Murray in 1858, four years after the death of the 3rd Marquess, noted several fields still required improved drainage, and repairs were needed to the roofs of the haysheds and the sawmill. He found one of the lodges at the Golden Gates in poor condition and recommended that Brierley Cottage be demolished. On his first visit, the Pleasure Grounds looked abandoned and the lake and ponds required cleaning. In Fanny's Glen, Close Wood and Bottle Hill plantation, a large number of trees had been felled and not replaced. In 1859, rabbits destroyed twenty eight acres of crops, a loss of £224.

Staffing the estate

Estate workers, William Baxter, baillif, is seated with a dog (Photographic Library Beamish Museum Ltd)

Estate loggers (Photographic Library Beamish Museum Ltd)

Before World War I, £200 paid the total weekly wage bill for fifty estate workers, excluding farmers. A register of workers on the estate in 1912 lists two cattlemen, two shepherds, four horsemen, two gamekeepers, five woodmen, four spademen, two masons, two carpenters and

Estate workers (Photographic Library Beamish Museum Ltd)

two blacksmiths, as well as a groom, a forester, a poultryman, a porter, a hall porter and two nightwatchmen. Mrs. Wallace, listed as dairymaid, would, no doubt, supervise several younger workers in the dairy. Pensions, army allowances and payment to extra labourers boosted the total weekly bill to £250, the responsibility of Alfred Bell, Head Clerk in the Estate Office from 1908-1956. Until the creation of the National Health Service in 1948, workers contributed five shillings per annum towards the costs of medical treatment they might require. Free housing, coal and milk helped to augment the undeniably low wages received for a six day working week.

Up to the 1950s and the advent of combine harvesters, threshing machines from Butterwick, Greatham and Wolviston came to Wynyard at harvest time, when all the farmers would work together gathering in the crop from each farm in turn. Much of the casual labour at Wynyard, especially at haymaking time, came from Ireland, making the sea crossing in April or May and returning home in late autumn. Before harvesting began, average weekly pay was 19 shillings, less than £1. The men usually worked from 7am till 5pm. During haymaking, they were given a pint of beer and some bread and cheese at four o'clock and another pint if they worked after 7 pm. A meal was provided at the end of the day's work. Labourers were provided with a rug and slept on the floor in the granary or empty cottages, on straw mattresses which they made themselves.

Awarding excellence

An advertising bill for a Show of Stock at Wynyard Park on Saturday 7 November 1857, during the time of the 4th Marquess, shows the family tradition continuing. Cash prizes ranging from £2 to £10 were awarded for the best six acres of swede turnips, the best kept hedges, the best dairy cow, the best brood sow and the best stock of poultry. Two prizes of £10 were awarded for the best three year old colts, one for agricultural purposes, the other for the road or field, both bred by the exhibitor. Lady Londonderry presented a silver cup, valued at £10, to the tenant possessing the largest and best breeds of cattle, while Frances Anne, the dowager Marchioness of Londonderry, gave a silver challenge cup, worth £20, to be awarded to the tenant considered to possess the most improving and best cultivated farm. If the same tenant won in three successive years, the trophy became his to keep. An early triple winner, a farmer named Darling, handed the trophy down as a family heirloom. His great great grandson Harold Boland retired as tenant of Middle Swainston farm in 1987. The trophy is still treasured by his family.

Agricultural shows continued at Wynyard into the first half of the 20th century. Durham County Agricultural Show, held at Wynyard on August 15 1907, had classes for horses, cattle, dairy cattle and dogs, as well as sheep dog trials and a milking competition. The band of the 1st Newcastle Royal Garrison Artillery performed and, in the afternoon, equestrian events took place in the large ring in front of the grandstand. During the show, competitors were invited, for one shilling, to guess the dead weight of a certain animal. Luncheon, served at 1pm, cost three shillings. The Marquess of Londonderry was president of the entire event, which ran from 9am till 7pm.

In August 1909, a vegetable and flower show held at Wynyard Park for the participation of Wynyard Estate Cottagers contained 47 classes, including best garden. Tenants and exhibitors were admitted free, visitors charged

Annual Show 1907 (George Nairn's collection)

Lord Londonderry's shepherd
(Photographic Library Beamish Museum Ltd)

one shilling between 10 am and 2pm, sixpence thereafter. Competitions for the best horses, cattle, sheep, poultry and dairy produce were held by the Tenants' Agricultural Society, Lord Londonderry providing £150 in prize money.

In more recent years, local people recall Stockton Show being held in the grounds. In the centre of this photograph, Tom Stephenson Ridley, shepherd on Wynyard estate is showing Suffolk cross Border Leicester heavy lambs.

The farms

By the beginning of the 20th century, Wynyard boasted a total of eighteen farms, including Warren Farm, Hurle, White House and Bottle Hill. A list of farms and their tenants from 1913-14, the time of the 6th Marquess, shows Ballands (or Boland) at Middle Swainston and High Burntofts, while

Miss Darling farmed at Low Burntofts. Other tenants were Musgrave at Embleton Old Hall, Applegarth at Old Acres and Sandersons at Amestone Hall. East Close Farm was tenanted by Trenholm and Elstob farmed at High Swainston.

In more recent times, Annigate and Woodside were farmed by Mr. A. Stonehouse and his son, the last tenant to be taken on by Lord Londonderry before the sale of Wynyard in 1987. As well as growing barley and wheat, the Stonehouses bred dairy cattle. Previous members of the family farmed at Embleton Old Hall, giving up the public house near Embleton church which they had previously run. Low Swainston Farm, run by the Kirk family from 1945-1989, covered 215 acres, growing wheat, oats and barley, with a dairy herd of approximately 50 milking cows and 100 heifers and calves.

For over 50 years, the Thompsons ran High Newton Hanzard, a farm of 130 acres, growing mainly barley and wheat, as well as breeding ewes and cows. Stan and David Hutchinson followed in the footsteps of their father Matthew Brown Hutchinson, farming at Low Newton Hanzard until the sale of the Wynyard estate in 1987. Run by the Hutchinson family for over 100 years, Low Newton Hanzard covered an area of approximately 214 acres. Crops of cereals and corn were grown in fields ploughed in the ridge and furrow method, allowing improved drainage and greater yield. The family also bred poultry, sheep, dairy cows and beef cattle. From 1968, for approximately 30 years, pupils from Manor Secondary School in Hartlepool, with their teacher Geoff Hainsworth, practised forestry skills on four acres of land at Newton Hanzard.

In 1964, Salter House, the home farm at Wynyard covered about 1,000 acres, mostly devoted to corn and stock, chiefly Aberdeen Angus, selling about 400 head a year to local butchers. By 1964, the 29 tenanted farms on the Wynyard estate, mixed in enterprise and ranging in size from 90 to 500 acres, yielded an annual rent which had risen from £5,000 in 1950 to £16,000 by 1964. Farm rents averaged 50 shillings an acre, £2.50 in today's currency. Just after World War II, farm rent averaged £3 per acre; by 1988 this had risen to £45. In the 1900s, William Fishburn, a Wynyard gamekeeper and tenant of a farm at Grindon, part of the Wynyard estate, paid monthly rent of one guinea, equivalent to £1 and 1 shilling, in modern currency £1.05 pence or £12.60 for the entire year.

Wynyard Mill

Built in the early 1500s, Blue Stone Mill was situated to the south of Bottle Hill Farm. As well as paying rents, early tenants were obliged to supply the owner with a portion of the corn produced. In more recent times, generations of the Crisp family lived and worked at the mill, which is no longer standing.

Members of the Crisp family at Wynyard Blue Stone Mill (with permission of Margaret Shepherd)

The old school at Wynyard c1890 from the Londonderry Album, with permission of Lord Londonderry

Wynyard School

At the turn of the century, Theresa, Marchioness of Londonderry, held a Sunday School each week in her boudoir (or study) at Wynyard Hall. In 1905, continuing the tradition established in the 1800s by Frances Anne, Theresa, Lady Londonderry provided a school in Wynyard Park. Housed since 1877 in the gardeners' bothy, the new school provided much better accommodation, its two classrooms catering for 50 pupils. Students housed at Wynyard from 1949-1961 also benefited from valuable teaching practice. In 1964, the school was extended at a cost of £16,000, partly funded by Lord Londonderry, officially opened by his wife and dedicated by the Bishop of Durham, Dr. Maurice Harland. One month later, after 21 years as headteacher,

Annie Heaton, daughter of Wynyard gamekeeper Henry Houliston, retired to live in North Lodge on the Sedgefield to Wolviston road. 'Wynyard Park Church of England School', officially named on April 1 1906, closed in 1985 due to dwindling numbers, its passing marked by a memorial service in the chapel. Modern housing, Scholars Green, now stands on the site of the former school. In 1888, Theresa, Lady Londonderry also provided, at Wynyard, almshouses capable of accommodating six poor women. In 1892, her husband, the 6th Marquess, ordered to be built, at his own expense, a red brick reading room, complete with caretaker's house, for the use of estate tenants and workers. Kelly's Trade Directory for 1902 lists as the secretary Francis Atkinson, who lived at Warren Farm.

A Christmas party in the school
(with permission of Margaret Shepherd)

Modern times

Having succeeded to the title in 1955 at the age of 18, in the 1960s, the 9th Marquess, turned his attentions to the management of the estate, which had been neglected in previous years. The Daily Telegraph of 16 June 1964 reported that the land surrounding Wynyard and another block at Long Newton totalled 9,000 acres, making the young Marquess the third largest private land-holder in County Durham. Since 1950, tenanted farms on the estate had benefitted from £100,000 worth of improvements, much of it on modernisation of houses and cottages. Electricity was installed in 1954 and, by 1964, all estate houses had hot and cold water and a bathroom. With the sale of the Wynyard estate in the 1980s, many of the farms ceased to exist, their memory preserved in the names of some of the roads on the housing development, including Burntoft, Annigate Close, Embleton Grove and Salter Houses.

The Reading Room photographed 2011

CHAPTER 25

THE END OF AN ERA

WYNYARD PARK, N. FRONT, STOCKTON-ON-TEES.

Death duties introduced in 1889 and augmented in 1894 had a catastrophic effect on families like the Londonderrys. By 1919, income tax on estate rentals rose to 30% and death duties to 40% on estates worth over £2 million. The 6th Marquess died in 1915 and, by 1919, the year marking the death of Theresa, Lady Londonderry, the Londonderrys had paid over £360,000 in death duties. Amongst the richest mine owners in Britain and one of just six millionaire peers during the years 1900-1949, the death of the 7th Marquess in 1949, followed by that of his son just six years later, dealt a heavy financial blow.

Nationalisation of the mines in 1947, although approved of by Robin, later to become 8th Marquess, removed a significant source of income. Up to that point, mining had continued at Seaham and at the collieries inherited from Frances Anne, Lady Londonderry. The 7th Marquess had invested in the sinking of a new pit as recently as 1928, the same year that Seaham Hall became a sanatorium. In 1939, to save paying rates of £4,000 per annum, Londonderry House was closed and the furniture removed. Requisitioned by the army during the war and taken over in 1946 by the Royal Aeronautical Club, in the 1960s, Londonderry House was sold. A week before its demolition to make way for a hotel,

300 guests joined the 9th Marquess to celebrate the life of a great house so important in an later era. Some years later, in 1977, the National Trust accepted responsibility for Mount Stewart, the Londonderry family home in Northern Ireland. Garron Tower, Frances Anne's castle on the Antrim coast, had long since ceased to be a Londonderry home. Only Wynyard remained.

As a young man, Alastair, Lord Londonderry did a great deal to restore the Hall to its former glory, converting one wing for the use of his growing family, and transforming the conservatory into an open-air swimming pool. Throughout his life, Lord Londonderry often worked alongside the estate staff, pruning trees and so on, indistinguishable from the tenantry. In the 1970s, in an effort to make Wynyard economically viable, he opened the Hall up for corporate events, dinner dances and conferences. In 1987, after agonising for many years, he took the difficult and heart-breaking decision to sell the estate. In a newspaper interview for the Evening Gazette of 26 January 1987, he explained, *'Wynyard began to die at the outbreak of World War One, suffering from under-investment and lack of inspiration. I tried hard to save it, but there comes a point when economic reality must prevail.'*

A NEW DAWN

13 May 1987 saw the arrival of Wynyard's new owner, Sir John Hall, knighted in 1991 for services to economic regeneration in the North-East of England. With family roots firmly fixed in the mining community of Northumberland, as chairman of Cameron Hall Developments, Sir John's working background, coupled with vision and determination, transformed a derelict area of Gateshead into an ultra-modern shopping mall, the Metro Centre, for many years the largest of its kind in Europe. Former owner and chairman of Newcastle United Football Club, now Life President, Sir John is an enthusiastic supporter of a vast array of organisations and initiatives. In 2011, he and his wife, Lady Mae, were granted the freedom of Gateshead for their services to leisure, retail, business and sport.

As relatively new custodians of Wynyard Hall, the Hall family recognise and respect the achievements of previous owners of Wynyard and the craftsmen they employed to design and create the magnificent Hall and grounds we can all enjoy today. High quality building development on part of the estate, followed by sensitive restoration and development of a superb country house hotel marks the beginning of a new era. *'Numb with misery'* over the sale of Wynyard, home to his family for over 160 years, Alastair, Lord Londonderry likened Sir John Hall to his illustrious ancestor, Charles Stewart, 3rd Marquess of Londonderry, both remarkable business men with outstanding entrepreneurial skills.

Bringing new ideas and economic reality to Wynyard, Sir John immediately embarked upon an ambitious programme of refurbishment, costing £8.5 million. Restored to the opulence of former days, the magnificent Entrance Hall and Statue Gallery, the Mirror Room, Ball Room and Library provided a luxurious home for the Hall family and impressive company offices for Cameron Hall Developments.

In 2007, the Hall family began to consider other uses of Wynyard Hall to ensure and improve its future economic viability. After considerable debate, it was agreed that the Hall should become a luxury 4-star hotel. A new company, Wynyard Hall Ltd., was created and Sir John's daughter, Allison Antonopoulos, appointed Managing Director to oversee the dawn of a new era.

Wynyard Hall Country House Hotel

In 2008, a nine month period of refurbishment, at a further cost of £3.5 million saw the transformation of Wynyard Hall into a beautiful country house hotel. History resonates in every part of Wynyard Hall. Portraits of eminent owners from Wynyard's illustrious past preside over the original dining room, now the stunning Wellington Restaurant. A team of outstanding chefs provide fine food and wine, enjoyed in magnificent rooms throughout the Hall and on the elegant terrace overlooking the beautiful landscape of the lake and parkland. Afternoon tea at Wynyard Hall, formerly a pleasure enjoyed only by certain members of society, has become a treat available to all.

Intimate yet sumptuous, the Brooks Chapel, its interior a testament to craftsmanship and artistry past and present, provides the perfect setting for a wedding to remember. Restored on a grand scale, the once derelict Conservatory hosts superb wedding receptions, each one given the privacy and importance essential to such an important day. A luxurious hotel with sixteen bedrooms, Wynyard Hall also hosts conferences, special events and smaller functions.

In order to survive into and beyond the 21st century, Wynyard Hall and its surrounding estate needed a sound economic base. Continuing housing development in Wynyard Village, undertaken by Cameron Hall Developments in recent years, will allow further investment in the fabric of the Hall itself, as well as the historic parkland and gardens. Beginning in 2012, a five year plan for the refurbishment of the grounds will include the creation of Sir John Hall's Rose Garden, one of the largest in England. As in former days, visitors will be welcome to enjoy the pleasures of the garden, as well as the glory of Wynyard Hall.

Determined to honour the proud tradition of illustrious predecessors, Sir John Hall and his family are dedicated to the continuing and future success of Wynyard Hall. Their vision, commitment and respect for Wynyard's history assured its sensitive transformation into a superb country house hotel. Another chapter in the fascinating history of this great house.

Wynyard Hall Country House Hotel 2011 (Photograph courtesy of Holden and Jones)

LONDONDERRY FAMILY TREE

LONDONDERRY FAMILY TREE

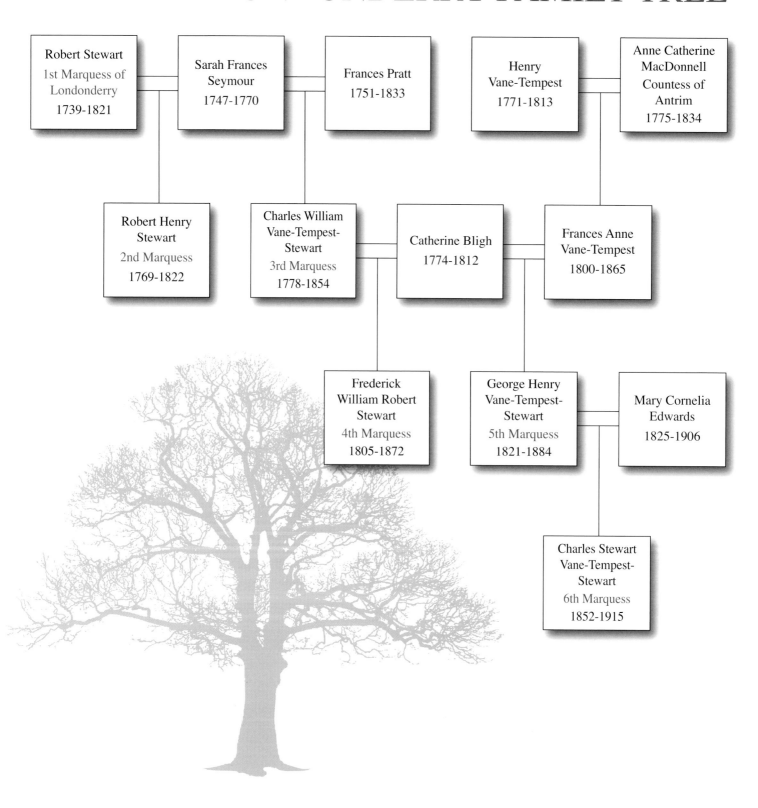

Robert Stewart
1st Marquess of Londonderry
1739-1821

Sarah Frances Seymour
1747-1770

Frances Pratt
1751-1833

Henry Vane-Tempest
1771-1813

Anne Catherine MacDonnell
Countess of Antrim
1775-1834

Robert Henry Stewart
2nd Marquess
1769-1822

Charles William Vane-Tempest-Stewart
3rd Marquess
1778-1854

Catherine Bligh
1774-1812

Frances Anne Vane-Tempest
1800-1865

Frederick William Robert Stewart
4th Marquess
1805-1872

George Henry Vane-Tempest-Stewart
5th Marquess
1821-1884

Mary Cornelia Edwards
1825-1906

Charles Stewart Vane-Tempest-Stewart
6th Marquess
1852-1915

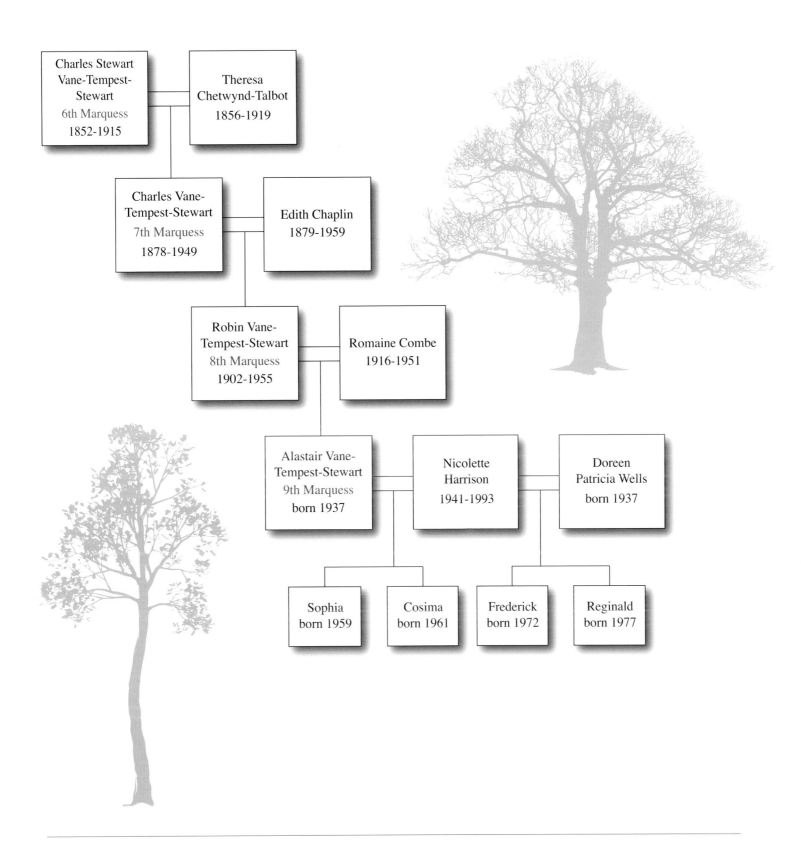

Charles Stewart Vane-Tempest-Stewart
6th Marquess
1852-1915

Theresa Chetwynd-Talbot
1856-1919

Charles Vane-Tempest-Stewart
7th Marquess
1878-1949

Edith Chaplin
1879-1959

Robin Vane-Tempest-Stewart
8th Marquess
1902-1955

Romaine Combe
1916-1951

Alastair Vane-Tempest-Stewart
9th Marquess
born 1937

Nicolette Harrison
1941-1993

Doreen Patricia Wells
born 1937

Sophia
born 1959

Cosima
born 1961

Frederick
born 1972

Reginald
born 1977

GLOSSARY OF ARCHITECTURAL TERMS

Apse – a semi-circular recess covered
with a hemispherical vault or semi-dome

Architrave – the lowest part of an entablature.
Resting directly on the capitals (tops) of the columns, the
architrave supports the frieze and the cornice. The term
can also refer to the moulding around a door or a window

Ashlar – dressed stone used in building

Balustrade – a row of decorative small posts
that support the upper rail of a railing

Boulle (or buhl) – a type of marquetry
using inlays of brass and tortoiseshell

Buttress – a projecting support built
on to the outside of a wall

Capital – the head or top part of a column

Chamfer – a bevelled edge connecting two surfaces

Clerestory – a high wall with a band
of narrow windows along the top

A coffered ceiling – divided into a grid
of recessed square or octagonal panels

Corinthian – the most ornate and elegant of the Greek
orders, characterized by a slender fluted column with an
ornate capital decorated with acanthus leaves and scrolls

Cornice – the upper slanting part
of an entablature located above the frieze

Crocketed pinnacles – ornamented pointed spires

Doric – one of the main styles of Greek architecture,
more formal and austere than Ionic

Enfilade – a series of rooms with adjoining doors,
allowing a view from one to the next

Entablature – the top part of a structure,
surmounting columns and resting upon capitals

Finial – decorative ornamentation,
often carved as foliage or fruit

Frieze – the wide central section
of an entablature (or upper part of a structure)

Greek architectural orders – In ascending elaboration -
Doric, Ionic, Corinthian

Hexastyle – having six columns at the front on a portico

Ionic – a style of Greek architecture, more elaborate
than Doric, less than Corinthian, its pillars bearing
ornamental scrolls or volutes on the capitals

Parapet – a low protective wall or railing
along the edge of a roof, balcony or bridge

Pediment – a triangular shape above the
entablature, typically supported by columns

Pilaster – a square column, partly built into,
partly projecting from a wall

Podium – a platform or base

Prostyle – a front portico of not more than four columns

Roundel – a circular decorative carving or design

Rusticated – large rough blocks separated by deep joints

Scagliola – Plasterwork in imitation of ornamental
marble, made from ground gypsum and glue,
coloured with marble or granite dust

Spandrel – the roughly triangular space between
the left or right exterior curve of an arch and the
rectangular framework

Stoothed (or stoothing) – a wall built with
a gap between its two faces

Tympanum – a semi-circular or pointed panel, sometimes
glazed, above a door or window, contained within an arch

ACKNOWLEDGEMENTS

We wish to express our gratitude for the invaluable help we have received in researching and compiling this book and for permission to use illustrations. Our thanks go to :-

Sir John Hall and Lady Mae of Wynyard Hall, their daughter Allison and her son Mark

Wynyard engineer Ken Olley, former MD of Cameron Hall Developments Russell Jones and all the staff at Wynyard Hall for their support, encouragement and interest

Alastair, Lord Londonderry and his retired agent, Raymond Wood

Lady Rose Lauritzen of Mount Stewart, who kindly gave permission to use material from the gardening album of her great grandmother, Theresa, Lady Londonderry

The staff at Mount Stewart, particularly manager Jon Kerr and Frances Bailey of The National Trust Northern Ireland

Also in Northern Ireland, Alec McKillop of Carnlough and Sinead Kinney at Garron Tower

Public Record Office of Northern Ireland

Durham County Record Office, for their help with enquiries and research of the Londonderry Papers

Julian Harrop, Assistant Registrar at Beamish Museum Ltd. Regional Resource Centre, who searched their database for photographs

Peter Rowe, Site and Monuments Officer, Tees Archaeology, for providing photographic material and reports

Stuart Pacitto of Teesside Archives, who searched their sources for information

Ward Philipson Photographic Collection

FPDSavills

Dawn Webster at Kiplin Hall

Elizabeth Conran, formerly of Bowes Museum

Holden and Jones, Photographers

Chapman Brown Photography

Focal Point Photography, Sunderland

Kim Ashton, photographer, Sedgefield

The National Portrait Gallery, London for permission to use portraits

The Ordnance Survey, for reproductions from OS maps of 1856, 1897, 1918, 1939 and 1940

RCHM – Royal Commission on the Historic Monuments of England for use of pictures

Olly Burton for information on stained glass and heraldry

George Nairn for his postcards of Wynyard

Irene Diependaal for explaining the Castlereagh connection with her country, the Netherlands

For their writing inspiration and expertise, Wendy Robertson, Avril Joy and Fadia Faqir

For their patience, skill and guidance with the publication, John Alderson and Steve Tolson of hpmgroup

Lillian Benson, Elizabeth Calvert, Valerie McLeod and Margaret Shepherd, who gave us invaluable information about life at Wynyard and kindly loaned photographs and documents

Also Olwyn Bragg, Geoff Hainsworth, Margaret Stewart, Ron Tempest and countless other people, local and distant, whose fond memories prove that Wynyard really is a special place.

BIBLIOGRAPHY

Annabel : An Unconventional Life – The memoirs of Lady Annabel Goldsmith (Weidenfeld and Nicholson 2004 ; Phoenix, an imprint of Orion Books 2005)

Aristocrat in Business: *The Third Marquess of Londonderry as Coalowner and Portbuilder* – R.W.Sturgess (Durham County Local History Society 1975)

An Atlas of the Peninsular War 1808-1814 – Ian Robertson with cartography by Martin Brown (Yale University Press 2010)

The Buildings of England County Durham - Nikolaus Pevsner (Yale University Press 1953; Second edition revised by Elizabeth Williamson 1983, reprinted 1985)

Character and Tradition – Edith, Marchioness of Londonderry (Macmillan 1934)

The Duke of Wellington - Matthew Shaw (The British Library – Historic Lives 2005)

El Tih and other poems - Frederick William Robert Stewart Londonderry (printed R.Born, London 1859, reproduced as a facsimile by Biblio Life, LLC 2009)

English Architecture – David Watkin (Thames & Hudson Ltd. 1979, revised 2001)

Frances Anne – The Life and Times of Frances Anne Marchioness of Londonderry and her husband Charles Third Marquess of Londonderry - Edith, Marchioness of Londonderry D.B.E. (Macmillan and Co. 1958)

Garron Tower, County Antrim – Paul Magill (Ulster Tatler Publications, Belfast 1990)

Glencloy, A Local History including Carnlough – Felix McKillop (Ulster Journals Ltd.1996)

Heraldry Explained – Arthur Charles Fox-Davies (The Burke Publishing Co. Ltd. 1906, reprinted 1925)

Henry Chaplin, a memoir – The Marchioness of Londonderry (Macmillan and Co. 1926, Kessinger Legacy Reprints 2010)

Henry Wilson, Practical Idealist - Cyndy Manton (Lutterworth Press 2009)

Historical, Topographical and Descriptive View of the County Palatine of Durham-E.Mackenzie and M. Ross (Mackenzie and Dent, Newcastle 1834)

The History & Antiquities of the County Palatine of Durham, Vol 2, 2nd edit., 1857 William Fordyce (within Kelly's Directory of Durham 1902)

History, Topography and Directory of Durham (William Whellan & Co. 1856)

An illustrated history of Wynyard Estate through the passage of time - Adrian Liddell (Printability Publishing, Wolviston 1989)

A Journal of a Three Months' Tour in Portugal, Spain, Africa etc. by the Marchioness of Londonderry – Frances Anne Vane Londonderry 1843 (reproduced by Biblio Life 2011)

A Journey to Damascus through Egypt, Nubia, Arabia Petra, Palestine and Syria Volume 1 - Viscount Castlereagh – (Originally published in two volumes 1847 by Henry Colburn, London 1847; Reproduced by Elibron Classics, Adamant Media Corporation 2005)

Kelly's Directory of Durham 1902

The Ladies of Londonderry – Diane Urquhart (I.B.Tauris 2007)

Letters from Benjamin Disraeli to Frances Anne Marchioness of Londonderry 1837-1861 Edited with an introduction by Edith, Marchioness of Londonderry (Macmillan and Co. 1938)

The Lives of Lord Castlereagh and Sir Charles Stewart - Sir Archibald Alison, Bart (William Blackwood and Sons 1861)

The Londonderry Album, Portraits from a Great House in the 1890s Introduced by the (9ᵗʰ) Marquess of Londonderry (Blond and Briggs 1978)

Londonderry House and its Pictures - H. Montgomery Hyde (The Cresset Press Ltd. 1937)

The Londonderrys : A Family Portrait – H. Montgomery-Hyde (Hamish Hamilton 1979)

The Londonderry Railway - George Hardy, edited and introduced by Charles Lee (Goose and Son Ltd., Norwich 1973)

The Magic Ink-pot – Edith, Marchioness of Londonderry (Macmillan and Co. 1928)

Making friends with Hitler – Lord Londonderry and Britain's Road to War - Ian Kershaw (Allen Lane 2004, Penguin Books 2005)

More Letters from Martha Wilmot – Impressions of Vienna 1819-1829 – edited and with an introduction and notes by Edith, Marchioness of Londonderry and H.Montgomery Hyde (Macmillan 1935)

Narrative of a Visit to the Courts of Vienna, Constantinople, Athens, Naples etc. – Frances Anne Vane, Marchioness of Londonderry (Henry Colburn 1844, reproduced by The BiblioLife Network 1995)

Narrative of the Peninsular War from 1808 to 1813- Charles William Vane, Marquess of Londonderry (Henry Colburn 1848; reproduced by Nabu Public Domain Reprints 2011)

Ourselves and Germany – The Marquess of Londonderry K.G. (First published by Robert Hale Ltd. 1938, Penguin 1938)

Retrospect – Edith, Marchioness of Londonderry (Frederick Muller Ltd. 1938)

Ribbentrop - Michael Bloch (Bantam Press 1994, revised Abacus 2003)

Robert Stewart, Viscount Castlereagh - Theresa Stewart Londonderry (Arthur L. Humphreys, London 1904, reprinted by Kessinger Legacy Reprints 2010)

Russian Journal of Lady Londonderry 1836-37 edited W.A.L.Seamand and J.R.Sewell (The History Book Club, London 1973)

Society's Queen : The Life of Edith, Marchioness of Londonderry – Anne de Courcy (Phoenix, an imprint of Orion Books Ltd. 2004; first published 1992 by Sinclair Stevenson Limited as *Circe : The Life of Edith, Marchioness of Londonderry*)

Thorpe Thewles of Grindon Parish – A History - Thorpe Thewles History Group (Printability Publishing Ltd., Wolviston 2007)

The Tides of War – a novel of the Peninsular War - Stella Tillyard (Chatto & Windus 2011)

The Viceroy's Daughters : The lives of the Curzon sisters – Anne de Courcy (first published by Weidenfeld and Nicholson 2000; Phoenix, an imprint of Orion Books 2001)

The Wild Garden, Expanded edition – William Robinson with new chapters and photography by Nick Darke (Timber Press 2009; original book first published 1870, fifth edition 1895)

Wings of Destiny – The Marquess of Londonderry (Macmillan and Co. Ltd. 1943)

Wynyard College and its Students – a continuing history - Joan Sims (Wynyard College Association 2008)

Wynyard Hall – D.Y.Davies Associates and Basil Constantatos Urban Design Unit (Cameron Hall Developments 1990)

Wynyard Hall and the Londonderry Family - Brian Masters (The Marquess of Londonderry 1973)

DOCUMENTS

Archaeological Building Recording and Desk Top Assessment of the Old School, The Wynd,Wynyard - Percival Turnbull and Deborah Walsh of The Brigantia Archaeological Practice for Bellway Homes October 2009

Brooks, James (1825-1901) - Geoffrey Tyacks Oxford Dictionary of National Biography (Oxford University Press 2004)

Building Recording at Wynyard Stables - Andrew Platell of Tees Archaeology August 2000

Harrison and Harrison, Organ Builders of Meadowfield, Durham – Mark Venning 2010

Latimer's Local Records 1857

The Londonderry Trust 1819-54 – R.W.Sturgess (Published by the Society of Antiquaries, Newcastle upon Tyne 1982)

Louis Davis - Nigel Hammond (Oxfordshire Local History Journal Vol 7 no 5 January 2006)

Notes regarding developments in the gardens and pleasure grounds at Wynyard Park- Caroline Backhouse (Undated, circa 2000)

The Role of Frances Anne, wife of the Third Marquis of Londonderry, as an economic entrepreneur between the years 1854-65 – Joseph Colby, M.A. dissertation Sunderland Polytechnic 1988

Wynyard Estate – L.Ellison and R.W.Sturgess 1987

Wynyard Parkland and Gardens Historic assessment – RPS Consultants January 2000

NEWSPAPERS

Belfast News (24 August 24 1849; 25 November 1828)

The Billingham Press (10 June 1949)

Country Life (28 August & 4 September 1986; 1 September 1988)

Daily Telegraph (16 June 1964; 21 June 2007; 12 February 2011)

Durham Advertiser (9 July 1937; 24 June 1938)

Freemans Journal & Daily Commercial Advertiser (11 November 1842)

The Guardian (17 March 2011, reporting from their archive of 17 March 1953)

Journal of Horticulture and Cottage Gardener (18 March 1889)

Lancaster Gazette and General Advertiser (7 November 1812)

Leeds Mercury 1885

London Gazette (18 June 1814; 29 March 1823)

Morning Chronicle (24 September 1827)

The Morning Post (28 August 1828; 26 February 1841; 13 October 1842; October 21 1845; 29 January 1852; 18 March 1854; 8 September 1884; 15 August 1885; 22 January 1802)

Newcastle Courant (25 April 1851; 18 January 1884)

Northern Echo (14 September 1996)

Seaham Weekly News (30 November 1928)

The York Herald (and General Advertiser) (3 October 1846; 11 March 1854)

The Yorkshire Herald and the York Herald (28 October 1890)

The Standard (24 April 1840; 3 November 1851)